INTELLIGENT DESIGN

INTELLIGENT DESIGN

SCIENCE OR RELIGION?
CRITICAL PERSPECTIVES

EDITED BY
ROBERT M. BAIRD & STUART E. ROSENBAUM

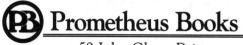 Prometheus Books

59 John Glenn Drive
Amherst, New York 14228–2197

Published 2007 by Prometheus Books

Inquiries should be addressed to
Prometheus Books
59 John Glenn Drive
Amherst, New York 14228–2197
VOICE: 716–691–0133, ext. 210
FAX: 716–691–0137
WWW.PROMETHEUSBOOKS.COM

11 10 09 08 07   5 4 3 2 1

Library of Congress Cataloging-in-Publication Data

Intelligent design : science or religion? critical perspectives / edited by Robert M. Baird and
    Stuart E. Rosenbaum.
        p. cm.
    ISBN 978–1–59102–445–3 (pbk. : alk. paper)
    1. Intelligent design (Teleology) 2. Religion and science. I. Baird, Robert M., 1937-
II. Rosenbaum, Stuart E.

BL262.I56 2006
231.7'652—dc22

                                                                        2006020264

Printed in the United States of America on acid-free paper

CONTENTS

PART TWO. INTELLIGENT DESIGN IN THE SCHOOLS: RESPONSES TO PRESIDENT GEORGE W. BUSH

PART THREE. ORIGINS OF THE DEBATE

PART FOUR. ONGOING CRITIQUE

PART FIVE. RELIGION AND EVOLUTION: COMPATIBILITY ISSUE

INTRODUCTION

American culture continues to struggle with evolution. On December 20, 2005, Federal District Court Judge John E. Jones III, in *Kitzmiller v. Dover*, delivered the most recent judicial decision involving these struggles.

Judge Jones's decision resulted from a suit brought by citizens of the Dover, Pennsylvania, school district against their own school board. The Dover board had adopted a policy that many of Dover's citizens believed illegitimately promoted religious beliefs in high school biology classes. The trial was a cultural event, much as the 1925 Scopes "monkey trial" in Tennessee had been.

As did the earlier Scopes trial, the 2005 Dover trial stood as testimony to the acrimony between some venues of American religion and mainstream biology. In the Dover trial, the main issue was whether intelligent design theory was a real scientific alternative to evolutionary theory or rather a covert effort to insert specific religious views into high school science classrooms. A subsidiary issue was whether or not the Dover School Board, in adopting the controversial policy, was motivated by a concern for the integrity of science education or by their religious views.

Here is part of the statement the Dover Board required to be read to students in biology classes:

> Because Darwin's theory is a theory, it continues to be tested as new evidence is discovered. The theory is not a fact. Gaps in the theory exist for which there is no evidence.
>
> Intelligent Design is an explanation of the origin of life that differs from Darwin's view. The reference book, *Of Pandas and People*, is available for students who might be interested in gaining an understanding of what Intelligent Design actually involves.
>
> With respect to any theory, students are encouraged to keep an open mind. The school leaves discussion of the origin of life to individual students and their families.[1]

Judge Jones's decision was unequivocal. Here is an excerpt:

> To be sure, Darwin's theory of evolution is imperfect. However, the fact that a scientific theory cannot yet render an explanation on every point should not be used as a pretext to thrust an untestable alternative hypothesis grounded in religion into the science classroom or to misrepresent well-established scientific propositions.
>
> The citizens of the Dover area were poorly served by the members of the board who voted for the I.D. policy. It is ironic that several of these individuals, who so staunchly and proudly touted their religious convictions in public, would time and again lie to cover their tracks and disguise the real purpose behind the I.D. policy. . . .
>
> Those who disagree with our holding will likely mark it as the product of an activist judge. If so, they will have erred as this is manifestly not an activist court. Rather, this case came to us as the result of the activism of an ill-informed faction on a school board, aided by a national public interest law firm eager to find a constitutional test case on I.D., who in combination drove the board to adopt an imprudent and ultimately unconstitutional policy.
>
> The breathtaking inanity of the board's decision is evident when considered against the factual backdrop which has now been fully revealed through this trial. The students, parents, and teachers of the Dover Area School District deserved better than to be dragged into this legal maelstrom, with its resulting utter waste of monetary and personal resources.[2]

The caustic tone of Judge Jones's decision may be difficult to understand. Indeed, upon reading his decision, one might wonder what could have motivated the almost derisive tone of some of Judge Jones's statements. The judge seems to have no respect for the Dover School Board members who were responsible for the intelligent design policy. Apparently, Judge Jones believed that the trial made quite obvious the "breathtaking inanity of the board's decision." And, Judge Jones's advance defense against the charge of judicial activism may serve as a reminder that he is a Republican and a Bush appointee.

— Polemical, prosaic pedantic political BS!

CHRISTIANITY OR SCIENCE: FAITHFULNESS OR ATHEISTIC NATURALISM

Judge Jones apparently became convinced during the course of the trial that some of the Dover School Board members were scientifically naïve, especially about biology. He apparently saw their adoption of the policy to commend to biology students intelligent design theory, along with the textbook *Of Pandas and People*, as an inept effort to be faithful to their Christian beliefs. Religious faithfulness was, for the Dover board, a commitment to be maintained at all costs, and public avowal of their faithfulness in board policy seemed simply a requirement for good stewardship of their Christianity. Board members in effect confessed in their testimonies that they were not well-informed about the theological, philosophical, or scientific issues involved in the controversy about evolutionary theory and intelligent design theory.[3] Judge Jones apparently thought that overwhelming evidence obvious in the testimonies of various experts confirmed the board's naiveté concerning issues about which they had rushed to public judgment. The board's willingness to adopt so controversial a policy in the face of what they might have suspected was their own naïveté signaled their willingness to appear foolish in order to be faithful to their Christian commitments.

In their willingness to risk public condemnation (or even scorn of the sort Judge Jones's decision comes close to expressing), members of the Dover board saw themselves as choosing to make their Christian commitments their first priority; they chose not to separate their personal commitments between their religion and their public roles as board members. They must have felt an almost palpable conflict between their Christianity and the scientific culture into which they were supposed to be leading students in the

Dover area schools. The conflict must have seemed to them to require a choice between their Christianity and the godless science of biology classrooms.

Faithfulness to one's religion is a (probably the) primary commitment for almost all American Christians. And such faithfulness is no vice.[4] How can it seem, how has it come to seem, that such faithfulness requires a negative judgment about a particular scientific view, evolutionary biology, which seems to a vast majority of biologists, geologists, paleontologists, along with many other specialists, to be as well-supported by evidence as any scientific theory in human history? What exactly is the religious objection to Darwinian evolution?

A rough account of the religious objection to Darwinism is that the scientific explanations Darwinian thinkers offer not only do not mention God but they also make God irrelevant to scientific thought about the origin and development of life. Within Darwinian evolution, God becomes irrelevant to understanding the development of human life on earth. More harshly, God may become a hindrance to scientific understanding of the complex phenomena of biology. Alvin Plantinga, in an important essay not included in this collection, quotes Richard Dawkins's remark to A.J. Ayer at an "elegant, candle-lit, bibulous" Oxford dinner that "although atheism might have been logically tenable before Darwin, . . . Darwin made it possible to be an intellectually fulfilled atheist."[5]

The fundamental problem for many religious people is that Darwinian evolution makes possible a way of thinking about the entire living world that has no need of God. Thus they see it as committed to scientific naturalism—a view they identify with secularism, relativism, and "might makes right" atheism—and as offering an invitation they fear might be especially attractive to the young people who study science in American classrooms. Roger Olson, a theology professor at Baylor University's Truett Seminary, expresses this problem succinctly in a guest column for the *Waco Tribune-Herald* after Judge Jones's decision:

> The concern many people (and not only fundamentalist Christians) have is whether it is really possible to be good without God. Of course, they know that there are atheists who are good people. That's not the point. The point is to ask whether in the long run society can hold onto objective values and morality such as respect and compassion for others without belief in God or something like God.

If God does not exist . . . what is the basis for objective right and wrong? Without God, wouldn't might make right? Wouldn't nature, the only reality, justify the survival of the fittest even among humans? Without God, why live anything but a totally selfish life? Why help the weak? Without appealing to something beyond ourselves and nature, how can we urge, even expect ourselves and others to be good?[6]

Many biologists, other scientists, theologians, philosophers, and many Christians who are not professional academics believe on the other hand that there need be no animosity, nor even any tension, between their Christian commitments and their commitments to Darwinian evolution. In addition to what Richard Dawkins calls "intellectually fulfilled atheists," many Christians find their religious beliefs fully compatible with their commitment to Darwinian evolution. Given that there are atheists among evolutionary biologists, the puzzle for many Christians like the Dover board members who adopted the intelligent design policy (who are probably pretty well represented by Roger Olson's commentary just cited) is how one can be *both* a good Christian *and* a committed evolutionary biologist, a Darwinian. How is such a combination possible?

CHRISTIANITY AND SCIENCE: FAITHFULNESS AND DARWINIAN EVOLUTION

Many people—biologists, theologians, philosophers and others—are in fact both Christians and Darwinians. Kenneth Miller, the Brown University biologist who offered expert testimony at the Dover trial, is a Catholic and a Darwinian; an excerpt from his testimony is included in this collection. Ernan McMullen, a Catholic priest and a philosopher of science at the University of Notre Dame, offers a critique of Alvin Plantinga's endorsement of "theistic science." And Pope John Paul II likewise endorses evolutionary biology in his statement near the end of this collection.

The position, however, that Christian faith and Darwinian science are compatible is also widespread among non-Catholic Christians. Nancey Murphy, a philosopher of science and a Baptist theologian who explicitly embraces both Christianity and Darwinian biology, offers a critique of Phillip Johnson in this collection. Others in this collection also see no incompatibility between earnest commitments both to Christian religion and to

Darwinian biology. Stephen Jay Gould, for example, while a practitioner neither of Christianity nor of his own Jewish tradition, argues strenuously for the legitimacy of all religious perspectives independently of Darwinian biology. In his essay, Gould seeks to mediate what he sees as needless controversy between some versions of Christianity and evolution. Others in this collection are non-committal about their own religious views but are generous in spirit toward those with whom they disagree. Michael Ruse, a strong advocate of Darwinian biology, speaks of Bill Dembski, a leading proponent of intelligent design, as a friend with whom he disagrees about basic issues in philosophy of science and biology, and Ruse evinces what might be thought of as religious reverence toward the biological mysteries of the natural world.

There is disagreement in this volume, but much of it is infused with charity toward intellectual opponents. But there remains the nagging original question: Why do some Christians think of Darwinian evolution as a direct challenge to their Christian commitments and others do not? This question is a genealogical one: How might we plausibly account for such deeply felt disagreement?

SOME HISTORICAL REMARKS

Nancey Murphy notes that Isaac Newton and Robert Boyle insisted on absolute separation between theology and science and that they did so for theological reasons. "Their Calvinistic doctrine of God's transcendence led them to make a radical distinction between God the Creator and the operation of the created universe, and hence to seek to protect *theology* from contamination *by science*."[7] Murphy's remark about Newton and Boyle suggests that they felt a need to bifurcate their intellectual world into a part where science does its work and a part where theology does its work. This bifurcation of our intellectual world into a religion part and a science part has a distinguished history.

Probably the most prominent thinker in that history is Immanuel Kant. Kant sought to answer Hume's empiricist skepticism by grounding scientific knowledge on synthetic *a priori* truths supplied by human nature, on "factual necessities" that govern human cognition of the natural world. Synthetic *a priori* intuitions and concepts "structure" our interactions with the world to make knowledge of that world possible, and they are sources of all the truths of mathematics and (Euclidean) geometry as well as all of the concepts—causation, substance, and others—involved in formulating (Newtonian) laws of nature.[8]

The price Kant willingly paid for his answer to Hume's skepticism was a price many thinkers have been unwilling to pay. Our human nature (in Kant's terminology our "transcendental ego") made proper use of these synthetic *a priori* structures to gain knowledge only of the empirical world. If humans sought to use these structures to gain knowledge of a transcendent (supernatural) world beyond the empirical world of scientific inquiry, they would inevitably become confused by equally legitimate arguments for contradictory conclusions; they would fall into "antinomies." The price of Kant's answer to Hume was to put knowledge of what transcends human experience—God, freedom and immortality—beyond human cognitive powers; knowledge of what is transcendent or supernatural is, in Kant, beyond human ken.

Kant made philosophically official the Calvinist theological perspective Nancey Murphy finds in Newton and Boyle. Although Kant was mistaken in thinking of Euclidean geometry and Newtonian physics as necessary or *a priori*, the spirit of his understanding of the relation between science and religion remains a prominent strand in Western intellectual culture; science gives us knowledge of our world and religion gives us the faith and values we live by. Each is an equally legitimate arena of human activity and inquiry, and each is a properly significant part of our lives. Neither may encroach on prerogatives of the other, though on some issues they may enter into constructive conversation.

The spirit of this Kantian perspective appears in many of the essays in this collection. Stephen Jay Gould's idea of "nonoverlapping magisteria" is conceived, even if unintentionally, in this Kantian spirit. John Paul's contribution in "Truth Cannot Contradict Truth" is also an expression of the same Kantian spirit. Perhaps it is only just to remark as well that there are resources specifically within the Catholic intellectual tradition, as Kant is not, who support John Paul's recognition of the autonomy of biology from Christian doctrine. Ernan McMullen makes explicit some of these resources.

Post-Kantian Western intellectual traditions, by and large, have turned away from Kant's bifurcation of human institutions into those that are cognitively accessible, where science may roam in unfettered pursuit of real knowledge, and those that are cognitively inaccessible, religion and morality, where knowledge is impossible but the human significance of which is guaranteed and unthreatened by scientific knowledge. Nevertheless, the Kantian intellectual spirit that sought to diminish the possibility that human institutions might "cannibalize" one another does find a vigorous expression in twentieth-century American pragmatism. John Dewey, in his Gifford Lectures, *The Quest for Certainty*, is a staunch advocate of an intellectual strategy similar to Kant's.[9]

The contemporary tendency to force confrontation between science and religion, between biology and creation, is unmistakable in intelligent design theorists, and that tendency depends upon strands of intellectual tradition that reject the Kantian spirit. For intelligent design theorists, including Michael Behe, Phillip Johnson, William Dembski and Stephen Meyer, evolutionary biology is inevitably committed to metaphysical materialism and metaphysical materialism is logically inconsistent with traditional Christian theism. In their view, and of many who share their commitment to intelligent design (probably including the members of the Dover School Board), conflict and confrontation are the only alternatives: God or matter-in-motion; God or godless science; God or materialistic mechanism; God or Chance; God or Darwin. The palpable absence of the Kantian spirit in these Christian thinkers underscores their reservations about Darwinian evolution.

The most philosophically sophisticated of thinkers who reject the spirit of Kantianism is Alvin Plantinga. Plantinga argues explicitly that truth is one, be it scientific truth or Christian truth, and that some scientific truth claims and Christian truth claims conflict in ways that no "accommodationist" (or Kantian) strategy can finesse.[10] Plantinga is sympathetic with intelligent design theorists who believe that confrontation and conflict are inevitable. His list of the metaphysical alternatives is a bit more extensive than theirs and includes three possibilities: Perennial Naturalism, Enlightenment Humanism, and Christian Theism. But Plantinga is as adamant about the alternatives as they are. As he puts it, "The stakes . . . are high; this is a battle for men's souls."[11] Elsewhere, he continues the metaphor of warfare: "The first thing to see . . . is that Christianity is indeed engaged in a conflict, a battle. There is indeed a battle between the Christian community and the forces of unbelief." Plantinga recommends to Christians engaged in this conflict that they find a way to win: "[W]e Christians must think about the matter at hand from a Christian perspective; we need Theistic Science. . . . What we need from our scientists and other academics . . . is both cultural criticism and Christian science."[12]

The principal fault line that philosophically divides intelligent design

Christians from Darwinian Christians is this Kantian tradition. Intelligent design Christians do not take that tradition seriously (and Plantinga even argues explicitly against it); Darwinian Christians do take it seriously. Attempting to adjudicate this particular philosophical disagreement is certainly beyond the scope of this volume, but taking note of it and bringing it to the focal attention of those on both sides of the fault line may be useful. Any serious effort to engage it constructively inevitably exposes many additional areas of philosophical disagreement inextricably tangled up with it. The concluding essay of this volume by Alfred Tauber represents and argues for a Kantian style perspective on issues of science and religion in general as well as on the particular issue of intelligent design and Darwinian evolution.

OTHER MATTERS

Other issues also turn up in these essays. Consider "methodological naturalism."

Plantinga notes that Dawkins remarked to Ayer that Darwin made it possible to be an "intellectually fulfilled atheist." Dawkins' remark suggests that he does not respect, any more than does Plantinga, the Kantian strategy of partition.[13] Is Darwinism atheistic? Perhaps it makes atheism possible as Dawkins remarked, but why would anyone think Darwinism makes evident, or even supports, atheism? This tendency of Dawkins and others to see naturalistic metaphysics in their biology is none other than the flip side of the same coin that Behe, Johnson, Dembski and Plantinga are looking at when they see Christianity at war with Darwinism. (Matt Cartmill, in his essay, addresses this issue.) Dawkins in effect agrees with Plantinga that truth is one and that there is, making use of Plantinga's conception, a war going on, a battle for men's souls, one that Dawkins and his atheist companions are as committed to winning as are Plantinga and the intelligent design theorists with whom he sympathizes.

The resort to the idea of "methodological naturalism," a way of thinking about science so as to give it at least temporary autonomy from religion, is an effort to call a truce in the war that Plantinga and Dawkins are training soldiers to fight. Each side thinks of methodological naturalism as a "cop out," a way to postpone the battle that each thinks must ultimately be fought to the death. In a battle for men's souls there is no place for half-hearted commitment, for anything other than a willingness to give one's all.

Still, even a truce about the metaphysical issue, perhaps pending more insight or greater wisdom about the Kantian strategy of partition that might lead to a negotiated settlement instead of continued bloodshed, is welcome. If a truce resting on methodological naturalism can be achieved, philosophical attention, including genealogical and historical attention, must be paid to the intellectual contexts in which the Kantian spirit thrives. Foremost among these intellectual contexts is that of American pragmatism, especially the work of William James and John Dewey. These American intellectuals had the breadth of spirit and mind that enabled them to see, in ways similar to those of Kant, beyond the intractable conflict still insisted on by Plantinga and Dawkins. We must take these American pragmatist thinkers seriously.[14]

Then there is of course the matter of the scientific evidence for Darwinian evolution. How good is it? Has significant progress been made in garnering scientific support for the theory since Darwin's 1859 publication? The answer to the latter question is a resounding *yes*! The answer to the former question is "pretty good, but not good enough." And there are unending disputes between the Darwinian faction and the intelligent design faction about how good "pretty good" is. On both of these questions, the discussion Nancey Murphy offers is quite good, as are also the discussions of Ernan McMullen and Kenneth Miller. Other selections also offer cogent discussions of the state of the evidence for Darwinism.

An interestingly different kind of evidence for Darwinian evolution has turned up in the last few years. Michael Ruse mentions it in his selection, as did Robert Pennock in his expert testimony at the Dover trial (though not in the selection by him included in this volume). Carl Zimmer offers a detailed account of this new evidence, provided strangely enough by a computer program designed to "mimic" the process of evolution, in "Testing Darwin." Whether or not the program mimics evolution or actually instantiates it is a matter of some controversy. Pennock and others directly involved in the research using the program are convinced that they are not showing merely how the process of Darwinian evolution can be imitated on a computer but are finding actual instances of evolution in progress. At the moment, it probably suffices to say that this new evidence looks promising, and it appears to undermine intelligent design objections to the possibility of natural selection and mutation as adequate sources of evolutionary change. Whether or not intelligent design theorists are able to produce an adequate response to this putative evidence remains to be seen. In the meantime, see Zimmer's account.

We have designed this collection of essays to capture critical dimensions of the controversy about intelligent design and Darwinian evolution. Each selection we believe deserves thoughtful attention, and we hope these selections capture the care and the passion with which each of these thinkers pursues issues in religion and biology.

(Note to readers: We had originally intended this volume to include important contributions from representatives of the intelligent design perspective. However, those representatives from whom we sought reprint permission denied it.)

Waco, Texas
October 2006

NOTES

1. These sentences are part of the focus of Kenneth Miller's Expert Statement at the trial. Miller is a Catholic professor of biology at Brown University and a portion of his expert statement appears in this collection.

2. A more extensive excerpt of Judge Jones's ruling appears in *The New York Times*, December 21, 2005, A21, along with more extensive coverage of the trial. The text of the entire ruling is available at the National Center for Science Education website, http://www.natcenscied.org/.

3. For an account of the trial that is more revealing of individual board members' characters and motivations see Matthew Chapman, "God or Gorilla: A Darwin Descendant at the Dover Monkey Trial," *Harper's Magazine*, February 2006, 54–63.

4. Such faithfulness can be a vice, though it need not be. See the essay by Daniel Dennett, "Common-Sense Religion," *The Chronicle of Higher Education*, January 20, 2006, B6–B8.

5. "When Faith and Reason Clash: Evolution and the Bible," *Christian Scholar's Review* XXI, no. 1 (1991): 17.

6 "We Need Intelligent Design," *Waco Tribune-Herald*, December 26, 2005, 9A.

7. Murphy essay, p. 194.

8. The most accessible account of Kant's view appears in *Prolegomena to Any Future Metaphysics* (Indianapolis: Bobbs-Merrill, 1950).; the full expression appears in *The Critique of Pure Reason*, trans. Norman Kemp Smith (New York: St. Martin's Press, 1929).

9. John Dewey, *The Later Works, 1925–1953, Volume 4: 1929, The Quest for*

Certainty, edited by Jo Ann Boydston (Carbondale: Southern Illinois University Press, 1988), especially chapters 3, 10, and 11. But see also William James's *The Varieties of Religious Experience* (New York: The Modern Library, 2002), James's own earlier Gifford Lectures and available in many editions; see especially chapters I and XVIII.

10. Plantinga addresses the issue of Kant's "segregation strategy" explicitly in his recent *Warranted Christian Belief* (New York: Oxford University Press, 2000), chapter 1, especially 18–30.

11. Plantinga, "When Faith and Reason Clash: Evolution and the Bible," *Christian Scholar's Review* XXI, no. 1 (September 1991): 8–33.

12. Plantinga, "When Faith and Reason Clash: Evolution and the Bible," 30.

13. For the origin of the use of "partition" in this context, see Dewey's *The Quest for Certainty*, chapter 3, especially page 47.

14. For an essay that explicitly makes this connection between American pragmatism and Kant, see Thomas Carlson, "James and the Kantian Tradition," *The Cambridge Companion to William James*, edited by Ruth Anna Putnam (Cambridge: Cambridge University Press, 1997), 363–83. Richard Rorty, too, suggests that Dewey came to this view; see "Dewey's Metaphysics," *Consequences of Pragmatism* (Minneapolis: University of Minnesota Press, 1982), 72–89.

PART ONE

THE DOVER DECISION

EXPERT STATEMENT AT THE DOVER, PENNSYLVANIA, TRIAL

KENNETH R. MILLER

March 30, 2005

LANGUAGE OF THE DOVER STATEMENT

It is my understanding that in January 2005 a statement was read to students in Dover schools which said, in part:

> Because Darwin's theory is a theory, it continues to be tested as new evidence is discovered. The theory is not a fact. Gaps in the theory exist for which there is no evidence. A theory is defined as a well-tested explanation that unifies a broad range of observations. Intelligent Design is an explanation of the origin of life that differs from Darwin's view. The reference book "Of Pandas and People" is available for students who might be interested in gaining an understanding of what Intelligent Design actually involves. With respect to any theory, students are encouraged to keep an open mind. The school leaves discussion of the origin of life to individual students and their families.

Kenneth Miller's Expert Statement, Dover, Pennsylvania Trial, March 30, 2005.

This statement contains a number of errors of fact, misrepresents the scientific standing of evolution, and serves, as far as I am able to tell, no scientific or educational purpose.

CALLING SPECIAL ATTENTION TO EVOLUTION

The Board statement correctly describes a theory as "as a well-tested explanation that unifies a broad range of observations," and it quite properly advises students that they should keep an open mind "with respect to any theory." Unfortunately, it disregards its own advice on these matters by calling special attention to just one scientific theory, the theory of evolution. The effect of citing evolution, and only evolution, in this way has the obvious effect of suggesting to students that the scientific support for evolution is weak, and that students should hold this particular theory up for special scrutiny.

In reality, evolutionary theory enjoys the same status as other well-tested explanations in science, and there is no rational basis for suggesting that it, and it alone, should be mentioned in the context of doubt and skepticism that pervades this statement from the Dover Board.

MISREPRESENTING THE MEANING OF A THEORY

The Board statement tells students that "The theory is not a fact," and that "it continues to be tested as new evidence is discovered." Both of these statements are clearly designed to mislead students about evolution.

The Board's emphasis that evolution is not a fact might be appropriate if they had pointed out instead that *no scientific theory* is a fact, and that *all scientific theories* continue to be tested in light of new scientific discoveries. Instead, their claim that evolution "is not a fact" is clearly designed to undermine the scientific standing of evolution by implying that if science were certain of the validity of evolutionary theory, it might some day be regarded as a fact. The important point to be made is that scientific theories don't ever become facts; rather, scientific theories explain facts. We do not expect, by reason of analogy, that atomic theory will ever become "atomic fact," regardless of the weight of evidence supporting it. The Board's language clearly has the effect of promoting student misunderstanding as to the nature and validity of scientific theories.

CITING UNNAMED "GAPS"

Students and teachers in Dover must be left to speculate as to what the Board might mean when it tells them that "gaps in the theory" [of evolution] "exist for which there is no evidence." If the Board wishes to tell students that evolution, like all of science, is necessarily incomplete, this admonition might serve a useful scientific purpose. Unfortunately, the Board's statement does distort scientific reality by telling students there are problems with evolutionary theory without ever stating what those problems ("gaps") might be. Because the "gaps" are unnamed, they cannot possibly be addressed in a factual manner, even by teachers well-versed in the scientific evidence for evolution.

MISREPRESENTING DARWIN'S THEORY

The Board seems to believe that our current understanding of evolution is the same as that of Charles Darwin, and this apparently has led them to statements such as "Intelligent Design is an explanation of the origin of life that differs from Darwin's view." This statement implies that "Darwin's view" of the origin of life is the one generally taught in biology classes (and textbooks), an implication that is completely incorrect.

In reality, Darwin never wrote in detail about the origin of life, beyond speculations in a personal letter to biologist Joseph Hooker that the conditions for life to appear on the early earth might have appeared in a "warm little pond." Since Darwin also speculated (in the final sentence of *On the Origin of Species*) that a Creator might have produced the first living things, it is not correct to tell students that Darwin had any particular view on "the origin of life."

The Board statement also misrepresents the "intelligent design" position by defining it merely as an idea on the origin of life. In reality, "intelligent design" argues that many features of living organisms, not just the origin of life, can be attributed to an intelligent agent acting outside the laws of nature.

LEAVING "THE ORIGIN OF LIFE" TO STUDENTS AND THEIR FAMILIES

The Dover statement contains a confusing contradiction that makes it nearly impossible to understand the Board's educational intent for the students of

Dover High School. After defining "intelligent design" as "an explanation of the origin of life," the Board explains that it will leave "discussion of the origin of life to individual students and their families." If "intelligent design" deals explicitly with the origin of life and if the School provides reference books (*Of Pandas and People*) presenting the "design" view of the origin of life, how can the Board possibly claim that this subject will be left to students and their families?

This internal contradiction leaves one to suspect that the Board hopes that evolutionary views of the origin of life will not be taught in classes, but that the "design" view that a supernatural designer intervened to create life on Earth will be adopted by students.

"INTELLIGENT DESIGN" AS A SCIENTIFIC ALTERNATIVE TO EVOLUTION

"Intelligent Design Theory" is a new anti-evolution movement that has been presented as an alternative to an older formulation known as "creation science." It differs from the older movement in that it maintains a studied neutrality on the scientific evidence from geology and astronomy on the ages of the earth and the universe, and seems to accept the fossil record. It argues, however, that an unnamed "designer" must have been responsible for much of the process, although it presents no evidence for the actions of such a designer. This means that "intelligent design" is an entirely negative concept, since the case for "design" is made entirely by assembling a selection of arguments that call the validity of evolutionary mechanisms into question.

"Intelligent design" advocates often cite the complexity of living cells as a reason to invoke the hypothesis of design. While this may seem to account for any unexplained problem in biology, it does so only by abandoning the scientific method and making "design" the solution to every such problem. An explanation of this sort, which can explain any conceivable evidence, in fact explains nothing. Since the "design" explanation is not testable, it falls outside the realm of science, and places it in the realm of theology, where non-natural explanations are an accepted part of the explanatory landscape. Theological explanations may be correct, of course (as when I believe that a loving God hears my prayers and acts in my life to answer them), but they cannot be tested by the methods of science—and therefore they are not science.

THE BIOCHEMICAL CHALLENGE TO EVOLUTION

One of the principal claims made by adherents of intelligent design is that they can detect the presence of "design" in complex biological systems. As evidence, they cite a number of specific examples, including the vertebrate blood clotting cascade, the eukaryotic cilium, and most notably, the eubacterial flagellum.[1]

Of all these examples, the flagellum has been presented so often as a counter-example to evolution that it might well be considered the "poster child" of the modern anti-evolution movement. To anti-evolutionists, the high status of the flagellum reflects the supposed fact that it could not possibly have been produced by an evolutionary pathway.

There is, to be sure, nothing new or novel in pointing to a complex or intricate natural structure, and professing skepticism that it could have been produced by the "random" processes of mutation and natural selection. Nonetheless, the "argument from personal incredulity," as such sentiment has been appropriately described, has been a weapon of little value. Anyone can state at any time that they cannot imagine how evolutionary mechanisms might have produced a certain species, organ, structure. Such statements, obviously, are personal, and not scientific.

The hallmark of the intelligent design movement, however, is that it purports to rise above the level of personal skepticism. It claims to have found a reason why evolution could not have produced a structure like the bacterial flagellum, a reason purportedly based on sound, solid scientific evidence.

Why does the intelligent design movement regard the flagellum as unevolvable? Because it is said to possesses a quality known as "irreducible complexity." Irreducibly complex structures, we are told, could not have been produced by evolution, or, for that matter, by any natural process. They do exist, however, and therefore they must have been produced by something.

That something could only be an outside intelligent agency operating beyond the laws of nature—an intelligent designer. That, simply stated, is the core of the new argument from design, and the intellectual basis of the intelligent design movement.

The great irony of the flagellum's increasing acceptance as an icon of anti-evolution is the fact that research had demolished its status as an example of irreducible complexity almost at the very moment it was first proclaimed.

The flagellum was cited in *Darwin's Black Box*,[2] a book by Michael Behe that employed it in a carefully crafted anti-evolution argument. Building upon William Paley's well-known "argument from design," Behe sought to bring the argument two centuries forward into the realm of biochemistry. Like Paley, Behe appealed to his readers to appreciate the intricate complexity of living organisms as evidence for the work of a designer. Unlike Paley, however, he claimed to have discovered a scientific principle that could be used to prove that certain structures could not have been produced by evolution. That principle goes by the name of "irreducible complexity."

An irreducibly complex structure is defined as ". . . a single system composed of several well-matched, interacting parts that contribute to the basic function, wherein the removal of any one of the parts causes the system to effectively cease functioning."[3]

> An irreducibly complex system cannot be produced directly by numerous, successive, slight modifications of a precursor system, because any precursor to an irreducibly complex system that is missing a part is by definition nonfunctional. . . . Since natural selection can only choose systems that are already working, then if a biological system cannot be produced gradually it would have to arise as an integrated unit, in one fell swoop, for natural selection to have anything to act on.[4]

Living cells are filled, of course, with complex structures which have only recently become accessible to scientific observation and study, and whose detailed evolutionary origins are therefore not known. Therefore, in fashioning an argument against evolution one might pick nearly any cellular structure, the ribosome for example, and claim—correctly—that its origin has not been explained in detail by evolution.

The utility of the bacterial flagellum is that it seems to rise above this "argument from ignorance." By asserting that it is a structure "in which the removal of an element would cause the whole system to cease functioning,"[5] the flagellum is presented as a "molecular machine" whose individual parts must have been specifically crafted to work as a unified assembly. The existence of such a multipart machine, it is argued, provides genuine scientific proof of the actions of an intelligent designer.

In the case of the flagellum, the assertion of irreducible complexity means that a minimum number of protein components, perhaps 30, are required to produce a working biological function. By the logic of irreducible complexity, these individual components should have no function until all 30 are put into place, at which point the function of motility appears. What this means, according to the argument, is that evolution could not have fashioned those components a few at a time, since they do not have functions that could be favored by natural selection. As Behe wrote: ". . . natural selection can only choose among systems that are already working,"[6] and an irreducibly complex system does not work unless all of its parts are in place. The flagellum is irreducibly complex, and therefore, it must have been designed.

The assertion that cellular machines are irreducibly complex, and therefore provide proof of design, has not gone unnoticed by the scientific community. A number of detailed rebuttals have appeared in the literature, and many have pointed out the poor reasoning of recasting the classic argument from design in the modern language of biochemistry.[7] I have suggested elsewhere that the scientific literature contains counter-examples to any assertion that evolution cannot explain biochemical complexity,[8] and other workers have addressed the issue of how evolutionary mechanisms allow biological systems to increase in information content.[9]

The most powerful rebuttals to the flagellum story, however, have emerged from the steady progress of scientific work on the genes and proteins associated with the flagellum and other cellular structures. Such studies have now established that the entire premise by which this molecular machine has been advanced as an argument against evolution is wrong—the bacterial flagellum is not irreducibly complex. As the evidence has shown, nature is filled with examples of "precursors" to the flagellum that are indeed "missing a part," and yet are fully-functional. Functional enough, in some cases, to pose a serious threat to human life.

Certain pathogenic bacteria attack human cells by means of specialized protein secretory systems that inject protein toxins into the cells of their hosts. The type III secretory system (TTSS) is such an example, allowing gram negative bacteria to translocate proteins directly into the cytoplasm of a host cell.[10] The proteins transferred through the TTSS include a variety of truly dangerous molecules, some of which are known as "virulence factors," and are directly responsible for the pathogenic activity of some of the most deadly bacteria in existence.[11]

Molecular studies of proteins in the TTSS have revealed a surprising fact—the proteins of the TTSS are directly homologous to the proteins in the basal portion of the bacterial flagellum. As Heuck has pointed out, these homologies extend to a cluster of closely-associated proteins found in both of these molecular "machines."[12] On the basis of these homologies, McNab has argued that the flagellum itself should be regarded as a type III secretory system.[13] Extending such studies with a detailed comparison of the proteins associated with both systems, Aizawa has seconded this suggestion, noting that the two systems "consist of homologous component proteins with common physico-chemical properties."[14] It is now clear, therefore, that a smaller subset of the full complement of proteins in the flagellum makes up the functional transmembrane portion of the TTSS.

Stated directly, the TTSS does its dirty work using a handful of proteins from the base of the flagellum. From the evolutionary point of view, this relationship is hardly surprising. In fact, it is to be expected that the opportunism of evolutionary processes would mix and match proteins to produce new and novel functions. According to the doctrine of irreducible complexity, however, this should not be possible. If the flagellum is indeed irreducibly complex, then removing just one part, let alone 10 or 15, should render what remains "by definition nonfunctional." Yet the TTSS is indeed fully-functional, even though it is missing most of the parts of the flagellum. The TTSS may be bad news for us, but for the bacteria that possess it, it is a truly valuable biochemical machine.

The existence of the TTSS in a wide variety of bacteria demonstrates that a small portion of the "irreducibly complex" flagellum can indeed carry out an important biological function. Since such a function is clearly favored by natural selection, the contention that the flagellum must be fully-assembled before any of its component parts can be useful is obviously incorrect. As a result, the principal biochemical argument for intelligent design, the contention that the bacterial flagellum is irreducibly complex, has failed.

As I noted in an article for *Natural History* magazine, similar analyses can be described for each of the other systems proposed as examples of intelligent design. The evolution of the vertebrate blood clotting cascade, for example, has been described in detail by Hanumanthaiah et al., Davidson et al. and Jiang and Doolittle. The evolution of antibody-based adaptive immunity, one of the most complex systems in the body, has been elucidated as well. This work has taken place in many laboratories, and representative reports have appeared in papers by Lewis and Wu, Market and Papavasiliou, DuPasquier et al., Zhou et al., and Klein and Nikolaidis. In addition, Nonanka and Yoshizaki were able to show how evolution produced the complement system, a complex and important part of the body's defenses against infection.[15]

More generally, Long et al. reviewed the origin of new genes with novel functions, and have described 22 examples of such genes. Krem and DiCera have described the ways in which evolution produces that complex cascade-like pathways that function in signaling pathways associated with functions from blood clotting to signal transduction in development. Intelligent design bases its critique of evolution on the claim that new information cannot be produced by Darwinian mechanisms, and yet this claim has been repeatedly disproved by observations of novel pathways and enzymes that have arisen in the recent past.[16]

THE INFORMATIONAL CHALLENGE TO EVOLUTION

At first glance, William Dembski's case for intelligent design seems to follow a distinctly different strategy in dealing with biological complexity. His recent book, *No Free Lunch*,[17] lays out this case, using information theory and mathematics to show that life is the result of intelligent design. Dembski makes the assertion that living organisms contain what he calls "complex specified information" (CSI), and claims to have shown that the evolutionary mechanism of natural selection cannot produce CSI. Therefore, any instance of CSI in a living organism must be the result of intelligent design. And living organisms, according to Dembski, are chock-full of CSI.

Dembski's arguments, couched in the language of information theory, are highly technical and are defended, almost exclusively, by reference to their utility in detecting information produced by human beings. These include phone and credit card numbers, symphonies, and artistic woodcuts, to name just a few. One might then expect that Dembski, having shown how the presence of CSI can be demonstrated in man-made objects, would then turn to a variety of biological objects. Instead, he turns to just one such object, the bacterial flagellum.

Dembski offers his readers a calculation showing that the flagellum could not have possibly have evolved. Significantly, he begins that calculation by linking his arguments to those of Behe, writing: "I want therefore in this section to show how irreducible complexity is a special case of specified complexity, and in particular I want to sketch how one calculates the relevant probabilities needed to eliminate chance and infer design for such systems."[18] Dembski then tells us that an irreducibly complex system, like the flagellum, is a "discrete combinatorial object." What this means, as he explains, is that the probability of assembling such an object can be calculated by determining the probabilities that each of its components might have originated by chance, that they might have been localized to the same region of the cell, and that they would be assembled in precisely the right order. Dembski refers to these three probabilities as **P**orig, **P**local, and **P**config, and he regards each of them as separate and independent.[19]

This approach overlooks the fact that the last two probabilities are actually contained within the first. Localization and self-assembly of complex protein structures in prokaryotic cells are properties generally determined by signals built into the primary structures of the proteins themselves. The same is likely true for the amino acid sequences of the 30 or so protein components of the flagellum and the approximately 20 proteins involved in the flagellum's assembly.[20] Therefore, if one gets the sequences of all the proteins right, localization and assembly will take care of themselves.

According to Dembski, evolution could still not construct the 30 proteins needed for the flagellum. His reason is that the probability of their assembly falls below what he terms the "universal probability bound." According to Dembski, the probability bound is a sensible allowance for the fact that highly improbable events do occur from time to time in nature. To allow for such events, he agrees that given enough time, any event with a probability larger than 10^{-150} might well take place. Therefore, if a sequence of events, such as a presumed evolutionary pathway, has a calculated probability less than 10^{-150}, we may conclude that the pathway is impossible. If the calculated probability is greater than 10^{-150}, it's possible (even if unlikely).

When Dembski turns his attention to the chances of evolving the 30 proteins of the bacterial flagellum, he makes what he regards as a generous assumption. Guessing that each of the proteins of the flagellum have about 300 amino acids, one might calculate that the chances of getting just one such protein to assemble from "random" evolutionary processes would be 20^{-300}, since there are 20 amino acids specified by the genetic code, Dembski, however, concedes that proteins need not get the exact amino acid sequence right in order to be functional, so he cuts the odds to just 20^{-30}, which he tells his readers is "on the order of 10^{-39}." Since the flagellum requires 30 such proteins, he explains that 30 such probabilities "will all need to be multiplied to form the origination probability."[21] That would give us an origination probability for the flagellum of 10^{-1170}, far below the universal probability bound. This is presented as proof that flagellum couldn't have evolved, and therefore must be the product of design.

In contrast to this confident conclusion, a careful analysis of the way in which Dembski calculates the probability of an evolutionary origin for the flagellum shows how little biology actually stands behind those numbers. His computation calculates only the probability of spontaneous, random assembly for each of the proteins of the flagellum. Having come up with a probability value on the order of 10^{-1170}, he assures us that he has shown the flagellum to be unevolvable. This conclusion, of course, fits comfortably with his view that "The Darwinian mechanism is powerless to produce irreducibly complex systems. . . ."[22]

However complex Dembski's analysis, the scientific problem with his calculations is almost too easy to spot. By treating the flagellum as a "discrete combinatorial object" he has shown only that it is unlikely that the parts of flagellum could assemble spontaneously. Unfortunately for his argument, no scientist has ever proposed that the flagellum or any other complex object evolved that way. Dembski, therefore, has constructed a classic "straw man" and addressed it away with an irrelevant calculation.

By treating the flagellum as a discrete combinatorial object he has assumed in his calculation that no subset of the 30 or so proteins of the flagellum could have biological activity. As we have already seen, this is wrong. Nearly a third of those proteins are closely related to components of the TTSS, which does indeed have biological activity. A calculation that ignores that fact has no scientific validity.

More importantly, Dembski's willingness to ignore the TTSS lays bare the underlying assumption of his entire approach towards the calculation of probabilities and the detection of "design." He *assumes what he is trying to prove.*

According to Dembski, the detection of "design" requires that an object display complexity that could not be produced by what he calls "natural causes." In order to do that, one must first examine all of the possibilities by which an object, like the flagellum, might have been generated naturally. Dembski and Behe, of course, come to the conclusion that there are no such natural causes. But how did they determine that? In fact, this "conclusion" is an unsupported assumption upon which all of his calculations depend. Suppose that there are such causes, but one simply happened not to think of them? Dembski actually seems to realize that this is a serious problem. He writes: "Now it can happen that we may not know enough to determine all the relevant chance hypotheses. Alternatively, we might think we know the relevant chance hypotheses, but later discover that we missed a crucial one. In the one case a design inference could not even get going; in the other, it would be mistaken."[23]

What Dembski is telling us is that in order to "detect" design in a biological object one must first come to the conclusion that the object *could not* have been produced by any "relevant chance hypotheses" (meaning evolution). Then, and only then, are Dembski's calculations brought into play. Stated more bluntly, what this really means is that the "method" first involves *assuming the absence* of an evolutionary pathway leading to the object, followed by a calculation "proving" the impossibility of spontaneous assembly. This faulty *a priori* reasoning is exactly the sort of logic upon which the new "science" of intelligent design has been constructed.

Not surprisingly, scientific reviewers have not missed this point—Dembski's arguments have been repeatedly criticized on this issue and on many others.[24]

THE ORIGIN OF BIOLOGICAL INFORMATION

Arguments in favor of "design" are often predicated on the statement that living organisms contain large quantities of biological information (which is true) and that no natural process can account for the presence of this information (which is false). They then conclude that the existence of such information is evidence for design.

Such arguments ignore a wealth of research and scholarship on the origins of biological information. In reality, evolutionary mechanisms that can generate increased complexity and biological information are very well understood, and are described in many research papers. Adami et al. described a carefully-controlled model system in which increases in information are driven by repeated rounds of reproduction, mutation, and selection, the same forces that drive evolutionary change in nature.[25] Adami's system mimics the evolutionary process in remarkable detail, as highlighted in a 2003 article in *Nature*.[26] Thomas Schneider of the National Institutes of Health has come to similar conclusions with respect to information based in nucleic acids.[27]

Specific experiments on a variety of living organisms have shown that information does indeed arise through distinctly Darwinian mechanisms. The supporting evidence includes a number of studies on gene duplication,[28] as well as experiments in which organisms have responded to adverse environmental conditions by increasing the information content of their DNA.[29]

The origin of biological information, as nearly all of these scientists have pointed out, is explained by the mechanism of evolution itself. Variation in the information content of living organisms arises by means of mutations, a few of which increase information content. Natural selection then chooses those variations best-suited to the environment, "fixing" the increased information in the genome. The energetic price that such increases in information entail is considerable, but is fully accounted for by the great cost of unsuccessful variants in the struggle for existence. To pretend otherwise, as the intelligent design movement has, is unfortunate and misleading.

OF PANDAS AND PEOPLE—A BRIEF ANALYSIS

Of Pandas and People,[30] which pretends to be an open, objective examination of the pros and cons of evolutionary biology, is actually nothing of the sort. It is, instead, a collection of half-truths, distortions, and outright falsehoods that attempts to misrepresent biology and mislead students as to the scientific status of evolutionary biology.

A complete critique of the many problems with *Pandas* would take almost as many pages as the book itself, but here are a few points of special concern:

THE AGE OF THE EARTH

Pandas claims to be a book that seeks to examine the "timeless question of biological origins." A truly scientific attempt to do exactly this would begin by examining the age of the earth and reviewing the scientific techniques used by geologists to determine the ages of rocks and fossils. Curiously, *Pandas* does nothing of the sort. In fact, not a word can be found anywhere in *Pandas* regarding the age of the earth or geological ages recognized by earth scientists. Ignoring the age of the earth while attempting to teach students natural history makes about as much sense as trying to teach American history without telling students that the American revolution began in 1775, which is to say, no sense at all.

Why does *Pandas* make this striking omission? Its authors have never been willing to say why they ignore such a crucial part of earth history, but I suspect that the answer is simple. If they were to bring authentic scientific evidence regarding earth history into play, it would immediately become clear to readers that the ages of rocks and fossils support, in dramatic fashion, the evolutionary history of life that geologists have recognized for many decades. Because this important mass of scientific evidence is at odds with their anti-evolutionary thesis, they choose to ignore it. They are free to do this, of course, but students who might attempt to use *Pandas* as a scientific textbook will be rightly baffled by its attempts to teach natural history without a time scale, and will surely ask their teachers what science can tell us about the geologic time scale. *Pandas* ignores this most basic question, perhaps because it does not like the answer that science provides.

THE FOSSIL RECORD

Pandas seriously misrepresents the nature of the fossil record. For example, the authors of *Pandas* have written:

> Intelligent design means that various forms of life began abruptly through an intelligent agency, with their distinctive features already intact—fish with fins and scales, birds with feathers, beaks, and wings, etc. Some scientists have arrived at this view since fossil forms first appear in the rock record with their distinctive features intact, rather than gradually developing.[31]

Actually, a close examination of the fossil record supplies scores of examples that show the gradual appearance of a wide variety of physical adaptations, including, for example, the vertebrate limb. *Pandas* wishes to claim that abrupt appearances of critical features (which might be taken to support design) characterize the fossil record. Unfortunately, this contention does not square with the facts. The earliest known fish, for example, were quite different from the fish we recognize today. The earliest fossil forms lacked many of the characteristics possessed by fish today, including jaws, paired limbs and bony internal skeletons, and yet *Pandas* wishes to tell students that fish (and all fossil forms) appear in the fossil record "with their distinctive features intact."

To take another example, strong fossil evidence indicates that the first land vertebrates evolved from lobe-finned fish. One of the very first land vertebrates, a species known as *Acanthostega gunnari*, illustrates the point. *Acanthostega*, although clearly a land-dwelling animal, retained an unmistakable sign of its aquatic ancestry: internal gills. No other amphibian possesses internal gills, and the gills preserved in key *Acanthostega* fossils make it clear that *Acanthostega* could breathe with its gills underwater, just like a fish, and could also breathe on land, using lungs. In other words, it was a true "transitional form." This first amphibian-like tetrapod was, as evolution would have predicted, more fish-like than any tetrapod to follow. As the discoverers of one of the most detailed *Acanthostega* fossils wrote: "Retention of fish-like internal gills by a tetrapod blurs the traditional distinction between tetrapods and fishes."[32]

Pandas implies that fossils such as these have never been discovered. If *Pandas'* goal was to engage students with authentic data, rather than to raise doubts and questions in the minds of its readers, it would surely present and discuss these fossil forms. Instead, it offers students a generalization that such fossils do not exist. Unfortunately, that generalization is wrong.

More recently, in 1997 paleontologists Edward B. Daeschler and Neil Shubin discovered a fossilized fin so well-preserved that its soft parts could be seen outside its underlying bony skeleton. The fin contained eight well-defined, recognizable digits. Incredibly, this fish had a fin with fingers, eight in number, just like the digits of *Acanthostega*. In other words, the limbs of land vertebrates did not appear suddenly (as if designed). They began to appear gradually, in the ancestors of land vertebrates, as if they evolved.[33] This evidence directly contradicts the "design" claim that such key morphological features appear fully-formed and complete.

MORE MISREPRESENTATIONS OF THE FOSSIL RECORD

On page 95 of *Pandas*, figure 4–2 attempts to show the abrupt appearance of most phyla in the Cambrian Period of geological history. Curiously, the diagram is a *schematic*, not a genuine diagram in which the individual phyla would be labeled and identified. Why not show the actual phyla and their names? I believe the reason is very simple. If the phyla were all labeled, the authors would not be able to make the suggestion that they do now, which is that most important groups of organisms alive today can trace their origins to this period, nor would they be able to pretend that all multicellular animal life first appeared in the Cambrian. In fact, if the dominant forms of plant and animal life on land were included in such a diagram (flowering plants and insects, respectively), students would learn that these organisms appeared hundreds of millions of years *after* the time shown in the graph. Furthermore, all of the great unicellular phyla (found in the kingdoms Eubacteria, Archaebacteria, and Protista) precede the Cambrian by hundreds of millions of years. And finally, the animals of the Cambrian were preceded by abundant soft-bodied animals known as Ediacaran fauna, which date at least a hundred million of years back into the Precambrian. Unfortunately, the readers of *Pandas* will never learn these facts because the authors are so intent on pretending that all major groups of organisms originated at just one period of time. And that is simply not true.

PANDAS IGNORES THE ISSUE OF EXTINCTION

Pandas shows a remarkable unwillingness to address the obvious questions raised by its own theories. For example, on page 99 . . . a graph showing a "face value" interpretation of the fossil record is presented. [Graph omitted.]

What question would any inquisitive 9th-grader ask of this graph after being instructed in "intelligent design" theory? Just this: If all organisms are intelligently designed, what are the forces that seem always to intervene and drive these organisms to extinction? Any theory that claims to see intelligence in these designs that have mysteriously appeared in living organisms over millions of years must also explain why these designs seem to fail nearly every time. Evolution, of course, can explain extinction quite easily. In fact, extinction is a major evolutionary mechanism. But *Pandas* avoids this embarrassing problem. Its authors cannot explain extinction, and therefore they short-change their student readers by stepping around the question.

PREDICTIONS MADE IN PANDAS ARE DRAMATICALLY INCORRECT

Pandas' predictions about future discoveries of fossils are wrong. To be sure, the text makes very few statements that could be subjected to scientific testing. However, when it does make a prediction, it fails miserably. Consider this statement from pages 101–102:

> The absence of unambiguous transitional fossils is illustrated by the fossil record of whales. The earliest forms of whales occur in rocks of Eocine age, dated some 50 million years ago, but little is known of their possible ancestors. By and large, Darwinists believe that whales evolved from a land

mammal. The problem is that there are no clear transitional fossils linking land mammals to whales. If whales did have land-dwelling ancestors, it is reasonable to expect to find some transitional fossils. Why? Because the anatomical differences between the two are so great that innumerable in-between stages must have paddled and swam the ancient seas.[34]

Yes, evolution predicts that there should have been transitional forms linking swimming mammals with land mammals. And their absence, *Pandas* argues, is good evidence that evolution is wrong. But in the past 20 years not one, not two, but three true intermediate forms have been discovered. Up until 1986, the oldest known fossil whale had been *Basilosaurus*, dating to about 40 million years before present (a sketch of *Basilosaurus* is shown in *Pandas*). However, fossil-hunters have now found 3 intermediates that link *Basilosaurus* to land-dwelling ancestors. They are:

Pakicetus inachus—52 myr.
Ambulocetus natans—50 myr.
Rodhocetus kasrani—46 myr.

The actual fossil forms were described in a 1994 article in the journal *Science*.[35] A less technical account of these intermediate forms and their importance for understanding cetacean evolution was written by Stephen Jay Gould in *Natural History* magazine.[36]

Pandas can certainly be forgiven for not including research that appeared *after* its publication date. However, in teaching students that such intermediate forms would, indeed, could never be found, *Pandas* compounds its earlier misrepresentations of fossil history with a demonstrably false prediction, a misperception of reality which has no place in authentic scientific education.

PANDAS MISREPRESENTS THE MOLECULAR EVIDENCE FOR EVOLUTION

Pandas' entire chapter 6 (Biochemical Similarities) is based on an incorrect representation of evolutionary theory. I do not know if this misrepresentation was done intentionally or out of simple misunderstanding, but either way, I would argue that the errors in this chapter are reason alone to disqualify the book from use in the science classroom.

Basically, the chapter repeatedly states that evolution predicts that amino acid sequences of key proteins (like cytochrome c) should be arranged in a linear sequence. For example, if one takes the sequences of, say, a worm, a frog, and a human, the frog sequence should be closer to the worm than the human sequence is. That is the claim that *Pandas* makes repeatedly as a "prediction" of evolutionary theory. However it is simply not true that any evolutionary biologist has ever made such a prediction (significantly, *Pandas* does not cite any references for its claims). *Pandas* then examines the data and shows that the frog and human sequences are equally distant from that of the worm. That, it argues, is contrary to the evolutionary prediction.

This is simply not true. The real story is that the fossil record clearly shows that the entire vertebrate group (including frogs and people) split off from the invertebrates (including worms) many hundreds of millions of years ago. Therefore, the protein sequences of every animal in that group should be *equidistant* from any single invertebrate. And that is exactly what the experimental data show, as the authors of *Pandas* ought to know.

The simple fact is that this chapter misrepresents evolutionary predictions on molecular sequences, and thereby covers up the fact that the sequences stand in stunning agreement with evolution. I cannot even imagine a greater misrepresentation of fundamental data to support an incorrect conclusion.

I could go on to document further misrepresentations of scientific fact and theory in *Of Pandas and People*. However, my criticisms of this text are not unique. In fact, the many errors and misleading statements in this text were immediately recognized almost from its first publication by a variety of scientists and educators. Reviews describing the errors and misrepresentations in *Pandas* have appeared in many publications, including *Scientific American*.[37]

Science is an open enterprise, and scientific inquiry thrives precisely because no scientific theory or idea is ever immune from criticism, examination, or testing in the crucibles of experiment and observation. When I first opened the pages of *Pandas* and read the fine words presented by its authors in the name of free and open inquiry, I expected a text that might genuinely challenge students to examine the assumptions of what they had learned and evaluate scientific theory in an objective manner. To say that I was disappointed is to put it mildly. What I found instead was a document that contrived not to teach, but to mislead.

Pandas misstates evolutionary theory, skims over the enormous wealth of the fossil record, and ignores the sophistication of radiometric dating. How sad it would be, given the need to improve the content and rigor of science instruction in this country, for this book to be offered as part of the educational solution. There is a great deal that we do not know about the origin of life on this planet, but that does not mean that science is obliged to pretend that it knows *nothing*, or to engage in a kind of scientific relativism, pretending that all speculations about the origin of our species are equally correct. The most compelling reason to keep this book out of the biology classroom is that it is bad science, pure and simple.

Science education today faces many challenges. Our teachers must deal with an ever-changing landscape of scientific advance and technological innovation that continually changes the ground upon which they educate their students. Biology education, in particular, will be the key for many of our students as they attempt to prepare themselves for the challenges of the next century, and therefore it is especially important that teachers be supported, not hindered, in their attempts to educate students in the life sciences. The many errors and misrepresentations that inhabit the pages in *Of Pandas and People* will, quite honestly, serve to hinder teachers as they attempt to cover the stunning range and diversity of contemporary biology. I believe it is best not to burden science faculty with the needless task of overcoming the many errors and misconceptions written into this book.

NOTES

1. Michael Behe, *Darwin's Black Box* (New York: The Free Press, 1996) and Michael Behe, "The Challenge of Irreducible Complexity," *Natural History* 111 (April 2002): 74.

2. Behe, *Darwin's Black Box.*

3. Ibid., 39.

4. Michael Behe, "Evidence for Intelligent Design from Biochemistry," (speech, Discovery Institute's God and Culture Conference, Seattle, WA, August 10, 1996), http://www.arn.org/docs/behe/mb_idfrombiochemistry.htm.

5. Behe, "The Challenge of Irreducible Complexity," 74.

6. Ibid.

7. See for example, Jerry A. Coyne, "God in the Details," *Nature* 383 (September 19, 1996): 227–28; Kenneth R. Miller, review of *Darwin's Black Box*, by Michael Behe, *Creation/Evolution* 16 (1996): 36–40; David J. Depew, "Intelligent Design and Irreducible Complexity: A Rejoinder," *Rhetoric and Public Affairs* 1

(1998): 571–78; and R. H. Thornhill and D. W. Ussery, "A Classification of Possible Routes of Darwinian Evolution," *Journal of Theoretical Biology* 203 (2000): 111–16.

8. Kenneth R. Miller, *Finding Darwin's God* (New York: HarperCollins, 1999), 147.

9. See T. D. Schneider, "Evolution of Biological Information," *Nucleic Acid Research* 28 (2000): 2794–99 and C. Adami, C. Ofria, and T. C. Collier, "Evolution of Biological Complexity," *Proceedings of the National Academy of Sciences* 97 (2000): 4463–68.

10. C. J. Hueck, "Type III Protein Secretion Systems in Bacterial Pathogens of Animals and Plants," *Microbiology and Molecular Biology Reviews* 62 (1998): 379–433.

11. Ibid., and D. Büttner and U. Bonas, "Port of Entry—The Type III Secretion Translocon," *Trends in Microbiology* 10 (2002): 186–91.

12. Hueck, *Microbiology and Molecular Biology Reviews* 62: 379–433.

13. R. M. McNab, "The Bacterial Flagellum: Reversible Rotary Propellor and Type III Export Apparatus," *Journal of Bacteriology* 181 (1999): 7149–53.

14. S. –I. Aizawa, "Bacterial Flagella and Type III Secretion Systems," *FEMS Microbiology Letters* 202 (2001): 157–64.

15. K. R. Miller, "Design Fails Biochemistry," *Natural History* 111 (April 2002): 75; R. Hanumanthaiah, K. Day, and P. Jagadeeswaran, "Comprehensive Analysis of Blood Coagulation Pathways in Teleostei: Evolution of Coagulation Factor Genes and Identification of Zebrafish Factor VIIi," *Blood Cells, Molecules, and Diseases* 29 (2002): 57–68; C. J. Davidson, E. J. Tuddenham, and J. H. McVey, "450 Million Years of Homeostasis," *Journal of Thrombosis and Haemostasis* 1 (2003): 1487–94; Y. Jiang and R. F. Doolittle, "The Evolution of Vertebrate Blood Coagulation as Viewed from a Comparison of Puffer Fish and Sea Squirt Genomes," *Proceedings of the National Academy of Sciences* 100 (2003): 7527–32; S. M. Lewis and G. E. Wu, "The Old and the Restless," *Journal of Experimental Medicine* 191 (2000): 1631–35; E. Market and F. N. Papavasiliou, "V(D)J Recombination and the Evolution of the Adaptive Immune System," *PloS Biology* 1 (2003) 24–27; L. DuPasquier, I. Zucchetti, and R. DeSantis, "Immunoglobin Superfamily Receptors in Protochordates: Before RAG Time," *Immunological Reviews* 198 (2004): 233–48; L. Zhou, R. Mitra, P. W. Atkinson, A. B. Hickman, F. Dyda, and N. L. Craig, "Transposition of *hAT* Elements Links Transposable Elements and V(D)J Recombination," *Nature* 432 (2004): 995–1001; J. Klein and N. Nikolaidis, "The Descent of the Anti-body Immune System by Gradual Evolution," *Proceedings of the National Academy of Sciences* 102 (2005): 169–74; and M. Nonaka and F. Yoshizaki, "Evolution of the Complement System," *Molecular Immunology* 40 (2004): 897–902.

16. M. Long, E. Betrán, K. Thornton, and W. Wang, "The Origin of New

Genes: Glimpses from the Young and Old," *Nature Reviews Genetics* 4 (2003): 865–75 and M. M. Krem and E. DiCera, "Evolution of Enzyme Cascades from Embryonic Development to Blood Coagulation," *Trends in Biochemical Sciences* 27 (2002): 67–74.

17. William Dembski, *No Free Lunch: Why Specified Complexity Cannot Be Purchased without Intelligence* (Lanham, MD: Rowan & Littlefield, 2002).

18. Ibid., 289.

19. Ibid., 291.

20. R. M. McNab, *Journal of Bacteriology* 181 (1999): 7149–53 and K. S. Yonekura, S. Maki, D. G. Morgan, D. J. DeRosier, F. Vonderviszt, K. Imada, and K. Namba, "The Bacterial Flagellar Cap as the Rotary Promoter of Flagellin Self-Assembly," *Science* 290 (2000): 2148–52.

21. Dembski, *No Free Lunch*, 301.

22. Ibid., 289.

23. Ibid., 123n80.

24. H. A. Orr, "The Return of Intelligent Design," *Boston Review* 27 (Summer 2002); B. Charlesworth, "Evolution by Design," *Nature* 418 (2002): 129; and K. Padian, "Waiting for the Watchmaker," *Science* 295 (2002): 2373–74.

25. C. Adami, C. Ofria, and T. C. Collier, "Evolution of Biological Complexity," *Proceedings of the National Academy of Sciences* 97 (2000): 4463–68.

26. R. E. Lenski, C. Ofria, and C. Adami, "The Evolutionary Origin of Complex Features," *Nature* 423 (2003): 139–44.

27. T. D. Schneider, "Evolution of Biological Information," *Nucleic Acid Research* 28 (2000): 2794–99.

28. C. J. Brown, K. M. Todd, and R. F. Rosenzweig, "Multiple Duplications of Yeast Hexose Transport Genes in Response to Selection in a Glucose-limited Environment," *Molecular Biology and Evolution* 15, no. 8 (1998): 931–42; T. Ohta, "Evolution by Gene Duplication Revisited: Differentiation of Regulatory Elements Versus Proteins," *Genetica* 118, nos. 2–3 (2003): 209–16; M. Lynch and J. S. Conery, "The Evolutionary Fate and Consequences of Duplicate Genes," *Science* 290 (2000): 1151–55; and A. L. Hughes and R. Friedman, "Parallel Evolution by Gene Duplication in the Genomes of Two Unicellular Fungi," *Genome Research* 13, no. 5 (2003): 794–99.

29. R. E. Lenski, "Evolution in Experimental Populations of Bacteria," in *Population Genetics of Bacteria: Fifty-second Symposium of the Society for General Microbiology*, edited by S. Baumberg, et al. (Cambridge: Cambridge University Press, 1995), 193–215; D. Papadopolous, D. Schneider, J. Meier-Eiss, W. Arber, R. E. Lenski, and M. Blot, "Genomic Evolution during a 10,000-Generation Experiment with Bacteria," *Proceedings of the National Academy of Sciences* 96 (1999): 3807–12; M. M. Riehle, A. F. Bennett, and A. D. Long, "Genetic Architecture of

Thermal Adaptation in Escherchia Coli," *Proceedings of the National Academy of Sciences* 98 (2001): 525–30.

30. Percival Davis and Dean H. Kenyon, *Of People and Pandas: The Central Question of Biological Origins* (Richardson, TX: Foundation for Thought and Ethics, 1993).

31. Ibid., 99–100.

32. M. I. Coates and J. A. Clack, "Fish-like Gills and Breathing in the Earliest Known Tetrapod," *Nature* 352 (1991): 234–36.

33. E. B. Daeschler and N. Shubin, "Fish with Fingers?" *Nature* 391 (1997): 133.

34. Davis and Kenyon, *Of Pandas and People*, 101–102.

35. J. G. M. Thewissen, E. M. Williams, L. J. Roe, and S. T. Hussein, "Skeletons of Terrestial Cetaeans and the Relationship to Whales to Artiodactyls," *Nature* 413 (2001): 277–81.

36. Stephen J. Gould, "Hooking Leviathan by Its Past," *Natural History* (April 1994): 12.

AN IDEA THAT PROVOKED, BUT DIDN'T DELIVER

KENNETH R. MILLER

I f there is such a thing as home-field advantage in a courtroom, intelligent design should have carried the day in the Dover evolution trial.

Advocates of ID had the support of the local school board, a case presented by experienced lawyers from the Thomas More Legal Foundation, expert witnesses with scientific credentials, and a conservative judge appointed by President George W. Bush. That judge gave them all the time they wanted to lay out the scientific case for ID. And lay it out they did.

But that was exactly the problem.

In the harsh light of the courtroom, ID shriveled and died. As Judge John E. Jones III noted in his opinion, he was forced to come to "the inescapable conclusion that ID is an interesting theological argument, but that it is not science." After six weeks of watching from the bench as ID's pseudoscientific arguments fell apart, as its advocates admitted they had no positive evidence for "design," and as school board members "testified inconsistently, or lied outright under oath," it was clear that the judge had seen enough.

Kenneth Miller, "An Idea That Provoked, But Didn't Deliver," *Philadelphia Inquirer*, December 25, 2005.

He slammed the Dover school board's "breathtaking inanity," and he enjoined the board from making ID a part of its curriculum at any time in the future. Jones' devastating opinion is written in clear and accessible language and should be required reading for every administrator, school board member, and science educator in the United States.

So, exposed, discredited and defeated, ID is finished as an anti-evolution movement, right? I wouldn't count on it.

As the Dover trial showed, ID is nothing more than old-fashioned creationism, distinguished only by its advocates' willingness to be disingenuous about its origins, motivations and goals. But that does little to detract from its appeal. Advocates of ID, such as Sen. Rick Santorum (R., Pa.), oppose evolution not because of its scientific flaws, but because they see it as a cultural and moral threat.

In an Aug. 4 interview on National Public Radio, Santorum stated that "if we are the result of chance, if we're simply a mistake of nature, then that puts a different moral demand on us. In fact, it doesn't put a moral demand on us—than if in fact we are a creation of a being that has moral demands." In other words, the problem with evolution, in his view, is that it invalidates morality because it does away with God.

Santorum, of course, has recently retracted his support of those involved in the Dover case. But his principled opposition to evolution remains.

That kind of visceral opposition isn't going to respond to scientific evidence, and it certainly isn't going to be affected by a judge's ruling—even from a judge whom the senator himself supported for the bench.

Nationwide, ID is on the march, and Dover notwithstanding, it's winning. The ID movement has rewritten science-education standards in Kansas, gained the support of legislators in more than a dozen states, and regularly pressures teachers, administrators and textbook publishers to weaken the coverage of evolution. Dover represents a substantial victory for science, but the greater war goes on. And, like many wars, this one results from a profound misunderstanding.

The great fiction that powers the ID movement is that evolution is inherently antireligious. By emphasizing the material nature of evolutionary science, ID advocates are convinced that they can force their antiscience ideas into the classroom in the name of balance and fairness. Once there, they are convinced, students in a society as religious as the United States will surely turn their backs on mainstream science, embracing ID and strengthening their faith in God. Any harm in that?

Why, none at all, if we are prepared to abdicate world leadership by raising a generation of young people so mistrustful of science that they turn their backs on the scientific community and abandon science as a way of knowing about the world and improving the human condition.

A deeper understanding of Western religion in general, and the Christian message in particular, would end this war and blunt the attempts of the anti-evolution movement to divide Americans along cultural lines. As conservative columnist Charles Krauthammer wrote last month, "How ridiculous to make evolution the enemy of God. What could be more elegant, more simple, more brilliant, more economical, more creative, indeed more divine than a planet with millions of life forms, distinct and yet interactive, all ultimately derived from accumulated variations in a single double-stranded molecule, pliable and fecund enough to give us mollusks and mice, Newton and Einstein?" What indeed? For just as Darwin said, there is "grandeur in this view of life," and a deeper understanding of the ways in which "endless forms most wonderful and most beautiful have been and are being evolved" can only deepen our faith and enhance our respect for the unity of scientific and spiritual knowledge.

On this Christmas season, I thank the Lord for the wonderful people of Dover who fought for this decision, and I hope the good news of its wisdom will spread throughout the land.

FAITH IN THEORY

Why "Intelligent Design" Simply Isn't Science

JAMES Q. WILSON

W hen a federal judge in Pennsylvania struck down the efforts of a local school board to teach "intelligent design," he rightly criticized the wholly unscientific nature of that enterprise. Some people will disagree with his view, arguing that evolution is a "theory" and intelligent design is a "theory," so students should look at both theories.

But this view confuses the meaning of the word "theory." In science, a theory states a relationship between two or more things (scientists like to call them "variables") that can be tested by factual observations. We have a "theory of gravity" that predicts the speed at which two objects will fall toward one another, the path on which a satellite must travel if it is to maintain a constant distance from the earth, and the position that a moon will keep with respect to its associated planet.

This theory has been tested rigorously, so much so that we can now launch a satellite and know exactly where it must be in space in order to keep

James Q. Wilson, "Faith in Theory: Why 'Intelligent Design' Simply Isn't Science," *Wall Street Journal,* December 26, 2005.

it rotating around the earth. It was not always that way. From classical times to the Middle Ages, many important thinkers thought that the speed with which an object falls toward the earth will depend on its weight. We now know that this view is false. In a vacuum, the two objects will fall at the same speed and, thanks to Newton, we know the formula with which to calculate that speed.

The other meaning of theory is the popular and not the scientific one. People use "theory" when they mean a guess, a faith or an idea. A theory in this sense does not state a testable relationship between two or more things. It is a belief that may be true, but its truth cannot be tested by scientific inquiry. One such theory is that God exists and intervenes in human life in ways that affect the outcome of human life. God may well exist, and He may well help people overcome problems or even (if we believe certain athletes) determine the outcome of a game. But that theory cannot be tested. There is no way anyone has found that we can prove empirically that God exists or that His action has affected some human life. If such a test could be found, the scientist who executed it would overnight become a hero.

Evolution is a theory in the scientific sense. It has been tested repeatedly by examining the remains of now-extinct creatures to see how one species has emerged to replace another. Even today we can see some kinds of evolution at work, as when scholars watch how birds on the Galapagos Islands adapt their beak size from generation to generation to the food supplies they encounter.

The theory of evolution has not been proved as fully as the theory of gravity. There are many gaps in what we know about prehistoric creatures. But all that we have learned is consistent with the view that the creatures we encounter today had ancestors from which they evolved. This view, which is literally the only scientifically defensible theory of the origin of species, does not by any means rule out the idea that God exists.

What existed before the Big Bang created the universe? Is there an afterlife of heaven (or hell) that awaits us after we die? Can a faith in God change our lives because of how God acts toward us? There are religious scientists who believe that God exists and operates on us today and there are scientists who reject the idea of God and his benign interventions.

Isaac Newton was a deeply religious man. No doubt he thought that the Newtonian laws he discovered existed because of God's handiwork. Charles Darwin, though he started his adult life as a deep believer and a student intending to enter the ministry, abandoned any belief that God has created animal species and replaced that view with his extraordinary, and largely correct, theory of evolution.

Proponents of intelligent design respond by saying that there are some things in the natural world that are so complex that they could not have been created by "accident." They often use the mousetrap as a simile. We can have all of the parts of a trap—a board, a spring, a clamp—but it will not be a mousetrap unless someone assembles it. The assembler is the "intelligent designer."

But since mousetraps are not created by nature but are manufactured by people, we must ask them what part of natural life is so irreducibly complex that it could not have evolved? Some have suggested that the human eye is an example. But the eye has been studied for decades in ways strongly suggesting that it has evolved. At first there were light-sensitive plates in prehistoric creatures that enabled them to move toward and away from illumination. For a few animals, these light-sensitive plates were more precise. This was the result of genetic differences: Just as a (very) few people today can see a baseball as well as Ted Williams could, so then some creatures were able not only to detect light but to see shapes or colors in the light.

When those talented creatures lived in a world that rewarded such precision, they reproduced and untalented creatures died out. Maybe the talented ones were better able to find food or avoid being eaten and the untalented ones could not. These first steps were followed, over millions of years, by more adaptations so that genetic accidents that made it possible for some creatures to see very tiny objects or see at great distances had an evolutionary advantage over ones that could not do these things.

But if an intelligent designer had created the human eye, He (or She) made some big mistakes. The eye has a blind spot in the middle that reduces the eye's capacity to see. Other creatures, more dependent on sharp eyesight than are we, do not have this blind spot. Some people are colorblind and others must start wearing glasses when they are small children. All of these variations and shortcomings are consistent with evolution. None is consistent with the view that the eye was designed by an intelligent being.

What schools should do is teach evolution emphasizing both its successes and its still unexplained limitations. Evolution, like almost every scientific theory, has some problems. But they are not the kinds of problems that can be solved by assuming that an intelligent designer (whom ID advocates will tell you privately is God) created life. There is not a shred of evidence to support this theory, one that has been around since the critics of Darwin began writing in the 19th century.

Some people worry that if evolution is a useful (and, so far, correct) theory, we should still see it at work all around us. We don't. But we can see it if we take a long enough time frame. Mankind has been on this earth for about 100,000 years. In that time there have been changes in how people appear, but they have occurred very slowly. After all, 1,000 centuries is just a blink in geological time.

Besides, the modern world has created an environment by means of public health measures, the reduction in crime rates, and improved levels of diet that have sharply reduced the environmental variation that is necessary to reward some genetic mutations and penalize others. But 100,000 years from now, will the environment change so much that people who now have quirky oddities will become the dominant group in society? Maybe.

PART TWO

INTELLIGENT DESIGN IN THE SCHOOLS

Responses to President George W. Bush

DEBATE ON INTELLIGENT DESIGN
BUILDS AFTER BUSH
STATES SUPPORT FOR IDEA

ELISABETH BUMILLER

A sharp debate between scientists and religious conservatives escalated . . . over comments by President Bush that the theory of intelligent design should be taught with evolution in the nation's public schools.

In an interview at the White House . . . with a group of Texas newspaper reporters, Mr. Bush appeared to endorse the push by many of his conservative Christian supporters to give intelligent design equal treatment with the theory of evolution.

Recalling his days as Texas governor, Mr. Bush said in the interview, according to a transcript, "I felt like both sides ought to be properly taught." Asked again by a reporter whether he believed that both sides in the debate between evolution and intelligent design should be taught in the schools, Mr. Bush replied that he did, "so people can understand what the debate is about."

Mr. Bush was pressed as to whether he accepted the view that intelligent design was an alternative to evolution, but he did not directly answer. "I think

Elisabeth Bumiller, "Debate on Intelligent Design Builds after Bush States Support for Idea," *New York Times*, August 3, 2005.

that part of education is to expose people to different schools of thought," he said, adding that "you're asking me whether or not people ought to be exposed to different ideas, and the answer is yes."

On Tuesday, the president's conservative Christian supporters and the leading institute advancing intelligent design embraced Mr. Bush's comments while scientists and advocates of the separation of church and state disparaged them. At the White House, where intelligent design has been discussed in a weekly Bible study group, Mr. Bush's science adviser, John H. Marburger 3rd, sought to play down the president's remarks as common sense and old news.

Mr. Marburger said in a telephone interview that "evolution is the cornerstone of modern biology" and "intelligent design is not a scientific concept." Mr. Marburger also said that Mr. Bush's remarks should be interpreted to mean that the president believes that intelligent design should be discussed as part of the "social context" in science classes.

Intelligent design, advanced by a group of academics and intellectuals and some biblical creationists, disputes the idea that natural selection—the force Charles Darwin suggested drove evolution—fully explains the complexity of life. Instead, intelligent design proponents say that life is so intricate that only a powerful guiding force, or intelligent designer, could have created it.

Intelligent design does not identify the designer, but critics say the theory is a thinly disguised argument for God and the divine creation of the universe. Invigorated by a recent push by conservatives, the theory has been gaining support in school districts in 20 states, with Kansas in the lead.

Mr. Marburger said it would be "over-interpreting" Mr. Bush's remarks to say that the president believed that intelligent design and evolution should be given equal treatment in schools.

But Mr. Bush's conservative supporters said the president had indicated exactly that in his remarks.

"It's what I've been pushing, it's what a lot of us have been pushing," said Richard Land, the president of the ethics and religious liberties commission of the Southern Baptist Convention. Dr. Land, who has close ties to the White House, said that evolution "is too often taught as fact," and that "if you're going to teach the Darwinian theory as evolution, teach it as theory. And then teach another theory that has the most support among scientists."

But critics saw Mr. Bush's comment that "both sides" should be taught as the most troubling aspect of his remarks.

"It sounds like you're being fair, but creationism is a sectarian religious viewpoint, and intelligent design is a sectarian religious viewpoint," said Susan Spath, a spokeswoman for the National Center for Science Education, a group that defends the teaching of evolution in public schools. "It's not fair to privilege one religious viewpoint by calling it the other side of evolution."

Ms. Spath added that intelligent design was viewed as more respectable and sophisticated than biblical creationism, but "if you look at their theological and scientific writings, you see that the movement is fundamentally anti-evolution."

The Rev. Barry W. Lynn, the executive director of Americans United for Separation of Church and State, called the president's comments irresponsible, and said that "when it comes to evolution, there is only one school of scientific thought, and that is evolution occurred and is still occurring." Mr. Lynn added that "when it comes to matters of religion and philosophy, they can be discussed objectively in public schools, but not in biology class."

The Discovery Institute in Seattle, a leader in developing intelligent design, applauded the president's words on Tuesday as a defense of scientists who have been ostracized for advancing the theory.

"We interpret this as the president using his bully pulpit to support freedom of inquiry and free speech about the issue of biological origins," said Stephen Meyer, the director of the institute's Center for Science and Culture. "It's extremely timely and welcome because so many scientists are experiencing recriminations for breaking with Darwinist orthodoxy."

At the White House, intelligent design was the subject of a weekly Bible study class several years ago when Charles W. Colson, the founder and chairman of Prison Fellowship Ministries, spoke to the group. Mr. Colson has also written a book, "The Good Life," in which a chapter on intelligent design features Michael Gerson, an evangelical Christian who is an assistant to the president for policy and strategic planning.

"It's part of the buzz of the city among Christians," Mr. Colson said in a telephone interview on Tuesday about intelligent design. "It wouldn't surprise me that it got to George Bush. He reads, he picks stuff up, he talks to people. And he's pretty serious about his own Christian beliefs."

SHOW ME THE SCIENCE

DANIEL C. DENNETT

P resident Bush, announcing this month that he was in favor of teaching about "intelligent design" in the schools, said, "I think that part of education is to expose people to different schools of thought." A couple of weeks later, Senator Bill Frist of Tennessee, the Republican leader, made the same point. Teaching both intelligent design and evolution "doesn't force any particular theory on anyone," Mr. Frist said. "I think in a pluralistic society that is the fairest way to go about education and training people for the future."

Is "intelligent design" a legitimate school of scientific thought? Is there something to it, or have these people been taken in by one of the most ingenious hoaxes in the history of science? Wouldn't such a hoax be impossible? No. Here's how it has been done.

First, imagine how easy it would be for a determined band of naysayers to shake the world's confidence in quantum physics—how weird it is!—or Einsteinian relativity. In spite of a century of instruction and popularization by physicists, few people ever really get their heads around the concepts

Daniel Dennett, "Show Me the Science," *New York Times*, August 28, 2005.

involved. Most people eventually cobble together a justification for accepting the assurances of the experts: "Well, they pretty much agree with one another, and they claim that it is their understanding of these strange topics that allows them to harness atomic energy, and to make transistors and lasers, which certainly do work."

Fortunately for physicists, there is no powerful motivation for such a band of mischief-makers to form. They don't have to spend much time persuading people that quantum physics and Einsteinian relativity really have been established beyond all reasonable doubt.

With evolution, however, it is different. The fundamental scientific idea of evolution by natural selection is not just mind-boggling; natural selection, by executing God's traditional task of designing and creating all creatures great and small, also seems to deny one of the best reasons we have for believing in God. So there is plenty of motivation for resisting the assurances of the biologists. Nobody is immune to wishful thinking. It takes scientific discipline to protect ourselves from our own credulity, but we've also found ingenious ways to fool ourselves and others. Some of the methods used to exploit these urges are easy to analyze; others take a little more unpacking.

A creationist pamphlet sent to me some years ago had an amusing page in it, purporting to be part of a simple questionnaire:

Test Two

Do you know of any building that didn't have a builder?	[YES] [NO]
Do you know of any painting that didn't have a painter?	[YES] [NO]
Do you know of any car that didn't have a maker?	[YES] [NO]

If you answered YES for any of the above, give details:

Take that, you Darwinians! The presumed embarrassment of the test-taker when faced with this task perfectly expresses the incredulity many people feel when they confront Darwin's great idea. It seems obvious, doesn't it, that there couldn't be any designs without designers, any such creations without a creator.

Well, yes—until you look at what contemporary biology has demonstrated beyond all reasonable doubt: that natural selection—the process in which reproducing entities must compete for finite resources and thereby engage in a tournament of blind trial and error from which improvements automatically emerge—has the power to generate breathtakingly ingenious designs.

Take the development of the eye, which has been one of the favorite challenges of creationists. How on earth, they ask, could that engineering marvel be produced by a series of small, unplanned steps? Only an intelligent designer could have created such a brilliant arrangement of a shape-shifting lens, an aperture-adjusting iris, a light-sensitive image surface of exquisite sensitivity, all housed in a sphere that can shift its aim in a hundredth of a second and send megabytes of information to the visual cortex every second for years on end.

But as we learn more and more about the history of the genes involved, and how they work—all the way back to their predecessor genes in the sightless bacteria from which multicelled animals evolved more than a half-billion years ago—we can begin to tell the story of how photosensitive spots gradually turned into light-sensitive craters that could detect the rough direction from which light came, and then gradually acquired their lenses, improving their information-gathering capacities all the while.

We can't yet say what all the details of this process were, but real eyes representative of all the intermediate stages can be found, dotted around the animal kingdom, and we have detailed computer models to demonstrate that the creative process works just as the theory says.

All it takes is a rare accident that gives one lucky animal a mutation that improves its vision over that of its siblings; if this helps it have more offspring than its rivals, this gives evolution an opportunity to raise the bar and ratchet up the design of the eye by one mindless step. And since these lucky improvements accumulate—this was Darwin's insight—eyes can automatically get better and better and better, without any intelligent designer.

Brilliant as the design of the eye is, it betrays its origin with a tell-tale flaw: the retina is inside out. The nerve fibers that carry the signals from the eye's rods and cones (which sense light and color) lie on top of them, and have to plunge through a large hole in the retina to get to the brain, creating the blind spot. No intelligent designer would put such a clumsy arrangement in a camcorder, and this is just one of hundreds of accidents frozen in evolutionary history that confirm the mindlessness of the historical process.

If you still find Test Two compelling, a sort of cognitive illusion that you can feel even as you discount it, you are like just about everybody else in the world; the idea that natural selection has the power to generate such sophisticated designs is deeply counterintuitive. Francis Crick, one of the discoverers of DNA, once jokingly credited his colleague Leslie Orgel with "Orgel's Second Rule": Evolution is cleverer than you are. Evolutionary biologists are often startled by the power of natural selection to "discover" an "ingenious" solution to a design problem posed in the lab.

This observation lets us address a slightly more sophisticated version of the cognitive illusion presented by Test Two. When evolutionists like Crick marvel at the cleverness of the process of natural selection they are not acknowledging intelligent design. The designs found in nature are nothing short of brilliant, but the process of design that generates them is utterly lacking in intelligence of its own.

Intelligent design advocates, however, exploit the ambiguity between process and product that is built into the word "design." For them, the presence of a finished product (a fully evolved eye, for instance) is evidence of an intelligent design process. But this tempting conclusion is just what evolutionary biology has shown to be mistaken.

Yes, eyes are for seeing, but these and all the other purposes in the natural world can be generated by processes that are themselves without purposes and without intelligence. This is hard to understand, but so is the idea that colored objects in the world are composed of atoms that are not themselves colored, and that heat is not made of tiny hot things.

The focus on intelligent design has, paradoxically, obscured something else: genuine scientific controversies about evolution that abound. In just about every field there are challenges to one established theory or another. The legitimate way to stir up such a storm is to come up with an alternative theory that makes a prediction that is crisply denied by the reigning theory— but that turns out to be true, or that explains something that has been baffling defenders of the status quo, or that unifies two distant theories at the cost of some element of the currently accepted view.

To date, the proponents of intelligent design have not produced anything like that. No experiments with results that challenge any mainstream biological understanding. No observations from the fossil record or genomics or biogeography or comparative anatomy that undermine standard evolutionary thinking.

Instead, the proponents of intelligent design use a ploy that works something like this. First you misuse or misdescribe some scientist's work. Then you get an angry rebuttal. Then, instead of dealing forthrightly with the charges leveled, you cite the rebuttal as evidence that there is a "controversy" to teach.

Note that the trick is content-free. You can use it on any topic. "Smith's work in geology supports my argument that the earth is flat," you say, misrepresenting Smith's work. When Smith responds with a denunciation of your misuse of her work, you respond, saying something like: "See what a controversy we have here? Professor Smith and I are locked in a titanic scientific debate. We should teach the controversy in the classrooms." And here is the delicious part: you can often exploit the very technicality of the issues to your own advantage, counting on most of us to miss the point in all the difficult details.

William Dembski, one of the most vocal supporters of intelligent design, notes that he provoked Thomas Schneider, a biologist, into a response that Dr. Dembski characterizes as "some hair-splitting that could only look ridiculous to outsider observers." What looks to scientists—and is—a knockout objection by Dr. Schneider is portrayed to most everyone else as ridiculous hair-splitting.

In short, no science. Indeed, no intelligent design hypothesis has even been ventured as a rival explanation of any biological phenomenon. This might seem surprising to people who think that intelligent design competes directly with the hypothesis of non-intelligent design by natural selection. But saying, as intelligent design proponents do, "You haven't explained everything yet," is not a competing hypothesis. Evolutionary biology certainly hasn't explained everything that perplexes biologists. But intelligent design hasn't yet tried to explain anything.

To formulate a competing hypothesis, you have to get down in the trenches and offer details that have testable implications. So far, intelligent design proponents have conveniently sidestepped that requirement, claiming that they have no specifics in mind about who or what the intelligent designer might be.

To see this shortcoming in relief, consider an imaginary hypothesis of intelligent design that could explain the emergence of human beings on this planet:

About six million years ago, intelligent genetic engineers from another galaxy visited Earth and decided that it would be a more interesting planet if there was a language-using, religion-forming species on it, so they sequestered some primates and genetically re-engineered them to give them the language instinct, and enlarged frontal lobes for planning and reflection. It worked.

If some version of this hypothesis were true, it could explain how and why human beings differ from their nearest relatives, and it would discon-firm the competing evolutionary hypotheses that are being pursued.

We'd still have the problem of how these intelligent genetic engineers came to exist on their home planet, but we can safely ignore that complica-tion for the time being, since there is not the slightest shred of evidence in favor of this hypothesis.

But here is something the intelligent design community is reluctant to discuss: no other intelligent-design hypothesis has anything more going for it. In fact, my farfetched hypothesis has the advantage of being testable in principle: We could compare the human and chimpanzee genomes, looking for unmistakable signs of tampering by these genetic engineers from another galaxy. Finding some sort of user's manual neatly embedded in the appar-ently functionless "junk DNA" that makes up most of the human genome would be a Nobel Prize–winning coup for the intelligent design gang, but if they are looking at all, they haven't come up with anything to report.

It's worth pointing out that there are plenty of substantive scientific con-troversies in biology that are not yet in the textbooks or the classrooms. The scientific participants in these arguments vie for acceptance among the rele-vant expert communities in peer-reviewed journals, and the writers and edi-tors of textbooks grapple with judgments about which findings have risen to the level of acceptance—not yet truth—to make them worth serious consid-eration by undergraduates and high school students.

So get in line, intelligent designers. Get in line behind the hypothesis that life started on Mars and was blown here by a cosmic impact. Get in line behind the aquatic ape hypothesis, the gestural origin of language hypothesis and the theory that singing came before language, to mention just a few of the enticing hypotheses that are actively defended but still insufficiently sup-ported by hard facts.

The Discovery Institute, the conservative organization that has helped to put intelligent design on the map, complains that its members face hostility from the established scientific journals. But establishment hostility is not the real hurdle to intelligent design. If intelligent design were a scientific idea whose time had come, young scientists would be dashing around their labs, vying to win the Nobel Prizes that surely are in store for anybody who can overturn any significant proposition of contemporary evolutionary biology.

Remember cold fusion? The establishment was incredibly hostile to that hypothesis, but scientists around the world rushed to their labs in the effort to explore the idea, in hopes of sharing in the glory if it turned out to be true.

Instead of spending more than $1 million a year on publishing books and articles for non-scientists and on other public relations efforts, the Discovery Institute should finance its own peer-reviewed electronic journal. This way, the organization could live up to its self-professed image: the doughty defenders of brave iconoclasts bucking the establishment.

For now, though, the theory they are promoting is exactly what George Gilder, a long-time affiliate of the Discovery Institute, has said it is: "Intelligent design itself does not have any content."

Since there is no content, there is no "controversy" to teach about in biology class. But here is a good topic for a high school course on current events and politics: Is intelligent design a hoax? And if so, how was it perpetrated?

PART THREE

ORIGINS OF THE DEBATE

SELECTIONS FROM *THE DESCENT OF MAN*

CHARLES DARWIN

INTRODUCTION

The nature of the following work will be best understood by a brief account of how it came to be written. During many years I collected notes on the origin or descent of man, without any intention of publishing on the subject, but rather with the determination not to publish, as I thought that I should thus only add to the prejudices against my views. It seemed to me sufficient to indicate, in the first edition of my *Origin of Species*, that by this work "light would be thrown on the origin of man and his history"; and this implies that man must be included with other organic beings in any general conclusion respecting his manner of appearance on this earth.

Now the case wears a wholly different aspect. . . . It is manifest that at least a large number of naturalists must admit that species are the modified descendants of other species; and this especially holds good with the younger and rising naturalists. The greater number accept the agency of nat-

Charles Darwin, *The Descent of Man* (selections).

ural selection; though some urge, whether with justice the future must decide, that I have greatly overrated its importance. Of the older and honored chiefs in natural science, many unfortunately are still opposed to evolution in every form. In consequence of the views now adopted by most naturalists, and which will ultimately, as in every other case, be followed by others who are not scientific, I have been led to put together my notes, so as to see how far the general conclusions arrived at in my former works were applicable to man. This seemed all the more desirable, as I had never deliberately applied these views to a species taken singly. When we confine our attention to any one form, we are deprived of the weighty arguments derived from the nature of the affinities which connect together whole groups of organisms—their geographical distribution in past and present times, and their geological succession. The homological structure, embryological development, and rudimentary organs of a species remain to be considered, whether it be man or any other animal, to which our attention may be directed; but these great classes of facts afford, as it appears to me, ample and conclusive evidence in favor of the principle of gradual evolution.

The strong support derived from the other arguments should, however, always be kept before the mind. The sole object of this work is to consider, firstly, whether man, like every other species, is descended from some pre-existing form; secondly, the manner of his development; and thirdly, the value of the differences between the so-called races of man. As I shall confine myself to these points, it will not be necessary to describe in detail the differences between the several races—an enormous subject which has been fully discussed in many valuable works. . . . Nor shall I have occasion to do more than to allude to the amount of difference between man and the anthropomorphous apes; for Prof. Huxley, in the opinion of most competent judges, has conclusively shown that in every visible character man differs less from the higher apes, than these do from the lower members of the same order of primates. This work contains hardly any original facts in regard to man; but as the conclusions at which I arrived, after drawing up a rough draft, appeared to me interesting, I thought that they might interest others. . . . The conclusion that man is the co-descendant with other species of some ancient, lower, and extinct form, is not in any degree new. Lamarck long ago came to this conclusion, which has lately been maintained by several eminent naturalists and philosophers. . . .

CHAPTER XXI. GENERAL SUMMARY AND CONCLUSION.

A brief summary will be sufficient to recall to the reader's mind the more salient points in this work. Many of the views which have been advanced are highly speculative, and some no doubt will prove erroneous; but I have in every case given the reasons which have led me to one view rather than to another. It seemed worth while to try how far the principle of evolution would throw light on some of the more complex problems in the natural history of man. False facts are highly injurious to the progress of science, for they often endure long; but false views, if supported by some evidence, do little harm, for every one takes a salutary pleasure in proving their falseness: and when this is done, one path towards error is closed and the road to truth is often at the same time opened.

The main conclusion here arrived at, and now held by many naturalists who are well competent to form a sound judgment is that man is descended from some less highly organized form. The grounds upon which this conclusion rests will never be shaken, for the close similarity between man and the lower animals in embryonic development, as well as in innumerable points of structure and constitution, both of high and of the most trifling importance—the rudiments which he retains, and the abnormal reversions to which he is occasionally liable—are facts which cannot be disputed. They have long been known, but until recently they told us nothing with respect to the origin of man. Now when viewed by the light of our knowledge of the whole organic world, their meaning is unmistakable. The great principle of evolution stands up clear and firm, when these groups or facts are considered in connection with others, such as the mutual affinities of the members of the same group, their geographical distribution in past and present times, and their geological succession. It is incredible that all these facts should speak falsely. He who is not content to look, like a savage, at the phenomena of nature as disconnected, cannot any longer believe that man is the work of a separate act of creation. He will be forced to admit that the close resemblance of the embryo of man to that, for instance, of a dog—the construction of his skull, limbs and whole frame on the same plan with that of other mammals, independently of the uses to which the parts may be put—the occasional re-appearance of various structures, for instance of several muscles, which man does not normally possess, but which are common to the Quadrumana [primates other than humans]—and a crowd of analogous facts—all point in the plainest manner to the conclusion that man is the co-descendant with other mammals of a common progenitor.

We have seen that man incessantly presents individual differences in all parts of his body and in his mental faculties. These differences or variations seem to be induced by the same general causes, and to obey the same laws as with the lower animals. In both cases similar laws of inheritance prevail. Man tends to increase at a greater rate than his means of subsistence; consequently he is occasionally subjected to a severe struggle for existence, and natural selection will have effected whatever lies within its scope. . . .

It must not be supposed that the divergence of each race from the other races, and of all from a common stock, can be traced back to any one pair of progenitors. On the contrary, at every stage in the process of modification, all the individuals which were in any way better fitted for their conditions of life, though in different degrees, would have survived in greater numbers than the less well-fitted. The process would have been like that followed by man, when he does not intentionally select particular individuals, but breeds from all the superior individuals, and neglects the inferior. He thus slowly but surely modifies his stock, and unconsciously forms a new strain. . . .

By considering the embryological structure of man,—the homologies which he presents with the lower animals,—the rudiments which he retains,—and the reversions to which he is liable, we can partly recall in imagination the former condition of our early progenitors; and can approximately place them in their proper place in the zoological series. We thus learn that man is descended from a hairy, tailed quadruped, probably arboreal in its habits, and an inhabitant of the Old World. This creature, if its whole structure had been examined by a naturalist, would have been classed amongst the Quadrumana, as surely as the still more ancient progenitor of the Old and New World monkeys. The Quadrumana and all the higher mammals are probably derived from an ancient marsupial animal [lower mammal], and this through a long series of diversified forms, from some amphibian-like creature, and this again from some fish-like animal. In the dim obscurity of the past we can see that the early progenitor of all the Vertebrata must have been an aquatic animal provided with branchiae, with the two sexes united in the same individual, and with the most important organs of the body (such as the brain and heart) imperfectly or not at all developed. This animal seems to have been more like the larvae of the existing marine ascidians than any other known form.

The high standard of our intellectual powers and moral disposition is the greatest difficulty which presents itself, after we have been driven to this conclusion on the origin of man. But every one who admits the principle of evolution must see that the mental powers of the higher animals, which are the same in kind with those of man, though so different in degree, are capable of advancement. Thus the interval between the mental powers of one of the higher apes and of a fish, or between those of an ant and scale-insect, is immense; yet their development does not offer any special difficulty; for with our domesticated animals, the mental faculties are certainly variable, and the variations are inherited. No one doubts that they are of the utmost importance to animals in a state of nature. Therefore the conditions are favorable for their development through natural selection.

The same conclusion may be extended to man; the intellect must have been all-important to him, even at a very remote period, as enabling him to invent and use language, to make weapons, tools, traps, &c., whereby with the aid of his social habits, he long ago became the most dominant of all living creatures. A great stride in the development of the intellect will have followed, as soon as the half-art and half-instinct of language came into use; for the continued use of language will have reacted on the brain and produced an inherited effect; and this again will have reacted on the improvement of language. As Mr. Chauncey Wright[1] has well remarked, the largeness of the brain in man relatively to his body, compared with the lower animals, may be attributed in chief part to the early use of some simple form of language—that wonderful engine which affixes signs to all sorts of objects and qualities, and excites trains of thought which would never arise from the mere impression of the senses, or if they did arise could not be followed out. The higher intellectual powers of man, such as those of ratiocination, abstraction, self-consciousness, &c., probably follow from the continued improvement and exercise of the other mental faculties.

The development of the moral qualities is a more interesting problem. The foundation lies in the social instincts, including under this term the family ties. These instincts are highly complex, and in the case of the lower animals give special tendencies towards certain definite actions; but the more important elements are love, and the distinct emotion of sympathy. Animals endowed with the social instincts take pleasure in one another's company, warn one another of danger, defend and aid one another in many ways. These instincts do not extend to all the individuals of the species, but only to those of the same community. As they are highly beneficial to the species, they have in all probability been acquired through natural selection.

A moral being is one who is capable of reflecting on his past actions and their motives—of approving of some and disapproving of others; and the fact that man is the one being who certainly deserves this designation, is the greatest of all distinctions between him and the lower animals. But in the fourth chapter I have endeavored to show that the moral sense follows, firstly, from the enduring and ever-present nature of the social instincts; secondly, from man's appreciation of the approbation and disapprobation of his fellows; and thirdly, from the high activity of his mental faculties, with past impressions extremely vivid; and in these latter respects he differs from the lower animals. Owing to this condition of mind, man cannot avoid looking both backwards and forwards, and comparing past impressions. Hence after some temporary desire or passion has mastered his social instincts, he reflects and compares the now weakened impression of such past impulses with the ever-present social instincts; and he then feels that sense of dissatisfaction which all unsatisfied instincts leave behind them, he therefore resolves to act differently for the future,—and this is conscience. Any instinct, permanently stronger or more enduring than another, gives rise to a feeling which we express by saying that it ought to be obeyed. A pointer dog, if able to reflect on his past conduct, would say to himself, I ought (as indeed we say of him) to have pointed at that hare and not have yielded to the passing temptation of hunting it.

Social animals are impelled partly by a wish to aid the members of their community in a general manner, but more commonly to perform certain definite actions. Man is impelled by the same general wish to aid his fellows; but has few or no special instincts. He differs also from the lower animals in the power of expressing his desires by words, which thus become a guide to the aid required and bestowed. The motive to give aid is likewise much modified in man: it no longer consists solely of a blind instinctive impulse, but is much influenced by the praise or blame of his fellows. The appreciation and the bestowal of praise and blame both rest on sympathy; and this emotion, as we have seen, is one of the most important elements of the social instincts. Sympathy, though gained as an instinct, is also much strengthened by exercise or habit. As all men desire their own happiness, praise or blame is bestowed on actions and motives, according as they lead to this end; and as happiness is an essential part of the general good, the greatest-happiness principle indirectly serves as a nearly safe standard of right and wrong. As the reasoning powers advance and experience is gained, the remoter effects of certain lines of conduct on the character of the individual, and on the general good, are perceived; and then the self-regarding virtues come within the scope of public opinion, and receive praise, and their opposites blame. But with the less civilized nations reason often errs, and many bad customs and base superstitions come within the same scope, and are then esteemed as high virtues, and their breach as heavy crimes.

The moral faculties are generally and justly esteemed as of higher value than the intellectual powers. But we should bear in mind that the activity of the mind in vividly recalling past impressions is one of the fundamental though secondary bases of conscience. This affords the strongest argument for educating and stimulating in all possible ways the intellectual faculties of every human being. No doubt a man with a torpid mind, if his social affections and sympathies are well developed, will be led to good actions, and may have a fairly sensitive conscience. But whatever renders the imagination more vivid and strengthens the habit of recalling and comparing past impressions, will make the conscience more sensitive, and may even somewhat compensate for weak social affections and sympathies.

The moral nature of man has reached its present standard, partly through the advancement of his reasoning powers and consequently of a just public opinion, but especially from his sympathies having been rendered more tender and widely diffused through the effects of habit, example, instruction, and reflection. It is not improbable that after long practice virtuous tendencies may be inherited. With the more civilized races, the conviction of the existence of an all-seeing Deity has had a potent influence on the advance of morality. Ultimately man does not accept the praise or blame of his fellows as his sole guide, though few escape this influence, but his habitual convictions, controlled by reason, afford him the safest rule. His conscience then becomes the supreme judge and monitor. Nevertheless the first foundation or origin of the moral sense lies in the social instincts, including sympathy; and these instincts no doubt were primarily gained, as in the case of the lower animals, through natural selection.

The belief in God has often been advanced as not only the greatest, but the most complete of all the distinctions between man and the lower animals. It is however impossible, as we have seen, to maintain that this belief is innate or instinctive in man. On the other hand a belief in all-pervading spiritual agencies seems to be universal; and apparently follows from a considerable advance in man's reason, and from a still greater advance in his faculties of imagination, curiosity and wonder. I am aware that the assumed instinctive belief in God has been used by many persons as an argument for His existence. But this is a rash argument, as we should thus be compelled to believe in the existence of many cruel and malignant spirits, only a little more powerful than man; for the belief in them is far more general than in a beneficent Deity. The idea of a universal and beneficent Creator does not seem to arise in the mind of man, until he has been elevated by long-continued culture. He who believes in the advancement of man from some low organized form, will naturally ask how does this bear on the belief in the immortality of the soul. The barbarous races of man . . . possess no clear belief of this kind; but arguments derived from the primeval beliefs of savages are, as we have just seen, of little or no avail. Few persons feel any anxiety from the impossibility of determining at what precise period in the development of the individual, from the first trace of a minute germinal vesicle, man becomes an immortal being; and there is no greater cause for anxiety because the period cannot possibly be determined in the gradually ascending organic scale. . . .

I am aware that the conclusions arrived at in this work will be denounced by some as highly irreligious; but he who denounces them is bound to show why it is more irreligious to explain the origin of man as a distinct species by descent from some lower form, through the laws of variation and natural selection, than to explain the birth of the individual through the laws of ordinary reproduction. The birth both of the species and of the individual are equally parts of that grand sequence of events, which our minds refuse to accept as the result of blind chance. The understanding revolts at such a conclusion, whether or not we are able to believe that every slight variation of structure,—the union of each pair in marriage, the dissemination of each seed,—and other such events, have all been ordained for some special purpose. . . .

Man scans with scrupulous care the character and pedigree of his horses, cattle, and dogs before he matches them; but when he comes to his own marriage he rarely, or never, takes any such care. He is impelled by nearly the same motives as the lower animals, when they are left to their own free choice, though he is in so far superior to them that he highly values mental charms and virtues. On the other hand he is strongly attracted by mere wealth or rank. Yet he might by selection do something not only for the bodily constitution and frame of his offspring, but for their intellectual and moral qualities. Both sexes ought to refrain from marriage if they are in any marked degree inferior in body or mind; but such hopes are Utopian and will never be even partially realized until the laws of inheritance are thoroughly known. Everyone does good service, who aids towards this end. When the principles of breeding and inheritance are better understood, we shall not hear ignorant members of our legislature rejecting with scorn a plan for ascertaining whether or not consanguineous marriages are injurious to man.

The advancement of the welfare of mankind is a most intricate problem: all ought to refrain from marriage who cannot avoid abject poverty for their children; for poverty is not only a great evil, but tends to its own increase by leading to recklessness in marriage. On the other hand, as Mr. Galton has remarked, if the prudent avoid marriage, whilst the reckless marry, the inferior members tend to supplant the better members of society. Man, like every other animal, has no doubt advanced to his present high condition through a struggle for existence consequent on his rapid multiplication; and if he is to advance still higher, it is to be feared that he must remain subject to a severe struggle. Otherwise he would sink into indolence, and the more gifted men would not be more successful in the battle of life than the less gifted. Hence our natural rate of increase, though leading to many and obvious evils, must not be greatly diminished by any means. There should be open competition for all men; and the most able should not be prevented by laws or customs from succeeding best and rearing the largest number of offspring. Important as the struggle for existence has been and even still is, yet as far as the highest part of man's nature is concerned there are other agencies more important. For the moral qualities are advanced, either directly or indirectly, much more through the effects of habit, the reasoning powers, instruction, religion, &c., than through natural selection; though to this latter agency may be safely attributed the social instincts, which afforded the basis for the development of the moral sense.

The main conclusion arrived at in this work, namely, that man is descended from some lowly organized form, will, I regret to think, be highly distasteful to many. But there can hardly be a doubt that we are descended from barbarians. The astonishment which I felt on first seeing a party of Fuegians on a wild and broken shore will never be forgotten by me, for the reflection at once rushed into my mind—such were our ancestors. These men were absolutely naked and bedaubed with paint, their long hair was tangled, their mouths frothed with excitement, and their expression was wild, startled, and distrustful. They possessed hardly any arts, and like wild animals lived on what they could catch; they had no government, and were merciless to every one not of their own small tribe. He who has seen a savage in his native land will not feel much shame, if forced to acknowledge that the blood of some more humble creature flows in his veins. For my own part I would as soon be descended from that heroic little monkey, who braved his dreaded enemy in order to save the life of his keeper, or from that old baboon, who descending from the mountains, carried away in triumph his young comrade from a crowd of astonished dogs—as from a savage who delights to torture his enemies, offers up bloody sacrifices, practices infanticide without remorse, treats his wives like slaves, knows no decency, and is haunted by the grossest superstitions.

Man may be excused for feeling some pride at having risen, though not through his own exertions, to the very summit of the organic scale; and the fact of his having thus risen, instead of having been aboriginally placed there, may give him hope for a still higher destiny in the distant future. But we are not here concerned with hopes or fears, only with the truth as far as our reason permits us to discover it; and I have given the evidence to the best of my ability. We must, however, acknowledge, as it seems to me, that man with all his noble qualities, with sympathy which feels for the most debased, with benevolence which extends not only to other men but to the humblest living creature, with his god-like intellect which has penetrated into the movements and constitution of the solar system—with all these exalted powers—Man still bears in his bodily frame the indelible stamp of his lowly origin.

NOTE

1. Chauncey Wright, "On the Limits of Natural Selection," *North American Review* (October 1870): 295.

SELECTIONS FROM *NATURAL THEOLOGY*

WILLIAM PALEY

CHAPTER ONE: STATE OF THE ARGUMENT

In crossing a heath, suppose I pitched my foot against a stone and were asked how the stone came to be there, I might possibly answer that for anything I knew to the contrary it had lain there forever; nor would it, perhaps, be very easy to show the absurdity of this answer. But suppose I had found a watch upon the ground, and it should be inquired how the watch happened to be in that place, I should hardly think of the answer which I had before given, that for anything I knew the watch might have always been there. Yet why should not this answer serve for the watch as well as for the stone; why is it not as admissible in the second case as in the first? For this reason, and for no other, namely, that when we come to inspect the watch, we perceive—what we could not discover in the stone—that its several parts are framed and put together for a purpose, e.g., that they are so formed and adjusted as to produce motion, and that motion so regulated as to point out the hour of the day; that

William Paley, *Natural Theology* (selections).

if the different parts had been differently shaped from what they are, or placed after any other manner or in any other order than that in which they are placed, either no motion at all would have been carried on in the machine, or none which would have answered the use that is now served by it. To reckon up a few of the plainest of these parts and of their offices, all tending to one result: we see a cylindrical box containing a coiled elastic spring, which, by its endeavor to relax itself, turns round the box. We next observe a flexible chain—artificially wrought for the sake of flexure—communicating the action of the spring from the box to the fusee. We then find a series of wheels, the teeth of which catch in and apply to each other, conducting the motion from the fusee to the balance and from the balance to the pointer, and at the same time, by the size and shape of those wheels, so regulating that motion as to terminate in causing an index, by an equable and measured progression, to pass over a given space in a given time. We take notice that the wheels are made of brass, in order to keep them from rust; the springs of steel, no other metal being so elastic; that over the face of the watch there is placed a glass, a material employed in no other part of the work, but in the room of which, if there had been any other than a transparent substance, the hour could not be seen without opening the case. This mechanism being observed—it requires indeed an examination of the instrument, and perhaps some previous knowledge of the subject, to perceive and understand it; but being once, as we have said, observed and understood—the inference we think is inevitable, that the watch must have had a maker—that there must have existed, at some time and at some place or other, an artificer or artificers who formed it for the purpose which we find it actually to answer, who completely comprehended its construction and designed its use.

I. Nor would it, I apprehend, weaken that conclusion, that we had never seen a watch made—that we had never known an artist capable of making one—that we were altogether incapable of executing such a piece of workmanship ourselves, or of understanding in what manner it was performed. . . .

II. Neither, secondly, would it invalidate our conclusion, that the watch sometimes went wrong or that it seldom went exactly right. . . .

III. Nor, thirdly, would it bring any uncertainty into the argument, if there were a few parts of the watch, concerning which we could not discover or had not yet discovered in what manner they conduced to the general affect; or even some parts, concerning which we could not ascertain whether they conduced to that effect in any manner whatever. . . .

IV. Nor, fourthly, would any man in his senses think the existence of the watch with its various machinery accounted for, by being told that it was one out of possible combinations of material forms; that whatever he had found in the place where he found the watch, must have contained some internal configuration or other; and that this configuration might be the structure now exhibited, namely, of the works of a watch, as well as a different structure.

V. Nor, fifthly, would it yield his inquiry more satisfaction, to be answered that there exists in things a principle of order, which had disposed the parts of the watch into their present form and situation. He never knew a watch made by the principle of order; nor can he even form to himself an idea of what is meant by a principle of order distinct from the intelligence of the watchmaker.

VI. Sixthly, he would be surprised to hear that the mechanism of the watch was no proof of contrivance, only a motive to induce the mind to think so.

VII. And not less surprised to be informed that the watch in his hand was nothing more that the result of the laws of metallic nature. It is a perversion of language to assign any law as the efficient, operative cause of any thing. A law presupposes an agent, for it is only the mode according to which an agent proceeds: it implies a power, for it is the order according to which that power acts. Without this agent, without this power, which are both distinct from itself, the law does nothing, is nothing. . . .

VIII. Neither, lastly, would our observer be driven out of his conclusion or from his confidence in its truth by being told that he knew nothing at all about the matter. He knows enough for his argument; he knows the utility of the end; he knows the subserviency and adaptation of the means to the end. These points being known, his ignorance of other points, his doubts concerning other points affect not the certainty of his reasoning. The consciousness of knowing little need not beget a distrust of that which he does know.

CHAPTER TWO: STATE OF THE ARGUMENT CONTINUED

Suppose, in the next place, that the person who found the watch should after some time discover that, in addition to all the properties which he had hitherto observed in it, it possessed the unexpected property of producing in the course of its movement another watch like itself—the thing is conceivable; that it contained within it a mechanism, a system of parts—a mold, for instance, or a complex adjustment of lathes, files, and other tools—evidently and separately calculated for this purpose; let us inquire what effect ought such a discovery to have upon his former conclusion.

I. The first effect would be to increase his admiration of the contrivance, and his conviction of the consummate skill of the contriver. . . .

II. He would reflect that, though the watch before him were in some sense the maker of the watch which was fabricated in the course of its movements, yet it was in a very different sense from that in which a carpenter, for instance, is the maker of a chair—the author of its contrivance, the cause of the relation of its parts to their use. With respect to these, the first watch was no cause at all to the second; in no such sense as this was it the author of the constitution and order, either of the parts which the new watch contained, or of the parts by the aid and instrumentality of which it was produced. . . . Therefore,

III. Though it be now no longer probable that the individual watch which our observer had found was made immediately by the hand of an artificer, yet this alteration does not in anywise affect the inference that an artificer had been originally employed and concerned in the production. The argument from design remains as it was. Marks of design and contrivance are no more accounted for now than they were before. . . .

IV. Nor is anything gained by running the difficulty farther back, that is, by supposing the watch before us to have been produced from another watch, that from a former, and so on indefinitely. Our going back ever so far brings us no nearer to the least degree of satisfaction upon the subject. Contrivance is still unaccounted for. We still want a contriver. . . . The machine which we are inspecting demonstrates, by its construction, contrivance and design. Contrivance must have had a contriver, design a designer, whether the machine immediately proceeded from another machine or not. . . .

V. Our observer would further also reflect that the maker of the watch before him was in truth and reality the maker of every watch produced from it: there being no difference, except that the latter manifests a more exquisite skill, between the making of another watch with his own hands, by the mediation of files, lathes, chisels, etc., and the disposing, fixing, and inserting of these instruments, or of others equivalent to them, in the body of the watch in the course of the movements which he had given to the old one. It is only working by one set of tools instead of another. The conclusion which the first examination of the watch, of its works, construction, and movement, suggested, was that it must have had, for cause and author of that construction, an artificer who understood its mechanism and designed its use. This conclusion is invincible. A second examination presents us with a new discovery. The watch is found, in the course of its movement, to produce another watch similar to itself; and not only so, but we perceive in it a system or organization separately calculated for that purpose. What effect would this discovery have or ought it to have upon our former inference? What, as has already been said, but to increase beyond measure our admiration of the skill which had been employed in the formation of such a machine? Or shall it, instead of this, all at once turn us round to an opposite conclusion, namely, that no art or skill whatever has been concerned in the business, although all other evidences of art and skill remain as they were, and this last and supreme piece of art be now added to the rest? Can this be maintained without absurdity? Yet this is atheism.

CHAPTER TWENTY-SEVEN: CONCLUSION

In all cases wherein the mind feels itself in danger of being confounded by variety, it is sure to rest upon a few strong points, or perhaps upon a single instance. Among a multitude of proofs it is one that does the business. If we observe in any argument that hardly two minds fix upon the same instance, the diversity of choice shows the strength of the argument because it shows the number and competition of the examples. There is no subject in which the tendency to dwell upon select or single topics is so usual because there is no subject of which, in its full extent, the latitude is so great as that of natural history applied to the proof of an intelligent Creator. For my part, I take my stand in human anatomy; and the examples of mechanism I should be apt to draw out from the copious catalogue which it supplies are the pivot upon which the head turns, the ligaments within the socket of the hip-joint, the pulley or trochlear muscles of the eye, the epiglottis, the bandages which tie down the tendons of the wrist and instep, the slit or perforated muscles at the hands and feet, the knitting of the intestines to the mesentery, the course of the chyle into the blood, and the constitution of the sexes as extended throughout the whole of animal creation. To these instances the reader's memory will go back, as they are severally set forth in their places: there is not one of the number which I do not think decisive—not one which is not strictly mechanical; nor have I read or heard of any solution of these appearances, which in the smallest degree shakes the conclusion that we build upon them.

But of the greatest part of those who, either in this book or any other, read arguments to prove the existence of a God, it will be said that they leave off only where they began; that they were never ignorant of this great truth, never doubted of it; that it does not therefore appear what is gained by researches from which no new opinion is learned, and upon the subject of which no proofs were wanted. Now, I answer that by investigation the following points are always gained in favor of doctrines even the most generally acknowledged, supposing them to be true, namely, stability, and impression. Occasions will arise to try the firmness of our most habitual opinions. And upon these occasions it is a matter of incalculable use to feel our foundation, to find a support in argument for what we had taken up upon authority. In the present case the arguments upon which the conclusion rests are exactly such as a truth of universal concern ought to rest upon. "They are sufficiently open to the views and capacities of the unlearned, at the same time that they acquire new strength and luster from the discoveries of the learned." If they had been altogether abstruse and recondite, they would not have found their way to the understandings of the mass of mankind; if they had been merely popular, they might have wanted solidity.

But, secondly, what is gained by research in the stability of our conclusion is also gained from it in impression. Physicians tell us that there is a great deal of difference between taking a medicine and the medicine getting into the constitution; a difference not unlike which, obtains with respect to those great moral propositions which ought to form the directing principles of human conduct. It is one thing to assent to a proposition of this sort; another, and a very different thing, to have properly imbibed its influence. I take the case to be this: perhaps almost every man living has a particular train of thought, into which his mind glides and falls, when at leisure from the impressions and ideas that occasionally excite it; perhaps, also, the train of thought here spoken of, more than any other thing, determines the character. It is of the utmost consequence, therefore, that this property of our constitution be well regulated. Now it is by frequent or continued meditation upon a subject, by placing a subject in different points of view, by induction of particulars, by variety of examples, by applying principles to the solution of phenomena, by dwelling upon proofs and consequences, that mental exercise is drawn into any particular channel. It is by these means, at least, that we have any power over it. The train of spontaneous thought, and the choice of that train, may be directed to different ends, and may appear to be more or less judiciously fixed, according to the purpose in respect of which we consider it; but, in a moral view, I shall not, I believe, be contradicted when I say that, if one train of thinking be more desirable than another, it is that which regards the phenomena of nature with a constant reference to a supreme intelligent Author. To have made this the ruling, the habitual sentiment of our minds, is to have laid the foundation of everything which is religious. The world thenceforth becomes a temple, and life itself one continued act of adoration. The change is no less than this: that whereas formerly God was seldom in our thoughts, we can now scarcely look upon anything without perceiving its relation to Him. Every organized natural body, in the provisions which it contains for its sustentation and propagation, testifies a care, on the part of the Creator, expressly directed to these purposes: We are on all sides surrounded by such bodies: examined in their parts, wonderfully diversified. So that the mind, as well as the eye, may either expatiate in variety and multitude or fix itself down to the investigation of particular divisions of the science. And in either case it will rise up from its occupation, possessed by the subject in a very different manner, and with a very different degree of influence, from what a mere assent to any verbal proposition which can be formed concerning the existence of the Deity—at least that merely complying assent with which those about us are satisfied, and with which we are too apt to satisfy ourselves—will or can produce upon the thoughts. More especially may this difference be perceived in the degree of admiration and of awe with which the Divinity is regarded, when represented to the understanding by its own remarks, its own reflections, and its own reasonings, compared with what is excited by any language that can be used by others. The works of nature want only to be contemplated. When contemplated, they have everything in them which can astonish by their greatness; for, of the vast scale of operation through which our discoveries carry us, at one end we see an intelligent Power arranging planetary systems, fixing, for instance, the trajectory of Saturn, or constructing a ring of two hundred thousand miles diameter, to surround His body, and be suspended like a magnificent arch over the heads of His inhabitants; and at the other, bending a hooked tooth, concerting and providing an appropriate mechanism for the clasping and reclasping of the filaments of the feather of the hummingbird. We have proof not only of both these works proceeding from an intelligent agent but of their proceeding from the same agent: for, in the first place, we can trace an identity of the plan, a connection of system, from Saturn to our own globe; and when arrived upon our globe, we can, in the second place pursue the connection though all the organized, especially the animated bodies which it supports. We can observe marks of a common relation, as well to one another as to the elements of which their habitation is composed. Therefore, one mind has planned or at least has prescribed a general plan for all these productions. One Being has been concerned in all.

Under this stupendous Being we live. Our happiness, our existence, is in His hand. All we expect must come from Him. Nor ought we to feel our situation insecure. In every nature, and in every portion of nature which we can descry, we find attention bestowed upon even the minutest parts. The hinges in the wings of an earwig, and the joints of its antennae, are as highly wrought as if the Creator had had nothing else to finish. We see no signs of diminution of care by multiplicity of objects, or of distraction of thought by variety. We have no reason to fear, therefore, our being forgotten, or overlooked, or neglected.

The existence and character of the Deity is, in every view, the most interesting of all human speculations. In none, however, is it more so than as it facilitates the belief of the fundamental articles of revelation. It is a step to have it proved that there must be something in the world more than what we see. It is a further step to know, that among the invisible things of nature there must be an intelligent mind concerned in its production, order, and support. These points being assured to us by natural theology, we may well leave to revelation the disclosure of many particulars which our research cannot reach respecting either the nature of this Being as the original cause of all things, or His character and designs as a moral governor; and not only so, but the more full confirmation of other particulars, of which, though they do not lie altogether beyond our reasonings and our probabilities, the certainty is by no means equal to the importance. The true theist will be the first to listen to any credible communication of divine knowledge. Nothing which he has learnt from natural theology will diminish his desire of further instruction, or his disposition to receive it with humility and thankfulness. He wishes for light, he rejoices in light. His inward veneration of this great Being will incline him to attend with the utmost seriousness, not only to all that can be discovered concerning Him by researches into nature, but to all that is taught by a revelation which gives reasonable proof of having proceeded from Him.

INTELLIGENT DESIGN

Creationism's Trojan Horse

A CONVERSATION WITH BARBARA FORREST

*I*n *your new book,* Creationism's Trojan Horse: The Wedge of Intelligent Design, *you focus on The Wedge strategy pioneered by Phillip Johnson. For those not familiar with it, what is "The Wedge" strategy and what it its ultimate goal?*

The Wedge strategy is the intelligent design movement's tactical plan for promoting intelligent design (ID) creationism as an alternative to evolutionary theory in the American cultural mainstream and public school science classes. The movement's 5-, 10- and 20-year goals are outlined in a document on the Internet entitled "The Wedge Strategy." Informally known as the "Wedge Document," it was a fundraising tool used by the Discovery Institute to raise money for its creationist subsidiary, the Center for the Renewal of Science and Culture (CRSC), which was established in 1996 and is now called the Center for Science and Culture. According to the Wedge

---

Intelligent Design: Creationism's Trojan Horse, A Conversation with Barbara Forrest, Americans United for Separation of Church and State, www.au.org.

Document, the strategy is designed to defeat "Darwinism" and to promote an idea of science "consonant with Christian and theistic convictions." The ultimate goal of the Wedge strategy is to "renew" American culture by shaping public policy to reflect conservative Christian values.

The intelligent design creationists who are executing this strategy collectively refer to themselves as "the Wedge." Phillip Johnson, the architect of the strategy and the group's de facto leader, invokes the metaphor of a wood-splitting wedge to illustrate his goal of splitting apart the concepts of science and naturalism. A fundamental part of the Wedge strategy is the rejection of naturalism as unnecessary to science. Of course, the only alternative to naturalism is supernaturalism. But ID proponents avoid this word when speaking to mainstream audiences, substituting thinly disguised euphemisms such as "non-natural." They believe that such semantic subterfuge will enable them to skirt the constitutional prohibitions against promoting religion in public schools. They have not always avoided mentioning the supernatural, however. In the movement's early years, when Johnson brought together the Wedge's younger members, they had to build a base of religious, political, and financial support. This required revealing the true nature of their program. The CRSC's early website announced that new developments in the sciences were "raising serious doubts about scientific materialism and re-opening the case for the supernatural." This was a clear signal to potential supporters that the CRSC was open for business as a religious organization dedicated to opposing evolution.

Science, however, is a naturalistic enterprise. Scientists cannot appeal to supernatural explanations because there is neither a methodology for testing them nor an epistemology for knowing the supernatural. Science has a naturalistic methodology, known less controversially as "scientific method." That simply means that scientists seek natural explanations for natural phenomena. Science also has an epistemology, namely, the use of human sensory faculties to collect empirical data about the world and the use of our rational faculties to draw conclusions and construct explanations of this data. This is the only successful way to do science, and the pragmatic success of this naturalistic methodology is the only reason scientists use it. There is neither a conspiracy by scientists to prohibit "alternative explanations" nor an arbitrary commitment to naturalism, as ID proponents charge. Scientists use this naturalistic methodology because it works. Period.

Yet ID proponents argue that science need not be naturalistic but can—indeed must—appeal to an intelligent designer, i.e., a supernatural being, in order to explain the natural world adequately. In short, since the ID movement cannot really influence the way science is actually done (even the scientists among them do not use the concept of ID in their professional scientific work), they want to influence the way science is understood by the American public and by policymakers. But the idea they are promoting is nothing more than a return to the pre-modern concept of science in which the religious beliefs of its practitioners shaped their explanation of the natural world.

What is the relationship between advocates of The Wedge and the older school of creationists who promote a literal reading of the Bible and think Earth is only 6,000 years old? Wedge advocates like Johnson and Michael Behe say they reject young-Earth creationism, yet many young-Earthers seem to have endorsed the Wedge strategy. What is going on here?

There is a marriage of convenience between young-Earth creationists (YECs) and ID creationists. The fundamentalist YECs insist on the literal interpretation of Genesis, which includes the view that Earth is only 6,000–10,000 years old. Most ID proponents are evangelicals who allow a little more room for biblical interpretation than fundamentalists do. They are not literalists but accept modern scientific evidence that Earth is several billion years old. This is a source of conflict between the two groups, but YECs have had their day in court (quite a few of them, in fact) and have lost every time. They know that they have no hope of getting their own views into public school science classes. Phillip Johnson knows this, too, but he also needs the YECs' political support. And there are YECs in the ID movement such as Paul Nelson, a philosopher, and Nancy Pearcey, a Christian writer and commentator. Both are longtime CRSC fellows. YECs and ID proponents are united by their social and political conservatism, so Johnson has tried to construct a "big tent," a coalition of YECs and ID creationists, hoping to use the strength of their combined numbers as a political force. The YECs have gone along, grudgingly at times, eager to profit from the Wedge's hoped-for success at getting ID into public schools. For them, ID is now the only game in town.

But the strategy and arguments ID proponents use are the same ones the YECs have always used. ID terminology is somewhat more scientifically sophisticated and religiously sanitized, but not so much that YECs cannot recognize its true identity as creationism. In chapter 9 of *Creationism's Trojan Horse*, my co-author and I catalogue the parallels between ID and the "creation science" of well-known YECs Henry Morris and Duane Gish. For instance, both Morris and Gish have stated that in promoting creationism, discussions of the Bible should be strategically avoided. Johnson says exactly the same thing. One of the "evidences" Morris and Gish offer for their antievolutionism is the supposed absence of transitional fossils. Philosopher/mathematician/Christian apologist William Dembski, the chief Wedge intellectual, makes the same charge in *Mere Creation: Science, Faith and Intelligent Design*, where he hits all the same antievolutionist notes that YECs traditionally do. We list a number of such similarities in our book and could have included even more.

Despite occasional carping by the YECs about ID's not being biblical enough, they carefully avoid criticizing it too harshly and sometimes publicize their alliance with it. Young-Earther Ashby Camp, writing for the Creation Research Society's *Creation Matters*, has said, "If the science establishment can be forced to acknowledge the scientific case for intelligent design, theism will become part of the 'post-Christian' cultural air. . . . If ID is successful in changing the culture, the presumption against the supernatural will be eliminated." YECs clearly think they have something to gain from this partnership. However, there are signals from within ID ranks that they do not hold their fundamentalist allies in high esteem. One of the Wedge Document's goals is for seminaries to "increasingly recognize and repudiate naturalistic presuppositions." Dembski and his Wedge colleague Jay Wesley Richards, in a 2001 book they co-edited, *Unapologetic Apologetics*, seek to "transform mainline seminaries in particular and the secular academic world in general." But they consider fundamentalism a problem: "One obstacle is fundamentalism, which assumes all conceptual problems facing Christianity are easily resolved. . . . Fundamentalism prevents us from doing the quality work that's needed to deserve the respect of the secular academic world." Yet Wedge members do not hesitate to appear in public with their fundamentalist allies. The YEC/ID political marriage will likely last as long as both sides think there is hope of some headway in furthering the ID agenda.

Advocates of intelligent design argue that their ideas are not necessarily religious. Yet it would seem that if humans were intelligently designed, the designer must have been God. In light of this, how do ID proponents argue that their ideas are not religious in nature?

ID creationists contend that the work of an intelligent designer can be empirically detected in nature, but they evade questions about the designer's identity and the mechanisms through which it works by insisting that detecting its activity does not require knowing its identity. They argue that ID is based on cutting-edge science. Yet even ID proponents with legitimate science credentials have never produced one iota of original scientific data to support these claims. Biochemist Michael Behe never invokes ID in any of his professional publications. He surely would do this if he really believed that ID is a genuine scientific theory. In his role as an ID proponent, he claims that biological structures such as bacterial flagella are "irreducibly complex," meaning that their parts could not have been assembled over time by natural selection and that the absence of one part would by definition make the entire structure nonfunctional. Yet he admits that his definition of irreducible complexity is flawed and has not so far produced a promised revision of it. Dembski, who has no science credentials, claims to have developed a test for detecting intelligently designed complexity in biological systems, but he has never made a successful attempt to show how it works and ignores requests to produce data that might enable others to do it. So despite their argument that ID is not religious, it certainly is not science.

As to whether ID is religious, we can go straight to the horse's mouth to verify this. Fortunately, members of the Wedge themselves have made the task very easy by confirming unambiguously on numerous occasions that ID is fundamentally a religious belief. Insisting that their concerns are scientific and educational, they complain that their motives are irrelevant to the merits of their arguments. But in the absence of scientific accomplishment, the ID movement rests only on its proponents' religious motives and goals, revealed through their own pronouncements. As early as 1992, Dembski stipulated that when he spoke of an intelligent designer, he was referring to a "supernatural intelligence." The "Wedge Strategy," written between 1996 and 1998, states that "the proposition that human beings are created in the image of God" has been under "wholesale attack" by people like "Charles Darwin, Karl Marx, and Sigmund Freud." It states further that "the cultural consequences of this triumph of materialism were devastating." So much for the Wedge's non-religious motives. Furthermore, according to this document, "Discovery Institute's Center for the Renewal of Science and Culture seeks nothing less than the overthrow of materialism and its cultural legacies." Once materialism is dead, the Wedge hopes to reinstate a "broadly theistic understanding of nature." So much for non-religious goals. The Discovery

Institute has tried to downplay the significance of this document, but it is the Wedge's own statement of their strategy, and they are stuck with it. And contrary to their posturing as a secular, scientific organization, they have continued to provide a great deal more evidence of ID's religious identity.

Phillip Johnson confirmed that ID is a religious belief in 1996, the year the Center for the Renewal of Science and Culture was established, when the Wedge had to make its religious identity known in order to attract support. Johnson stated, "My colleagues and I speak of 'theistic realism'—or sometimes, 'mere creation'—as the defining concept of our movement. This means that we affirm that God is objectively real as Creator, and that the reality of God is tangibly recorded in evidence accessible to science, particularly in biology." He clearly wants people to see ID as an idea that can supplant naturalistic science with divine revelation: "If life is not simply matter evolving by natural selection, but is something that had to be designed by a creator who is *real*, then the nature of that creator, and the possibility of revelation, will become a matter of widespread interest among thoughtful people who are currently being taught that evolutionary science has shown God to be a product of the human imagination." He referred to the Wedge's religious goals in a 2001 speech before an audience of supporters when he explained that Wedge leaders founded the ID movement to explain the evidence for "a Creator" and to "unify the religious world." In an interview that same year, Johnson predicted that "with the success of intelligent design," people would understand that "the Christians have been right all along—at least on major elements of the story, like divine creation." That realization, according to Johnson, would forestall the argument that Christian ideas have "no legitimate place in public education, in public lawmaking, in public discussion generally."

Yet despite Wedge members' claim that ID is a scientific alternative to evolution, they don't dare carry this charade too far. In order to maintain their standing with conservative religious supporters—and fend off fundamentalist criticisms that ID is not sufficiently biblical—they have to show that ID is indeed biblically based. But they also want to avoid divisive arguments over the age of Earth, etc., so they simply substitute the Book of John for the Book of Genesis. Johnson says that the biblical basis for ID is John 1: "In the beginning was the Word, and the Word was with God, and the Word was God. / The same was in the beginning with God. / All things were made by him; and without him was not anything made that was made." Johnson appeals to this minimalist account of divine creation instead of Genesis, which invokes a literalist interpretation of the Bible that many ID proponents do not share and introduces a source of contention into the "big tent."

In a 1999 article for the Christian magazine *Touchstone*, Dembski confirmed the foundation of ID in John 1 when he assured readers that "[i]ndeed, intelligent design is just the Logos theology of John's Gospel restated in the idiom of information theory." And in *Intelligent Design: The Bridge Between Science and Theology*, the 1999 book in which Dembski explains ID for his Christian audience, he makes it clear that "divine Logos" is God's own language, "the Word that in Christ was made flesh." He seals the connection between the concept of divine creation and ID as "Logos theology" when he asserts that "God speaks the *divine Logos* to create the world." He even specifies in this book about ID that God must be male!

There is a wealth of such statements. So Wedge leaders' argument that ID is not religious is a complete sham. ID proponents use it with mainstream audiences for public relations and legal purposes. It does not reflect the true essence of ID creationism.

Is there a conflict between what ID backers tell the public through the media and what they say before conservative Christian audiences?

There is a noticeable conflict, but it is studied and deliberate. When speaking to a mainstream audience and to the media, ID proponents must pretend that ID is a secular, scientific theory. In short, they actually have to deny the religious foundation of their own ideas. Philosopher of science Robert Pennock, who has written extensively about ID, says, "When lobbying for ID in the public schools, Wedge members sometimes deny that ID makes any claims about the identity of the designer. It is ironic that their political strategy leads them to deny God in the public square more often than Peter did." Moreover, Wedge members are now disavowing their own terminology because the term "intelligent design" has become a liability for them. They are doing this for two reasons. First, because of the Discovery Institute's successful public relations campaign to make "intelligent design" a household word, more people now also recognize it as the religious concept of creationism. Second, the Wedge is waging an unrelenting campaign to get ID into public school sciences classes in some form. They have come close to doing that in Ohio, where they succeeded in getting the State Board of Education to adopt a creationist lesson plan. So they are now using euphemisms to refer to ID in an attempt to craft a workable legal defense should there be a lawsuit in Ohio or elsewhere.

They claim not to be promoting the teaching of "intelligent design," but rather the teaching of the "controversy" over evolution, or the "strengths and weaknesses" of evolutionary theory, or "arguments against evolution."

But when speaking to what the Wedge Document calls their "natural constituency, namely [conservative] Christians," ID creationists express themselves unambiguously in religious language, as I have shown above. They know that they cannot afford to do *too* good a job of disguising their true religious loyalties, since only by maintaining their conservative Christian base can they also maintain their political momentum—and their major funding sources, virtually all of which are religious organizations and individuals such as Howard Ahmanson.

Intelligent design supporters often portray it in the media as some new, ground-breaking idea. But isn't it true that the argument from design is an old, discredited idea that actually pre-dates Charles Darwin? What are the origins of what is now called intelligent design?

The argument from design is indeed very old and illustrates how pre-scientific people constructed explanations of the cosmos that reflect their own experience as intelligent agents. Thomas Aquinas used it as one of his arguments for God's existence, noting that many natural objects function as though they are aiming toward "the best result." Thomas reasoned that since an object lacking intelligence cannot do this without external guidance from an intelligent being, there must be such a being by whom unintelligent things are purposefully directed. The idea of intelligent design is also central to William Paley's 1802 book, *Natural Theology*, where he presents his famous watchmaker analogy. Although ID proponents, particularly Dembski, deny that ID is natural theology, the resemblance between what Paley said in 1802 and what Dembski says today is striking. Reading Paley is like reading works by ID creationists in many ways.

The Foundation for Thought and Ethics published "Of Pandas and People," a popular ID volume. The name of this group sounds innocuous. What did your research turn up about the Foundation?

The Foundation for Thought and Ethics (FTE) is a publishing company headquartered in Richardson, Texas. The founder and president is Jon A. Buell, whom the FTE website describes as an "author, editor, and lecturer."

Although the website is registered under the organizational name, William Dembski is the administrative contact, and the FTE mailing address is actually Dembski's. FTE has been an integral partner in the Wedge strategy since Phillip Johnson first organized the Wedge in the early 1990s. FTE also holds the copyright to the creationist textbook, *Of Pandas and People*, which it markets to teachers and tried unsuccessfully to have adopted by the Plano, Texas, school district in 1995. It also co-sponsored the ID movement's first conference in 1992, which its website touts with overblown rhetoric as "a historic event" that was "soon felt at even the top levels of science in America." FTE published the conference proceedings and sells other "educational resources" on its website; these include all the major ID books. Dembski is the FTE's "Academic Editor." FTE's true mission is to put materials into the hands of parents, students, and teachers that promote a conservative Christian worldview. One of its most recent efforts is described in a fundraising letter in which FTE promotes its book, *Sex and Character*, apparently attempting to cash in on rising interest in abstinence education in public schools, or, as FTE puts it, to "increase the cleansing tonic we are sending into the classrooms of our country's youngest citizens."

Your book contains a lot of information about the Discovery Institute. What is this organization, and what tactics does it use to promote the spread of ID in public schools?

The Discovery Institute is a conservative think tank in Seattle, Washington. Its founder and president is Bruce Chapman, a former member of the Reagan administration. The organization has several interests centering around transportation and other issues in the Pacific Northwest, but it functions primarily as the headquarters of the ID movement. Although it purports to be a secular organization, its religious moorings are clearly recognizable. Patricia O'Connell Killen, a religion professor at Pacific Lutheran University in Tacoma whose work centers around the regional religious identity of the Pacific Northwest, recently wrote that "religiously inspired think tanks such as the conservative evangelical Discovery Institute" are part of the "religious landscape" of that area.

Discovery Institute's most important subsidiary is its creationist arm, the Center for Science and Culture (CSC), established in 1996 as the Center for the Renewal of Science and Culture in order to advance the Wedge strategy. Chapman calls the center "our No. 1 project." Although the CSC website advertises lucrative fellowships of up to $50,000 a year for "support of significant and original research in the natural sciences, the history and philosophy of science, cognitive science and related fields," none of the center's fellows has ever produced the scientific research which the Wedge Document says is to form the foundation of the Wedge strategy.

Instead of producing original scientific data to support ID's claims, the Discovery Institute has promoted ID politically to the public, education officials and public policymakers. In 2000, the Wedge held a congressional briefing in Washington, D.C., to promote ID to lawmakers. ID creationists have tried to influence the content of state and local science standards, the content of state-approved science textbooks, and even the No Child Left Behind Act. Senator Rick Santorum of Pennsylvania inserted a sense of the Senate resolution into the bill calling for students to be taught why evolution "generates so much continuing controversy." The resolution was actually a pro-ID subterfuge designed to bolster the Wedge's claim to have congressional support for their efforts. Few of the senators who voted to support the "Santorum amendment" actually could have recognized the resolution for what it truly was, however. Pro-science organizations succeeded in having the resolution removed from the bill, but Wedge supporters on the conference committee preserved it in the bill's legislative history. The item is not federal law, but just as its author Phillip Johnson planned, it is constantly cited by ID supporters as providing federal sanction for their pro-ID agenda.

ID proponents are the first creationists to establish such high-level political influence in the nation's capitol. Senator Santorum is their most vocal supporter there, but there are others. Representatives John Boehner and Steve Chabot of Ohio and Senator Judd Gregg of New Hampshire, along with Santorum, have signed letters supporting the Discovery Institute's interpretation of the Santorum amendment. One of those letters was sent to the president and vice-president of the Ohio Board of Education; the other was sent to the Texas Board of Education.

Discovery Institute's efforts have caused problems in a number of states, notably Kansas, Montana, Texas and Ohio. (Only 10 states have not had problems with ID.) And there are two additional de facto Wedge subsidiaries. Access Research Network (ARN), headquartered in Colorado Springs, serves as a clearinghouse and marketer for ID books, videotapes, etc. The Intelligent Design Network (IDnet), which does a great deal of the footwork with state and local boards of education, is headquartered in Kansas but has extended the Wedge's reach through branches in New Mexico and Minnesota. IDnet operatives also worked closely with Science Excellence for All Ohioans, which spearheaded the highly publicized effort to insert ID into the science standards in Ohio.

Discovery Institute also employs staff at its Seattle headquarters whose main task is to advance the Wedge strategy through an aggressive public relations campaign. One of their most disturbing public relations coups was convincing PBS to sell a creationist video, *Unlocking the Mystery of Life*, as a science film in its online store for two years. Fortunately, but only after misleading unsuspecting customers for all this time, PBS has stopped selling the video. But the Wedge public relations campaign continues. Apparently unhappy with unfavorable media coverage, Discovery Institute now features a weblog, "Evolution News & Views." Rob Crowther, CSC director of communications, explains this initiative: "We're going to use this blog [to] inform, analyze, and expose how the news media cover—and fail to cover— the scientific controversy over Darwinian evolution. . . . We not only plan to offer critiques and corrections to major news stories, we will also offer behind-the-scenes glimpses at journalists and how they operate when they report on this issue." The media must be quaking in their boots.

The Center for Science and Culture has also announced the establishment of the "CSC Discovery Society," which its website bills as a "select grassroots mobilization force designed to support the work—and disseminate the message—of Discovery Institute's Center for Science and Culture." Members are assured that they will be supporting "cutting-edge research that challenges Darwinian evolution and validates the intelligent design of life and the universe." The $300 annual membership fee may help keep the Discovery Society *very* select.

You teach at the university level and your coauthor, Paul Gross, has a Ph.D. in general physiology. Based on your knowledge of higher education in America, is intelligent design commonly taught in university-level biology courses as a serious alternative to Darwinian theory?

No. Respectable university science departments teach evolution because it is the only scientific theory that explains the development of Earth's life forms. The Wedge does have a following in academia, however. The cultivation of support in higher education is one of the most active parts of their strategy. I don't think it is a stretch to say that they have faculty supporters on every university campus in this country, including at Ivy League schools. Some, such as Alvin Plantinga at Notre Dame and Frank Tipler at Tulane University, are high-profile figures in academia.

There are certainly religious schools that teach ID. Biola University and Oklahoma Baptist University are listed on the Access Research Network website as "ID Colleges." In addition, the Intelligent Design and Evolution Awareness (IDEA) Center, which began as a student organization at the University of California at San Diego, helps establish student IDEA clubs on university and high school campuses. The Intelligent Design and Undergraduate Research Center, ARN's student division, also cultivates followers at universities. Campus youth ministries play an active role in bringing ID to university campuses through lectures by Wedge leaders Phillip Johnson, William Dembski, Jonathan Wells, Michael Behe and other ID figures. But this activity takes place outside university science departments. No science program worth its salt is going to teach ID.

At a number of public universities, including the University of California at Berkeley and the University of New Mexico, sympathetic faculty have slipped ID courses under the radar as freshman seminars, honors courses and other courses outside required curricula in which instructors have wider latitude regarding course content. I predict that this will increase, and university administrators should be paying closer attention to what college students are getting in such classes. This is a question of professional competence. Students should not pay the price for dereliction of duty by instructors who are either not qualified to teach classes purporting to be about science or have subordinated scientific integrity to personal religious loyalties.

Scientists publish the results of their research in peer-reviewed journals that are subject to rigorous scrutiny from other researchers working in the field. How do ID proponents disseminate their ideas? Are there peer-reviewed ID journals?

The major vehicle for the dissemination of ID is the roughly three dozen books its proponents have published and marketed aggressively. The Wedge strategy called for publication of 30 books by 2003, and that deadline was almost met. It probably has been met by now. Wedge members also write numerous op-eds and magazine articles and have made masterful use of the Internet. Two issues of *Touchstone* magazine have been devoted to ID. *Christianity Today*, which I had always considered a credible magazine, has unfortunately given ID a very high profile. Focus on the Family, in addition to co-publishing the creationist videotape *Unlocking the Mystery of Life,* which features the major Wedge leaders, publishes pro-ID articles on its website and in its *Citizen* magazine. Focus on the Family employee Mark Hartwig is also a CSC fellow, a connection which has helped to publicize ID extensively. James Dobson often features ID proponents on his Focus on the Family radio program.

ID creationists have published what they call "peer-reviewed" ID journals, but their peers consist of their own network of supporters. *Origins and Design,* which was formerly *Origins Research,* a publication by the creationist Students for Origins Research, was published by ARN for a number of years but is now apparently defunct. Dembski publishes *Progress in Complexity, Information, and Design,* an electronic journal featuring articles by supporters of his online organization, the International Society for Complexity, Information, and Design (ISCID). But the publication standards of Dembski's on-line journal are a bit lax. The editorial board consists of Dembski's close associates. Most of the articles are by Wedge members and ID supporters, some of whom are only students. The articles are posted to ISCID's discussion forum, which Dembski calls an "archive." Once an article meets "basic scholarly standards" and is accepted into the archive, it is considered suitable for publication upon approval by one (it used to be two) of ISCID's 58 fellows, who constitute the editorial advisory board. Describing standard procedures of scientific peer review as geared toward censorship, Dembski recently loosened his on-line journal's publication standards even more for the sake of "novelty and creativity."

ID proponents have long sought to stifle criticism that they publish no genuinely scientific, peer-reviewed articles on ID. They recently got a little help from a friend. A pro-ID article by CSC program director Stephen C. Meyer was published in a legitimate science journal, *Proceedings of the Biological Society of Washington.* The article, a review essay which presents no original ID research, is a revised version of a 2001 article on the "Cambrian explosion" that was first posted on the Intelligent Design and Undergraduate Research Center website. A later version also appeared in the book Meyer co-edited, *Darwinism, Design and Public Education.* The editor, Richard V. Sternberg, a creationist himself who left his position shortly after the article appeared, published it without allowing the journal's associate editors to review it. The Biological Society of Washington Council has since repudiated the article and vowed that proper review procedures will henceforth be followed. The Wedge claimed a similar victory when an article by Michael

Behe and David W. Snoke was published in *Protein Science*. But the paper has been critiqued by qualified scientists, who point out that "it contains no 'design theory,' makes no attempt to model an 'intelligent design' process, and proposes no alternative to evolution." Neither article gives the Wedge the credibility they claim. As far as publishing original scientific data to support ID is concerned, their scorecard is still blank.

To many people, this may seem like an esoteric debate over obtuse scientific questions. Why should parents be concerned? How will the outcome of this debate affect our children?

The debate is esoteric only in the sense that it involves science, which most Americans understand poorly despite their love of technology. But even though the average American's scientific literacy is rather low, there are aspects of the issue that parents can and should understand. Americans insist that education is one of their chief priorities, but the United States is the world's only industrialized country in which people are still fighting over evolution. Even developing countries are not doing this. Americans look like fools to the rest of the world.

The Wedge's primary target audience is politically and religiously conservative people who hold the mistaken view that evolution threatens their moral and religious values, believe that ID is a real scientific theory and will support anyone who shares that view. Their secondary target is sincere but scientifically uninformed people who fall for ID proponents' argument that all sides of an issue deserve a hearing. Desiring to encourage "critical thinking," they are susceptible to the Wedge's proposal that schools balance evolution with "teaching the controversy," or "the strengths and weaknesses of evolution," or "evidence against evolution"—all well-known Wedge euphemisms for ID. But to teach ID in any of its guises is to balance truth with lies. There is no scientific controversy about the fact of biological evolution. There is only the fake controversy the Discovery Institute manufactured to advance its political and religious agenda. ID proponents know that few people in their audiences are willing or able to do the research that exposes ID as the sham it is. (Hence the need for books like *Creationism's Trojan Horse.*) The unavoidable conclusion is that Wedge strategists are exploiting their audiences' fears, religious loyalties and gullibility. This shows little respect for the people they convince to petition school board officials on behalf of ID.

Parents should be concerned about the resurgence of creationism as ID because it threatens the quality of their children's education. It diminishes their chances for competing in the job market, making informed choices as consumers of medical care, and making responsible contributions as citizens. Not the least of people's concerns should be the enormous amounts of time and money being wasted on this issue. Science is one of the weakest areas of American education, and the resistance many teachers face when teaching evolution discourages them, especially those who are under prepared, from bothering with it. Parents should support teachers and insist that schools offer quality science instruction. If a school's science instruction is good, it's a pretty good bet that everything else is, too. Every day and every tax dollar spent fighting creationists, paying the costs of inevitable lawsuits, etc., is a day and a dollar not spent on decently educating children, and that should make parents fighting mad.

Creationists have for years labored to undermine the teaching of evolution in the public schools. What is different about this new ID strategy? In what ways is it more sophisticated?

First, I want to stress that there is virtually nothing different about ID in terms of its identity as creationism. The "new" ID creationists use virtually the same arguments, employ the same tactics, and have the same agenda as the earlier "creation scientists." That is clearly documented in our book.

The difference is that the creationists at the Discovery Institute's Center for Science and Culture are more aggressive and more politically connected and sophisticated than earlier creationists. The core group in the Wedge has the luxury of devoting themselves to these efforts, unlike their opponents, who do not have the benefit of wealthy benefactors to bankroll clerical staff, expensive advertising campaigns and political networking, as Wedge members do.

Finally—and I cannot stress this point strongly enough—Americans who value their Constitution and religious freedom should be concerned about the larger problem of which ID is a prominent symptom. Americans need to know about the darker side of the Wedge strategy, which few people except its supporters have seen. ID is more than just creationism's Trojan horse; it is a stalking horse for the Religious Right's effort to steamroll its way into American education and public policy. The core of this issue is really about power, who controls education and thus the minds of children, and who controls the policy that shapes American culture and public life. ID proponents share the Religious Right's dislike of secular education. They also share its theocratic vision for our country. Their most vocal supporters include powerful Religious Right leaders: James Dobson, Phyllis Schlafly, Beverly LaHaye and D. James Kennedy.

The vision Wedge strategists have for American culture is not pretty. In addressing their conservative Christian audience, both Phillip Johnson and William Dembski promote a disturbing religious exclusionism and anti-secularism. Johnson has made comments that could be interpreted as anti-Muslim. Referring to Americans' fear of "these Muslim terrorists" after September 11, he paints a picture of American professors who are "afraid of what the Muslim students will do" on their campuses. Commenting that he never thought "our country would descend to this level," he implies that Muslims worship a false God: "We once knew who the true God was and were able to proclaim it frankly." Dembski favors reviving the religious transgression of heresy even for fellow Christians. He recognizes the question his view might provoke: "Can't we all just get along and live together in peace?" His answer should have all Americans worried: "Unfortunately, the answer is no."

PART FOUR

ONGOING CRITIQUE

BELIEVING WHERE WE CANNOT PROVE

PHILIP KITCHER

OPENING MOVES

S imple distinctions come all too easily. Frequently we open the way for later puzzlement by restricting the options we take to be available. So, for example, in contrasting science and religion, we often operate with a simple pair of categories. On one side there is science, proof, and certainty; on the other, religion, conjecture, and faith.

The opening lines of Tennyson's *In Memoriam* offer an eloquent statement of the contrast:

> Strong Son of God, immortal love,
> Whom we, that have not seen Thy face,
> By faith, and faith alone, embrace,
> Believing where we cannot prove.

Philip Kitcher, "Believing Where We Cannot Prove," *Abusing Science: The Case Against Creationism* (Cambridge, MA: MIT Press, 1982), chapter 2.

A principal theme of Tennyson's great poem is his struggle to maintain faith in the face of what seems to be powerful scientific evidence. Tennyson had read a popular work by Robert Chambers, *Vestiges of the Natural History of Creation*, and he was greatly troubled by the account of the course of life on earth that the book contains. *In Memoriam* reveals a man trying to believe where he cannot prove, a man haunted by the thought that the proofs may be against him.

Like Tennyson, contemporary Creationists accept the traditional contrast between science and religion. But where Tennyson agonized, they attack. While they are less eloquent, they are supremely confident of their own solution. They open their onslaught on evolutionary theory by denying that it is a science. *In The Troubled Waters of Evolution*, Henry Morris characterizes evolutionary theory as maintaining that large amounts of time are required for evolution to produce "new kinds." As a result, we should not expect to see such "new kinds" emerging. Morris comments, "Creationists in turn insist that this belief is not scientific evidence but only a statement of faith. The evolutionist seems to be saying, Of course, we cannot really *prove* evolution, since this requires ages of time, and so, therefore, you should accept it as a proved fact of science! Creationists regard this as an odd type of logic, which would be entirely unacceptable in any other field of science."[1] David Watson makes a similar point in comparing Darwin with Galileo; "So here is the difference between Darwin and Galileo: Galileo set a demonstrable fact against a few words of Bible poetry which the Church at that time had understood in an obviously naive way; Darwin set an unprovable *theory* against eleven chapters of straightforward history which cannot be reinterpreted in any satisfactory way."[2]

The idea that evolution is conjecture, faith, or "philosophy" pervades Creationist writings. It is absolutely crucial to their case for equal time for "scientific" Creationism. This ploy has succeeded in winning important adherents to the Creationist cause. As he prepared to defend Arkansas law 590, Attorney General Steven Clark echoed the Creationist judgment. "Evolution," he said, "is just a theory." Similar words have been heard in Congress. William Dannemeyer, a congressman from California, introduced a bill to limit funding to the Smithsonian with the following words: "If the theory of evolution is just that—a theory—and if that theory can be regarded as a religion . . . then it occurs to this Member that other Members might prefer it not to be given exclusive or top billing in our Nation's most famous museum but equal billing or perhaps no billing at all."

In their attempt to show that evolution is not science, Creationists receive help from the least likely sources. Great scientists sometimes claim that certain facts about the past evolution of organisms are "demonstrated" or "indubitable." But Creationists also can (and do) quote scientists who characterize evolution as "dogma" and contend that there is no conclusive proof of evolutionary theory. Evolution is not part of science because, as evolutionary biologists themselves concede, science demands proof, and, as other biologists point out, proof of evolution is not forthcoming.

The rest of the Creationist argument flows easily. We educate our children in evolutionary theory as if it were a proven fact. We subscribe officially, in our school system, to one faith—an atheistic, materialistic faith—ignoring rival beliefs. Antireligious educators deform the minds of children, warping them to accept as gospel a doctrine that has no more scientific support than the true Gospel. The very least that should be done is to allow for both alternatives to be presented.

We should reject the Creationists' gambit. Eminent scientists notwithstanding, science is not a body of demonstrated truths. Virtually all of science is an exercise in believing where we cannot prove. Yet, scientific conclusions are not embraced by faith alone. Tennyson's dichotomy was too simple.

INCONCLUSIVE EVIDENCE

Sometimes we seem to have conclusive reasons for accepting a statement as true. It is hard to doubt that $2 + 2 = 4$. If, unlike Lord Kelvin's ideal mathematician, we do not find it obvious that at least the elementary parts of mathematics appear to command our agreement. The direct evidence of our senses seems equally compelling. If I see the pen with which I am writing, holding it firmly in my unclouded view, how can I doubt that it exists? The talented mathematician who has proved a theorem and the keen-eyed witness of an episode furnish our ideals of certainty in knowledge. What they tell us can be engraved in stone, for there is no cause for worry that it will need to be modified.

Yet, in another mood, one that seems "deeper" or more "philosophical," skeptical doubts begin to creep in. Is there really anything of which we are so certain that later evidence could not give us reason to change our minds? Even when we think about mathematical proof, can we not imagine that new discoveries may cast doubt on the cogency of our reasoning? (The history of mathematics reveals that sometimes what seems for all the world like a proof may have a false conclusion.) Is it not possible that the most careful observer may have missed something? Or that the witness brought preconceptions to the observation that subtly biased what was reported? Are we not *always* fallible?

I am mildly sympathetic to the skeptic's worries. Complete certainty is best seen as an ideal toward which we strive and that is rarely, if ever, attained. Conclusive evidence always eludes us. Yet even if we ignore skeptical complaints and imagine that we are sometimes lucky enough to have conclusive reasons for accepting a claim as true, we should not include scientific reasoning among our paradigms of proof. Fallibility is the hallmark of science.

This point should not be so surprising. The trouble is that we frequently forget it in discussing contemporary science. When we turn to the history of science, however, our fallibility stares us in the face. The history of the natural sciences is strewn with the corpses of intricately organized theories, each of which had, in its day, considerable evidence in its favor. When we look at the confident defenders of those theories we should see anticipations of ourselves. The eighteenth-century scientists who believed that heat is a "subtle fluid," the atomic theorists who maintained that water molecules are compounded out of one atom of hydrogen and one of oxygen, the biochemists who identified protein as the genetic material, and the geologists who thought that continents cannot move were neither unintelligent nor ill informed. Given the evidence available to them, they were eminently reasonable in drawing their conclusions. History proved them wrong. It did not show that they were unjustified.

Why is science fallible? Scientific investigation aims to disclose the general principles that govern the workings of the universe. These principles are not intended merely to summarize what some select groups of humans have witnessed. Natural science is not just natural history. It is vastly more ambitious. Science offers us laws that are supposed to hold universally, and it advances claims about things that are beyond our power to observe. The nuclear physicist who sets down the law governing a particular type of radioactive decay is attempting to state a truth that holds throughout the entire cosmos and also to describe the behavior of things that we cannot even see. Yet, of necessity, the physicist's ultimate evidence is highly restricted. Like the rest of us, scientists are confined to a relatively small region of space and time and equipped with limited and imperfect senses.

How is science possible at all? How are we able to have any confidence about the distant regions of the cosmos and the invisible realm that lies behind the surfaces of ordinary things? The answer is complicated. Natural science follows intricate and ingenious procedures for fathoming the secrets of the universe. Scientists devise ways of obtaining especially revealing evidence. They single out some of the things we are able to see as crucial clues to the way that nature works. These clues are used to answer questions that cannot be addressed by direct observation. Scientific theories, even those that are most respected and most successful, rest on indirect arguments from the observational evidence. New discoveries can always call those arguments into question, showing scientists the way that they have misread their evidence.

But scientists often forget the fallibility of their enterprise. This is not just absentmindedness or wishful thinking. During the heyday of a scientific theory, so much evidence may support the theory, so many observational clues may seem to attest to its truth, that the idea that it could be overthrown appears ludicrous. In addition, the theory may provide ways of identifying quickly what is inaccessible to our unaided senses. Electron microscopes and cloud chambers are obvious examples of those extensions of our perceptual system that theories can inspire. Trained biochemists will talk quite naturally of seeing large molecules, and it is easy to overlook the fact that they are presupposing a massive body of theory in describing what they "see." If that theory were to be amended, even in subtle ways, then the descriptions of the "observed characteristics" of large molecules might have to be given up. Nor should we pride ourselves that the enormous successes of contemporary science secure us against future amendments. No theory in the history of science enjoyed a more spectacular career than Newton's mechanics. Yet Newton's ideas had to give way to Einstein's.

When practicing scientists are reminded of these straightforward points, they frequently adopt what the philosopher George Berkeley called a "forlorn skepticism." From the idea of science as certain and infallible, they jump to a cynical description of their endeavors. Science is sometimes held to be a game played with arbitrary rules, an irrational acceptance of dogma, an enterprise based ultimately on faith. Once we have appreciated the fallibility of natural science and recognized its sources, we can move beyond the simple opposition of proof and faith. Between these extremes lies the vast field of cases in which we believe something on the basis of good—even excellent—but inconclusive evidence.

If we want to emphasize the fact that what scientists believe today may have to be revised in the light of observations made tomorrow, then we can describe all our science as "theory." But the description should not confuse us. To concede that evolutionary biology is a theory is not to suppose that there are alternatives to it that are equally worthy of a place in our curriculum. All theories are revisable, but not all theories are equal. Even though our present evidence does not prove that evolutionary biology—or quantum physics, or plate tectonics, or any other theory—is true, evolutionary biologists will maintain that the present evidence is overwhelmingly in favor of their theory and overwhelmingly against its supposed rivals. Their enthusiastic assertions that evolution is a proven fact can be charitably understood as claims that the (admittedly inconclusive) evidence we have for evolutionary theory is as good as we ever obtain for any theory in any field of science.

Hence the Creationist try for a quick Fools' Mate can easily be avoided. Creationists attempt to draw a line between evolutionary biology and the rest of science by remarking that large-scale evolution cannot be observed. This tactic fails. Large-scale evolution is no more inaccessible to observation than nuclear reactions or the molecular composition of water. For the Creationists to succeed in divorcing evolutionary biology from the rest of science, they need to argue that evolutionary theory is less well supported by the evidence than are theories in, for example, physics and chemistry. It will come as no surprise to learn that they try to do this. To assess the merits of their arguments we need a deeper understanding of the logic of inconclusive justification. We shall begin with a simple and popular idea: Scientific theories earn our acceptance by making successful predictions.

PREDICTIVE SUCCESS

Imagine that somebody puts forward a new theory about the origins of hay fever. The theory makes a number of startling predictions concerning connections that we would not have thought worth investigating. For example, it tells us that people who develop hay fever invariably secrete a particular substance in certain fatty tissues and that anyone who eats rhubarb as a child never develops hay fever. The theory predicts things that initially appear fantastic. Suppose that we check up on these predictions and find that they are borne out by clinical tests. Would we not begin to believe—and believe reasonably—that the theory was *at least* on the right track?

This example illustrates a pattern of reasoning that is familiar in the history of science. Theories win support by producing claims about what can be observed, claims that would not have seemed plausible prior to the advancement of the theory, but that are in fact found to be true when we make the appropriate observations. A classic (real) example is Pascal's confirmation of Torricelli's hypothesis that we live at the bottom of an ocean of air that presses down upon us. Pascal reasoned that if Torricelli's hypothesis were true, then air pressure should decrease at higher altitudes (because at higher altitudes we are closer to the "surface" of the atmosphere, so that the length of the column of air that presses down is shorter). Accordingly, he sent his brother-in-law to the top of a mountain to make some barometric measurements. Pascal's clever working out of the observational predictions of Torricelli's theory led to a dramatic predictive success for the theory.

The idea of predictive success has encouraged a popular picture of science. (We shall see later that this picture, while popular, is not terribly accurate.) Philosophers sometimes regard a theory as a collection of claims or statements. Some of these statements offer generalizations about the features of particular, recondite things (genes, atoms, gravitational force, quasars, and the like). These statements are used to infer statements whose truth or falsity can be decided by observation. (This appears to be just what Pascal did.) Statements belonging to this second group are called the *observational consequences* of the theory. Theories are supported when we find that their observational consequences (those that we have checked) are true. The credentials of a theory are damaged if we discover that some of its observational consequences are false.

We can make the idea more precise by being clearer about the inferences involved. Those who talk of inferring observational predictions from our theories think that we can *deduce* from the statements of the theory, and from those statements alone, some predictions whose accuracy we can check by direct observation. Deductive inference is well understood. The fundamental idea of deductive inference is this: We say that a statement S is a valid deductive consequence of a group of statements if and only if it is *impossible* that all the statements in the group should be true and that S should be false; alternatively, S is a valid deductive consequence (or, more simply, a valid consequence) of a group of statements if and only if it would be self-contradictory to assert all the statements in the group and to deny S.

It will be helpful to make the idea of valid consequence more familiar with some examples. Consider the statements "All lovers of baseball dislike

George Steinbrenner" and "George Steinbrenner loves baseball." The statement "George Steinbrenner dislikes himself" is a deductively valid consequence of these two statements. For it is impossible that the first two should be true and the third false. However, in claiming that this is a case of deductively valid consequence, we do not commit ourselves to maintaining that any of the statements is true. (Perhaps there are some ardent baseball fans who admire Steinbrenner. Perhaps Steinbrenner himself has no time for the game.) What deductive validity means is that the truth of the first two statements would guarantee the truth of the third; that is, *if* the first two *were* true, then the third would have to be true.

Another example will help rule out other misunderstandings. Here are two statements: "Shortly after noon on January 1, 1982, in the Oval Office, a jelly bean was released from rest more than two feet above any surface"; "Shortly after noon on January 1, 1982, in the Oval Office, a jelly bean fell." Is the second statement a deductively valid consequence of the first? You might think that it is, on the grounds that it would have been impossible for the unfortunate object to have been released and not to have fallen. In one sense this is correct, but that is not the sense of impossibility that deductive logicians have in mind. Strictly speaking, it is not *impossible* for the jelly-bean to have been released without falling; we can imagine, for example, that the law of gravity might suddenly cease to operate. We do not *contradict* ourselves when we assert that the jellybean was released but deny that it fell; we simply refuse to accept the law of gravity (or some other relevant physical fact).

Thus, S is a deductively valid consequence of a group of statements if and only if there is *absolutely no possibility* that all the statements in the group should be true and S should be false. This conception allows us to state the popular view of theory and prediction more precisely. Theories are collections of statements. The observational consequences of a theory are statements that have to be true if the statements belonging to the theory are all true. These observational consequences also have to be statements whose truth or falsity can be ascertained by direct observation.

My initial discussion of predictive success presented the rough idea that, when we find the observational consequences of a theory to be true, our findings bring credit to the theory. Conversely, discovery that some observational consequences of a theory are false was viewed as damaging. We can now make the second point much more precise. Any theory that has a false observational consequence must contain some false statement (or statements). For if all the statements in the theory were true, then, according to the standard definitions of *deductive validity* and *observational consequence*, any observational consequence would also have to be true. Hence, if a theory is found to have a false observational consequence, we must conclude that one or more statements of the theory is false.

This means that theories can be conclusively falsified, through the discovery that they have false observational consequences. Some philosophers, most notably Sir Karl Popper,[3] have taken this point to have enormous significance for our understanding of science. According to Popper, the essence of a scientific theory is that it should be *falsifiable*. That is, if the theory is false, then it must be possible to show that it is false. Now, if a theory has utterly no observational consequences, it would be extraordinarily difficult to unmask that theory as false. So, to be a genuine scientific theory, a group of statements must have observational consequences. It is important to realize that Popper is not suggesting that every good theory must be false. The difference between being falsifiable and being false is like the difference between being vulnerable and actually being hurt. A good scientific theory should not be false. Rather, it must have observational consequences that could reveal the theory as mistaken if the experiments give the wrong results.

While these ideas about theory testing may seem strange in their formal attire, they emerge quite frequently in discussions of science. They also find their way into the creation-evolution debate.

PREDICTIVE FAILURE

From the beginning, evolutionary theory has been charged with just about every possible type of predictive failure. Critics of the theory have argued that (a) the theory makes no predictions (it is unfalsifiable and so fails Popper's criterion for science), (b) the theory makes false predictions (it is falsified), (c) the theory does not make the kinds of predictions it ought to make (the observations and experiments that evolutionary theorists undertake have no bearing on the theory). Many critics, including several Creationists, manage to advance all these objections in the same work. This is somewhat surprising, since points (a) and (b) are, of course, mutually contradictory.

The first objection is vitally important to the Creationist cause. Their opponents frequently insist that Creationism fails the crucial test for a scientific theory. The hypothesis that all kinds of organisms were separately fashioned by some "originator" is unfalsifiable.[4] Creationists retort that they can play the same game equally well. *Any* hypothesis about the origins of life, including that advanced by evolutionary theory, is not subject to falsification. Hence we cannot justify a decision to teach evolutionary theory and not to teach Creationism by appealing to the Popperian criterion for genuine science.

The allegation that evolutionary theory fails to make any predictions is a completely predictable episode in any Creationist discussion of evolution. Often the point is made by appeal to the authority of Popper. Here are two sample passages:

> The outstanding philosopher of science, Karl Popper, though himself an evolutionist, pointed out cogently that evolution, no less than creation, is untestable and thus unprovable.[5]
>
> Thus, for a theory to qualify as a scientific theory, it must be supported by events, processes or properties which can be observed, and the theory must be useful in predicting the outcome of future natural phenomena or laboratory experiments. An additional limitation usually imposed is that the theory must be capable of falsification. That is, it must be possible to conceive some experiment, the failure of which would disprove the theory.
>
> It is on the basis of such criteria that most evolutionists insist that creation be refused consideration as a possible explanation for origins. Creation has not been witnessed by human observers, it cannot be tested experimentally, and as a theory it is unfalsifiable.
>
> The general theory of evolution also fails to meet all three of these criteria, however.[6]

These passages, and many others, draw on the picture of science sketched above. It is not clear that the Creationists really understand the philosophical views that they attempt to apply. Gish presents the most articulate discussion of the falsifiability criterion. Yet he muddles the issue by describing falsifiability as an "additional limitation" beyond predictive power. (The previous section shows that theories that make predictions are automatically falsifiable.) Nevertheless, the Creationist challenge is a serious one, and, if it could not be met, evolutionary theory would be in trouble.

Creationists buttress their charge of unfalsifiability with further objections. They are aware that biologists frequently look as though they are engaged in observations and experiments. Creationists would allow that researchers in biology sometimes make discoveries. What they deny is that the discoveries support evolutionary theory. They claim that laboratory manipulations fail to teach us about evolution in nature: "Even if modern scientists should ever actually achieve the artificial creation of life from non-life, or of higher kinds from lower kinds, in the laboratory, this would not *prove* in any way that such changes did, or even could, take place in the past by random natural processes."[7] The standards of evidence to be applied to evolutionary biology have suddenly been raised. In this area of inquiry, it is not sufficient that a theory yield observational consequences whose truth or falsity can be decided in the laboratory. Creationists demand special kinds of predictions, and will dismiss as irrelevant any laboratory evidence that evolutionary theorists produce.

Oddly enough, however, the most popular supplement to the charge that evolutionary theory is unfalsifiable is a determined effort to falsify it [point (b)]. Creationists cannot resist arguing that the theory is actually falsified. Some of them, Morris and Gish, for example, recognize the tension between the two objections. They try to paper over the problem by claiming that evolutionary theory and the Creationist account are both "models." Each "model" would "naturally" incline us to expect certain observational results. A favorite Creationist ploy is to draw up tables in which these "predictions" are compared. When we look at the tables we find that the evolutionary expectations are confounded. By contrast, the Creationist "model" leads us to anticipate features of the world that are actually there. Faced with such adverse results, the benighted evolutionary biologist is portrayed as struggling to "explain away" the findings by whatever means he can invent.

. . . "The data must be *explained* by the evolutionist, but they are *predicted* by the Creationist."[8]

The careful reader ought to be puzzled. If Morris really thinks that evolutionary theory has been falsified, why does he not say so? Of course, he would have to admit that the theory is falsifiable. Seemingly, however, a staunch Creationist should be delighted to abandon a relatively abstruse point about unfalsifiability in favor of a clear-cut refutation. The truth of the matter is that the alleged refutations fail. No evolutionary theorist will grant that (for example) the theory predicts that the fossil record should show "innumerable transitions." Instead, paleontologists will point out that we can deduce conclusions about what we should find in the rocks only if we make assumptions about the fossilization process. Morris makes highly dubious assumptions, hails them as "natural," and then announces that the "natural predictions" of the theory have been defeated.

To make a serious assessment of these broad Creationist charges, we must begin by asking some basic methodological questions. We cannot decide whether evolutionary biologists are guilty of trying to save their theory by using *ad hoc* assumptions (new and implausible claims dreamed up for the sole purpose of protecting some cherished ideas) unless we have some way of deciding when a proposal is ad hoc. Similarly, we cannot make a reasoned response to the charge that laboratory experiments are irrelevant, or to the fundamental objection that evolutionary theory is unfalsifiable, unless we have a firmer grasp of the relation between theory and evidence.

NAIVE FALSIFICATIONISM

The time has come to tell a dreadful secret. While the picture of scientific testing sketched above continues to be influential among scientists, it has been shown to be seriously incorrect. (To give my profession its due, historians and philosophers of science have been trying to let this particular cat out of the bag for at least thirty years.) Important work in the history of science has made it increasingly clear that no major scientific theory has ever exemplified the relation between theory and evidence that the traditional model presents.

What is wrong with the old picture? Answer: Either it debars most of what we take to be science from counting as science or it allows virtually anything to count. On the traditional view of "theory," textbook cases of scientific theories turn out to be unfalsifiable. Suppose we identify Newtonian mechanics with Newton's three laws of motion plus the law of gravitation. What observational consequences can we deduce from these four statements? You might think that we could deduce that if, as the (undoubtedly apocryphal) story alleges, an apple became detached from a branch above where Newton was sitting, the apple would have fallen on his head. But this does not follow at all. To see why not, it is only necessary to recognize that the failure of this alleged prediction would not force us to deny any of the four statements of the theory. All we need do is assume that some other forces were at work that overcame the force of gravity and caused the apple to depart from its usual trajectory. So, given this simple way of applying Popper's criterion, Newtonian mechanics would be unfalsifiable. The same would go for any other scientific theory. Hence none of what we normally take to be science would count as science. (I might note that Popper is aware of this problem and has suggestions of his own as to how it should be overcome. However, what concerns me here are the *applications* of Popper's ideas, that are made by Creationists, as well as by scientists in their professional debates.)

The example of the last paragraph suggests an obvious remedy. Instead of thinking about theories in the simple way just illustrated, we might take them to be far more elaborate. Newton's laws (the three laws of motion and the law of gravitation) are *embedded* in Newtonian mechanics. They form the core of the theory, but do not constitute the whole of it. Newtonian mechanics also contains supplementary assumptions, telling us, for example, that for certain special systems the effects of forces other than gravity are negligible. This more elaborate collection of statements *does* have observational consequences and is falsifiable.

But the remedy fails. Imagine that we attempt to expose some self-styled spiritual teacher as an overpaid fraud. We try to point out that the teacher's central message—"Quietness is wholeness in the center of stillness"—is unfalsifiable. The teacher cheerfully admits that, taken by itself, this profound doctrine yields no observational consequences. He then points out that, by themselves, the central statements of scientific theories are also incapable of generating observational consequences. Alas, if all that is demanded is that a doctrine be embedded in a group of statements with observational consequences, our imagined guru will easily slither off the hook. He replies, "You have forgotten that my doctrine has many other claims. For example, I believe that if quietness is wholeness in the center of stillness, then flowers bloom in the spring, bees gather pollen, and blinkered defenders of so-called science raise futile objections to the world's spiritual benefactors. You will see that these three predictions are borne out by experience. Of course, there are countless others. Perhaps when you see how my central message yields so much evident truth, you will recognize the wealth of evidence behind my claim. Quietness is wholeness in the center of stillness."

More formally, the trouble is that *any* statement can be coupled with other statements to produce observational consequences. Given any doctrine *D*, and any statement *O* that records the result of an observation, we can enable *D* to "predict" *O* by adding the extra assumption, "If *D*, then *O*." (In the example, *D* is "Quietness is wholeness in the center of stillness"; examples of *O* would be statements describing the blooming of particular flowers in the spring, the pollen gathering of specific bees, and so forth.)

The falsifiability criterion adopted from Popper—which I shall call the *naive falsificationist* criterion—is hopelessly flawed. It runs aground on a fundamental fact about the relation between theory and prediction: On their own, individual scientific laws, or the small groups of laws that are often identified as theories, do not have observational consequences. This crucial point about theories was first understood by the great historian and philosopher of science Pierre Duhem. Duhem saw clearly that individual scientific claims do not, and cannot, confront the evidence one by one. Rather, in his picturesque phrase, "Hypotheses are tested in bundles." Besides ruling out the possibility of testing an individual scientific theory (read, small group of laws), Duhem's insight has another startling consequence. We can only test relatively large bundles of claims. What this means is that when our experiments go awry we are not logically compelled to select any particular claim as the culprit. We can always save a cherished hypothesis from refutation by rejecting (however implausibly) one of the other members of the bundle. Of course, this is exactly what I did in the illustration of Newton and the apple above. Faced with disappointing results, I suggested that we could abandon the (tacit) additional claim that no large forces besides gravity were operating on the apple.

Creationists wheel out the ancient warhorse of naive falsificationism so that they can bolster their charge that evolutionary theory is not a science. The (very) brief course in deductive logic plus the whirlwind tour through naive falsificationism and its pitfalls enable us to see what is at the bottom of this seemingly important criticism. Creationists can appeal to naive falsificationism to show that evolution is not a science. But, given the traditional picture of theory and evidence I have sketched, one can appeal to naive falsificationism to show that *any* science is not a science. So, as with the charge that evolutionary change is unobservable, Creationists have again failed to find some "fault" of evolution not shared with every other science. (And, as we shall see, Creationists like some sciences, especially thermodynamics.) Consistent application of naive falsificationism can show that anybody's favorite science (whether it be quantum physics, molecular biology, or whatever) is not science. Of course, what this shows is that the naive falsificationist criterion is a very poor test of genuine science. To be fair, this point can cut both ways. Scientists who charge that "scientific" Creationism is unfalsifiable are not insulting the theory as much as they think.

SUCCESSFUL SCIENCE

Despite the inadequacies of naive falsificationism, there is surely something right in the idea that a science can succeed only if it can fail. An invulnerable "science" would not be science at all. To achieve a more adequate under-standing of how a science can succeed and how it runs the risk of failure, let us look at one of the most successful sciences and at a famous episode in its development.

Newtonian celestial mechanics is one of the star turns in the history of science. Among its numerous achievements were convincing explanations of the orbits of most of the known planets. Newton and his successors viewed the solar system as a collection of bodies subject only to gravitational inter-actions; they used the law of gravitation and the laws of motion to compute the orbits. (Bodies whose effects were negligible in any particular case would be disregarded. For example, the gravitational attraction due to Mer-cury would not be considered in working out the orbit of Saturn.) The results usually tallied beautifully with astronomical observations. But one case proved difficult. The outermost known planet, Uranus, stubbornly followed an orbit that diverged from the best computations. By the early nineteenth century it was clear that something was wrong. Either astronomers erred in treating the solar system as a Newtonian gravitational system or there was some particular difficulty in applying the general method to Uranus.

Perhaps the most naive of falsificationists would have recommended that the central claim of Newtonian mechanics—the claim that the solar system is a Newtonian gravitational system—be abandoned. But there was obvi-ously a more sensible strategy. Astronomers faced one problematical planet, and they asked themselves what made Uranus so difficult. Two of them, John Adams and Urbain Leverrier, came up with an answer. They proposed (inde-pendently) that there was a hitherto unobserved planet beyond Uranus. They computed the orbit of the postulated planet and demonstrated that the anom-alies of the motion of Uranus could be explained if a planet followed this path. There was a straightforward way to test their proposal. Astronomers began to look for the new planet. Within a few years, the planet—Neptune—was found.

I will extract several morals from this success story. The first concerns an issue we originally encountered in Morris's "table of natural predictions:" What is the proper use of auxiliary hypotheses? Adams and Leverrier saved the central claim of Newtonian celestial mechanics by offering an auxiliary hypothesis. They maintained that there were more things in the heavens than had been dreamed of in previous natural philosophy. The anomalies in the orbit of Uranus could be explained on the assumption of an extra planet. Adams and Leverrier worked out the exact orbit of that planet so that they could provide a detailed account of the perturbations—and so that they could tell their fellow astronomers where to look for Neptune. Thus, their auxiliary hypothesis was *independently testable*. The evidence for Neptune's existence was not just the anomalous motion of Uranus. The hypothesis could be checked independently of any assumptions about Uranus or about the correctness of Newtonian celestial mechanics—by making telescopic observations.

Since hypotheses are always tested in bundles, this method of checking presupposed other assumptions, in particular, the optical principles that justify the use of telescopes. The crucial point is that, while hypotheses are always tested in bundles, they can be tested in *different* bundles. An auxiliary hypothesis ought to be testable independently of the particular problem it is introduced to solve, independently of the theory it is designed to save.

While it is obvious in retrospect—indeed it was obvious at the time—that the problem with Uranus should not be construed as "falsifying" celestial mechanics, it is worth asking explicitly why scientists should have clung to Newton's theory in the face of this difficulty. The answer is not just that nothing succeeds like success, and that Newton's theory had been strikingly successful in calculating the orbits of the other planets. The crucial point concerns the way in which Newton's successes had been achieved. Newton was no opportunist, using one batch of assumptions to cope with Mercury, and then moving on to new devices to handle Venus. Celestial mechanics was a remarkably *unified* theory. It solved problems by invoking the same pattern of reasoning, or *problem-solving strategy*, again and again: From a specification of the positions of the bodies under study, use the law of gravitation to calculate the forces acting; from a statement of the forces acting, use the laws of dynamics to compute the equations of motion; solve the equations of motion to obtain the motions of the bodies. This single pattern of reasoning was applied in case after case to yield conclusions that were independently found to be correct.

At a higher level, celestial mechanics was itself contained in a broader theory. Newtonian physics, as a whole, was remarkably unified. It offered a strategy for solving a diverse collection of problems. Faced with *any* question about motion, the Newtonian suggestion was the same: Find the forces acting, from the forces and the laws of dynamics work out the equations of motion, and solve the equations of motion. The method was employed in a broad range of cases. The revolutions of planets, the motions of projectiles, tidal cycles and pendulum oscillations—all fell to the same problem-solving strategy.

We can draw a second moral. A science should be *unified*. A thriving science is not a gerrymandered patchwork but a coherent whole. Good theories consist of just one problem-solving strategy, or a small family of problem-solving strategies, that can be applied to a wide range of problems. The theory succeeds as it is able to encompass more and more problem areas. Failure looms when the basic problem-solving strategy (or strategies) can resolve almost none of the problems in its intended domain without the "aid" of untestable auxiliary hypotheses.

Despite the vast successes of his theory, Newton hoped for more. He envisaged a time when scientists would recognize other force laws, akin to the law of gravitation, so that other branches of physics could model themselves after celestial mechanics. In addition, he suggested that many physical questions that are not ostensibly about motion—questions about heat and about chemical combination, for example—could be reduced to problems of motion. *Principia*, Newton's masterpiece, not only offered a theory; it also advertised a program:

> I wish we could derive the rest of the phenomena of Nature by the same kind of reasoning from mechanical principles, for I am induced by many reasons to suspect that they may all depend upon certain forces by which the particles of bodies, by some causes hitherto unknown, are either mutually impelled towards one another, and cohere in regular figures, or are repelled and recede from one another. These forces being unknown, philosophers have hitherto attempted the search of Nature in vain; but I hope the principles here laid down will afford some light either to this or some truer method of philosophy.[9]

Newton's message was clear. His own work only began the task of applying an immensely fruitful, unifying idea.

Newton's successors were moved, quite justifiably, to extend the theory he had offered. They attempted to show how Newton's main problem-solving strategy could be applied to a broader range of physical phenomena. During the eighteenth and nineteenth centuries, the search for understanding of the forces of nature was carried into hydrodynamics, optics, chemistry, and the studies of heat, elasticity, electricity, and magnetism. Not all of these endeavors were equally successful. Nevertheless, Newton's directive fostered the rise of some important new sciences.

The final moral I want to draw from this brief look at Newtonian physics concerns *fecundity*. A great scientific theory, like Newton's, opens up new areas of research. Celestial mechanics led to the discovery of a previously unknown planet. Newtonian physics as a whole led to the development of previously unknown sciences. Because a theory presents a new way of looking at the world, it can lead us to ask new questions, and so to embark on new and fruitful lines of inquiry. Of the many flaws with the earlier picture of theories as sets of statements, none is more important than the misleading presentation of sciences as static and insular. Typically, a flourishing science is incomplete. At any time, it raises more questions than it can currently answer. But incompleteness is no vice. On the contrary, incompleteness is the mother of fecundity. Unresolved problems present challenges that enable a theory to flower in unanticipated ways. They also make the theory hostage to future developments. A good theory should be productive; it should raise new questions and presume that those questions can be answered without giving up its problem-solving strategies.

I have highlighted three characteristics of successful science. *Independent testability* is achieved when it is possible to test auxiliary hypotheses independently of the particular cases for which they are introduced. *Unification* is the result of applying a small family of problem-solving strategies to a broad class of cases. *Fecundity* grows out of incompleteness when a theory opens up new and profitable lines of investigation. Given these marks of successful science, it is easy to see how sciences can fall short, and how some doctrines can do so badly that they fail to count as science at all. A scientific theory begins to wither if some of its auxiliary assumptions can be saved from refutation only by rendering them untestable; or if its problem-solving strategies become a hodgepodge, a collection of unrelated methods, each designed for a separate recalcitrant case; or if the promise of the theory just fizzles, the few questions it raises leading only to dead ends.

When does a doctrine fail to be a science? If a doctrine fails sufficiently abjectly as a science, then it fails to be a science. Where bad science becomes egregious enough, pseudoscience begins. The example of Newtonian physics shows us how to replace the simple (and incorrect) naive falsificationist criterion with a battery of tests. Do the doctrine's problem-solving strategies encounter recurrent difficulties in a significant range of cases? Are the problem-solving strategies an opportunistic collection of unmotivated and unrelated methods? Does the doctrine have too cozy a relationship with auxiliary hypotheses, applying its strategies with claims that can be "tested" only in their applications? Does the doctrine refuse to follow up on unresolved problems, airily dismissing them as "exceptional cases"? Does the doctrine restrict the domain of its methods, forswearing excursions into new areas of investigation where embarrassing questions might arise? If all, or many, of these tests are positive, then the doctrine is not a poor scientific theory. It is not a scientific theory at all.

The account of successful science that I have given not only enables us to replace the naive falsificationist criterion with something better. It also provides a deeper understanding of how theories are justified. Predictive success is one important way in which a theory can win our acceptance. But it is not the only way. In general, theories earn their laurels by solving problems—providing answers that can be independently recognized as correct—and by their fruitfulness. Making a prediction is answering a special kind of question. The astronomers who used celestial mechanics to predict the motion of Mars were answering the question of where Mars would be found. Yet, very frequently, our questions do not concern what occurs, but *why* it occurs. We already *know* that something happens and we want an explanation. Science offers us explanations by setting the phenomena within a unified framework. Using a widely applicable problem-solving strategy, together with independently confirmed auxiliary hypotheses, scientists show that what happened was to be expected. It was known before Newton that the orbits of the planets are approximately elliptical. One of the great achievements of Newton's celestial mechanics was to apply its problem-solving strategy to deduce that the orbit of any planet will be approximately elliptical, thereby explaining the shape of the orbits. In general, science is at least as concerned with reducing the number of unexplained phenomena as it is with generating correct predictions.

The most global Creationist attack on evolutionary theory is the claim that evolution is not a science. If this claim were correct, then the dispute about what to teach in high school science classes would be over. Earlier . . . we saw how Creationists were able to launch their broad criticisms. If one accepts the idea that science requires proof, or if one adopts the naive falsificationist criterion, then the theory of evolution—and every other scientific theory—will turn out not to be a part of science. So Creationist standards for science imply that there is no science to be taught.

However, we have seen that Creationist standards rest on a very poor understanding of science. In light of a clearer picture of the scientific enterprise, I have provided a more realistic group of tests for good science, bad science, and pseudoscience. Using this more sophisticated approach, I now want to address seriously the global Creationist questions about the theory of evolution. Is it a pseudoscience? Is it a poor science? Or is it a great science? These are very important questions, for the appropriateness of granting equal time to Creation "science" depends, in part, on whether it can be regarded as the equal of the theory of evolution.

DARWIN'S DARING

The heart of Darwinian evolutionary theory is a family of problem-solving strategies, related by their common employment of a particular style of historical narrative. A *Darwinian history* is a piece of reasoning of the following general form. The first step consists in a description of an ancestral population of organisms. The reasoning proceeds by tracing the modification of the population through subsequent generations, showing how characteristics were selected, inherited, and became prevalent. (. . . Natural selection is taken to be the primary—but not the only—force of evolutionary change.)

Reasoning like this can be used to answer a host of biological questions. Suppose that we want to know why a contemporary species manifests a particular trait. We can answer that question by supplying a Darwinian history that describes the emergence of that trait. Equally, we can use Darwinian histories to answer questions about relationships among groups of organisms. One way to explain why two species share a common feature is to trace their descent from a common ancestor. Questions of biogeography can be addressed in a similar way. We can explain why we find contemporary organisms where we do by following the course of their historical modifications and migrations. Finally, we can tackle problems about extinction by showing how characteristics that had enabled organisms to thrive were no longer advantageous when the environment (or the competition) changed. In all these cases, we find related strategies for solving problems. The history of the development of populations, understood in terms of variation, competition, selection, and inheritance, is used to shed light on broad classes of biological phenomena.

The questions that evolutionary theory has addressed are so numerous that any sample is bound to omit important types. The following short selection undoubtedly reflects the idiosyncrasy of my interests: Why do orchids have such intricate internal structures? Why are male birds of paradise so brightly colored? Why do some reptilian precursors of mammals have enormous "sails" on their backs? Why do bats typically roost upside down? Why are the

hemoglobins of humans and apes so similar? Why are there no marsupial ana-
logues of seals and whales? Why is the mammalian fauna of Madagascar so
distinctive? Why did the large, carnivorous ground birds of South America
become extinct? Why is the sex ratio in most species one to one (although it
is markedly different in some species of insects)? Answers to these questions,
employing Darwinian histories, can be found in works written by contemporary Darwinian biologists. Those works contain answers to a myriad of other
questions of the same general types. Darwinian histories are constructed again
and again to illuminate the characteristics of contemporary organisms, to
account for the similarities and differences among species, to explain why the
forms preserved in the fossil record emerged and became extinct, to cast light
on the geographical distribution of animals and plants.

We can see the theory in action by taking a brief look at one of these
examples. The island of Madagascar, off the east coast of Africa, supports a
peculiar group of mammals. Many of these mammals are endemic. Among
them is a group of relatively small insectivorous mammals, the *tenrecs*. All
tenrecs share certain features that mark them out as relatively primitive mammals. They have very poor vision, their excretory system is rudimentary, the
testes in the male are carried within the body, their capacity for regulating
their body temperature is poor compared with that of most mammals. Yet, on
their simple and rudimentary body plan, specialized characteristics have often
been imposed. Some tenrecs have the hedgehog's method of defense. Others
have the forelimbs characteristic of moles. There are climbing tenrecs that
resemble the shrews, and there are tenrecs that defend themselves by
attempting to stick their quills into a would-be predator. Hedgehogs, moles,
tree shrews, and porcupines do not inhabit Madagascar. But they seem to have
their imitators. (These are examples of convergent evolution, cases in which
unrelated organisms take on some of the same characteristics.) Why are these
peculiar animals found on Madagascar, and nowhere else?

A straightforward evolutionary story makes sense of what we observe.
In the late Mesozoic or early Cenozoic, small, primitive, insectivorous mammals rafted across the Mozambique channel and colonized Madagascar.
Later the channel widened and Madagascar became inaccessible to the more
advanced mammals that evolved on the mainland. Hence the early colonists
developed without competition from advanced mainland forms and without
pressure from many of the normal predators who make life difficult for small
mammals. The tenrecs have been relatively protected. In the absence of rigorous competition, they have preserved their simple body plan, and they have

exploited unoccupied niches, which are filled elsewhere by more advanced creatures. Tenrecs have gone up the trees and burrowed in the ground because those are good ways to make a living and because they have had nobody but one another to contend with.

The same kind of story can be told again and again to answer all sorts of questions about all sorts of living things. Evolutionary theory is unified because so many diverse questions—questions as various as those I listed—can be addressed by advancing Darwinian histories. Moreover, these narratives constantly make claims that are subject to independent check. Here are four examples from the case of the triumphant tenrecs. (1) The explanation presupposes that Madagascar has drifted away from the east coast of Africa. That is something that can be checked by using geological criteria for the movement of landmasses, criteria that are independent of biology. (2) The account claims that the tenrecs would have been able to raft across the Mozambique channel, but that the present channel constitutes a barrier to more advanced mammals (small rodents). These claims could be tested by looking to see whether the animals in question can disperse across channels of the appropriate sizes. (3) The narrative assumes that the specialized methods of defense offered advantages against the predators that were present in Madagascar. Studies of animal interactions can test whether the particular defenses are effective against local predators. (4) Central to the explanatory account is the thesis that the tenrecs are related. If this is so, then studies of the minute details of tenrec anatomy should reveal many common features, and the structures of proteins ought to be similar. In particular, the tenrecs ought to be much more like one another than they are like hedgehogs, shrews, or moles.

Looking at one example, or even at a small number of examples, does not really convey the strength of evolutionary theory. The same patterns of reasoning can be applied again and again, in book after book, monograph after monograph, article after article. Yet the particular successes in dealing with details of natural history, numerous though they are, do not exhaust the accomplishments of the theory. Darwin's original theory—the problem-solving strategies advanced in the *Origin*, which are, in essence, those just described—gave rise to important new areas of scientific investigation. Evolutionary theory has been remarkably fruitful.

Darwin not only provided a scheme for unifying the diversity of life. He also gave a structure to our ignorance. After Darwin, it was important to resolve general issues about the presuppositions of Darwinian histories. The way in which biology should proceed had been made admirably plain, and it was clear that biologists had to tackle questions for which they had, as yet, no answers. How do new characteristics arise in populations? What are the mechanisms of inheritance? How do characteristics become fixed in populations? What criteria decide when a characteristic confers some advantage on its possessor? What interactions among populations of organisms affect the adaptive value of characteristics? With respect to all of these questions, Darwin was forced to confess ignorance. By raising them, his theory pointed the way to its further articulation.

Since Darwin's day, biologists have contributed parts of evolutionary theory that help to answer these important questions. Geneticists have advanced our understanding of the transmission of characteristics between generations and have enabled us to see how new characteristics can arise. Population geneticists have analyzed the variation present in populations of organisms; they have suggested how that variation is maintained and have specified ways in which characteristics can be fixed or eliminated. Workers in morphology and physiology have helped us to see how variations of particular kinds might yield advantages in particular environments. Ecologists have studied the ways in which interactions among populations can affect survival and fecundity.

The moral is obvious. Darwin gambled. He trusted that the questions he left open would be answered by independent biological sciences and that the deliverances of these sciences would be consistent with the presuppositions of Darwinian histories. Because of the breadth of his vision, Darwin made his theory vulnerable from a number of different directions. To take just one example, it could have turned out the mechanisms of heredity would have made it impossible for advantageous variations to be preserved and to spread. Indeed, earlier in this century, many biologists felt that the emerging views about inheritance did not fit into Darwin's picture, and the fortunes of Darwinian evolutionary theory were on the wane.

When we look at the last 120 years of the history of biology, it is impossible to ignore the fecundity of Darwin's ideas. Not only have inquiries into the presuppositions of Darwinian histories yielded new theoretical disciplines (like population genetics), but the problem-solving strategies have been extended to cover phenomena that initially appeared troublesome. One recent triumph has been the development of explanations for social interactions among animals. Behavior involving one animal's promotion of the good of others seems initially to pose a problem for evolutionary theory. How can we construct Darwinian histories for the emergence of such behavior? W. D.

Hamilton's concept of inclusive fitness, and the deployment of game-theoretic ideas by R. L. Trivers and John Maynard Smith, revealed how the difficulty could be resolved by a clever extension of traditional Darwinian concepts.

Yet puzzles remain. One problem is the existence of sex. When an organism forms gametes (sperm cells or egg cells) there is a meiotic division, so that in sexual reproduction only half of an organism's genes are transmitted to each of its progeny. Because of this "cost of meiosis," it is hard to see how genotypes for sexual reproduction might have become prevalent. (Apparently, they will spread only half as fast as their asexual rivals.) So why is there sex? We do not have a compelling answer to the question. Despite some ingenious suggestions by orthodox Darwinians there is no convincing Darwinian history for the emergence of sexual reproduction. However, evolutionary theorists believe that the problem will be solved without abandoning the main Darwinian insights—just as early nineteenth-century astronomers believed that the problem of the motion of Uranus could be overcome without major modification of Newton's celestial mechanics.

The comparison is apt. Like Newton's physics in 1800, evolutionary theory today rests on a huge record of successes. In both cases, we find a unified theory whose problem-solving strategies are applied to illuminate a host of diverse phenomena. Both theories offer problem solutions that can be subjected to rigorous independent checks. Both open up new lines of inquiry and have a history of surmounting apparent obstacles. The virtues of successful science are clearly displayed in both.

NOTES

1. Henry M. Morris, *The Troubled Waters of Evolution* (San Diego: Creation-Life Publishers, 1974), 16.

2. David C. C. Watson, *The Great Brain Robbery* (Chicago: Moody, 1976), 46.

3. Karl Popper, *The Logic of Scientific Discovery* (London: Hutchison, 1959) and Karl Popper, *Conjectures and Refutations* (New York: Harper, 1963).

4. Stephen J. Gould, "Evolution as Fact and Theory," *Discover* 2 (May 1981): 34–37.

5. Morris, *The Troubled Waters of Evolution*, 80.

6. Duane Gish, *Evolution? The Fossils Say No!* (San Diego: Creation-Life Publishers, 1979), 13.

7. Henry M. Morris, *Scientific Creationism*, general edition (San Diego: Creation-Life Publishers, 1974), 6.

8. Ibid., 13.

9. Isaac Newton, *The Mathematical Principles of Natural Philosophy*, ed. Florian Cajori, trans. Andrew Motte (Berkeley: University of California Press, 1960), xviii.

TURNING BACK THE CLOCK

MICHAEL RUSE

Although the fundamentalist movement went into decline after the Scopes trial, it never vanished. In the 1990s, a new group of evangelical Christians hostile to evolution took over the crusade. The rallying post was *Darwin on Trial* by Berkeley law professor Phillip Johnson, a work in which the author of the *Origin* was tried, convicted, and led away in chains.

As the decade matured, the fundamentalists switched from purely negative attacks on Darwinism to more positive claims. Ostensibly keeping their theological motives to a minimum, this group now directed its attention toward what they called an Intelligent Designer. The biochemist Michael Behe, in his best-selling book *Darwin's Black Box*, most fully articulated the empirical case. He focused on "irreducible complexity," which he defined as "a single system composed of several well-matched, interacting parts that contribute to the basic function, wherein the removal of any one of the parts

---

Michael Ruse, "Turning Back the Clock," *Darwin and Design: Does Evolution have a Purpose?* (Cambridge, MA: Harvard University Press, 2003), 315–36.

causes the system to effectively cease functioning." Behe added that any "irreducibly complex biological system, if there is such a thing, would be a powerful challenge to Darwinian evolution. Since natural selection can only choose systems that are already working, then if a biological system cannot be produced gradually it would have to arise as an integrated unit, in one fell swoop, for natural selection to have anything to act on."[1]

As an example of something irreducibly complex, Behe instanced the common mousetrap. This has various parts (five in a standard model—spring, base, and so forth), which are put together to produce a fatal snapping motion when the trigger is activated by a small rodent attempting to take the bait. Behe's point was that this mousetrap is an all-or-nothing phenomenon. Take away any one part and you have something that simply does not function at all. You could not have a mousetrap with four and a half parts or only four parts. "If the hammer were gone, the mouse could dance all night on the platform without becoming pinned to the wooden base. If there were no spring, the hammer and platform would jangle loosely, and again the rodent would be unimpeded."[2] And so on, through the various parts. The mousetrap functions only when it is entirely up and running. It could not have come about through gradual development—and of course, as we know, it did not. It came about through the conscious intent and actions of a human designer. It was planned and fabricated.

Now turn to the world of biology, and in particular turn to the microworld of the cell and of mechanisms that we find at that level. Take bacteria, which use a flagellum, driven by a kind of rotary motor, to move around. Every part is incredibly complex, and so are the various parts when combined. The external filament of the flagellum, for instance, is a single protein which makes a kind of paddle surface that contacts the liquid during swimming. Near the surface of the cell, one finds a thickening—just as needed, so that the filament can be connected to the rotor drive. This naturally requires a connector, known as a "hook protein." There is no motor in the filament, so that has to be somewhere else—at the base of the flagellum, according to Behe, where electron microscopy reveals several ring structures. All way too complex to have come into being gradually, in Behe's view. Only a one-step process would do, and this one-step process must have involved some sort of designing cause. Behe was careful not to identify this designer with the Christian God, but his implication was that it is a force from without the normal course of nature. Things happen through "the guidance of an intelligent agent."[3] More recently Behe has made his own commitment to the Christian God more explicit.

THE CONCEPTUAL ARGUMENT FOR INTELLIGENT DESIGN

Backing Behe's empirical argument was a conceptual argument presented by the philosopher-mathematician William Dembski. His aim was three-fold. First, to give us the criteria by which we can distinguish something that we would label "designed" rather than otherwise. Second, to show how we distinguish design from something produced naturally by law or something we would put down to chance. Third, to explain why it is impossible for any naturalistic process, including evolution by natural selection, to produce the organic world as we see around us today, that is, a world of design (or, not to prejudice the issue, design appearance).

To infer design, Dembski required three components: contingency, complexity, and specification. Contingency is the idea that something has happened that cannot be ascribed simply to blind law. Being hanged for murder is contingent; falling to the ground when I jump off a stool is not. Design requires contingency. The example Dembski used was the message received from outer space in the movie *Contact*. The series of dots and dashes, zeros and ones, could not be deduced from the laws of physics. They were contingent. But do they show evidence of design?

Here is where complexity comes in, according to Dembski. Suppose we can interpret the series in a binary fashion, and the initial yield is the number group 2, 3, 5. As it happens, these are the beginning of the prime number series, but with so small a yield no one is going to get very excited. It could just be chance, not design. But suppose now you keep going in the series, and it turns out that it yields, in exact and precise order, the prime numbers up to 101. At that point you would start to think that something is up, because the situation seems just too complex to be mere chance. It is highly improbable.

Although most of us would be happy to conclude, on the basis of the improbable prime number sequence, that there are extraterrestrials out there, in fact another component is needed: specification. "If I flip a coin 1000 times, I will participate in a highly complex (that is, highly improbable) event. Indeed, the sequence I end up flipping will be one in a trillion trillion trillion . . . where the ellipsis needs twenty-two more 'trillions.' This sequence of coin tosses will not, however, trigger a design inference. Though complex, this sequence will not exhibit a suitable pattern." Here, we have a contrast with the prime number sequence from 2 to 101. "Not only is this sequence complex, but it also embodies a suitable pattern. The SETI researcher in the movie *Contact* who discovered this sequence put it this way: 'This isn't noise, this has structure.'"[4]

What is going on here? According to Dembski, we recognize in design something that is not just arbitrary or random but rather something that was or could be in some way specified, insisted upon, at the outset. We know or could work out the sequence of prime numbers at any time before or after contact from space. The random sequence of penny tosses will come only after the event. "The key concept is that of 'independence.' I define a specification as a match between an event and an independently given pattern. Events that are both highly complex and specified (that is, that match an independently given pattern) indicate design."

This move puts Dembski in a position to go on to the second part of his argument, where we actually detect design. Here we have what he called an explanatory filter. We have a particular phenomenon; the question is, what caused it? Is it something that might not have happened, given the laws of nature? Is it contingent? Or was it necessitated? The moon goes endlessly around the earth. We know that it does this because of Newton's laws. End of discussion. No design here. However, now we have some rather strange new phenomenon, the causal origin of which is a puzzle. Suppose we have a mutation, where although we can predict occurrences over large numbers, we cannot predict a specific individual occurrence. Let us say, as supposedly happened in the extended royal family of Europe, there was a mutation to a gene, and this mutation was responsible for hemophilia. Is it complex? Obviously not, for it leads to breakdown rather than otherwise. Hence it is appropriate to talk here of chance rather than design. The hemophilia mutation was just an accident.

Suppose now that we have a complex mineral pattern where veins of precious metals are set in other materials, the whole being intricate and varied—certainly not a pattern one could simply deduce from the laws of physics or chemistry or geology or whatever. Nor would one think of it as being a breakdown mess, as one might a malmutation. Is this therefore design? Almost certainly not, for there is no way that one might pre-specify such a pattern. It is all a bit ad hoc and not something that comes across as the result of conscious intention.

But suppose finally that we have the microscopical biological apparatuses and processes discussed by Behe. They are contingent, they are irreducibly complex, and they are of pre-specified form. As such, they can survive the explanatory filter and be properly considered the product of real design.

Of course, the nature of their designer is another matter. Because one accepts Intelligent Design, one is certainly not thereby necessarily pushed into a literalistic reading of the early chapters of Genesis—six days, six thousand years, universal flood. Still, Dembski was explicit in his belief that evolution is ruled out by this analysis. Why is this? This is where the third, more recent, part of his argument kicked in. Dembski invoked what are known as "no free lunch" theorems, which claim essentially that you cannot get out what you do not put in. Garbage in, garbage out. Or in our specific case; No design in, no design out. In Dembski's opinion, even a guided "theistic" evolution of the Asa Gray variety is unacceptable.

Thinking of an "evolutionary algorithm" as some kind of automatic selection process or rule (like "choose black over white two times out of three"), Dembski writes: "The No Free Lunch theorems underscore the fundamental limits of the Darwinian mechanism. Up until their proof, it was thought that because the Darwinian mechanism could account for all of biological complexity, evolutionary algorithms (i.e., their mathematical underpinnings) must be universal problems solvers. The No Free Lunch theorems show that evolutionary algorithms, apart from careful fine-tuning by a programmer, are no better than blind search and thus no better than pure chance. Consequently, these theorems cast doubt on the power of the Darwinian mechanism to account for all of biological complexity."[5]

INTELLIGENT DESIGN CRITICIZED

Irreducible complexity supposedly could not have come about through unbroken law, and especially not through the agency of natural selection, according to Behe and Dembski. Behe's example of a mousetrap is somewhat unfortunate, however, for it is simply not the case that the trap will work only with all five pieces in place. For a start, one could reduce the number to four by removing the base and fixing the trap to the floor. It might be better if you could move it around, but selection never claimed to produce perfection— simply to produce something that functions better than the immediate alternatives. In fact, . . . it may even be possible to reduce the number of components down to one! Not a great trap, but a trap nevertheless.

Rather more significant, though, is that Behe's mousetrap shows a misunderstanding of the way natural selection works. No Darwinian would deny that in organisms there are parts which, if removed, would lead at once to the malfunctioning or nonfunctioning of the systems in which they occur. The point is not whether the parts now in place could be removed without collapse but whether they could have been put in place by natural selection.

To counter Behe's artifactual analogy, we can think of other artifactual analogies that show precisely how the apparently impossible could be achieved. Consider an arched bridge made from cut stone, without cement, held in place only by the force of the stones against one another. If you tried to build the bridge from scratch, upward and then inward, you would fail— the stones would keep falling to the ground. Indeed, the whole bridge now would collapse if you were to remove the keystone or any stone surrounding it. What you must do to construct an arch is, first, build a supporting structure (possibly an earthen embankment) on which you lay the stones of the bridge, until they are all in place. Then you remove the structure, which is now no longer needed and in fact is in the way of walking under the bridge. Likewise, one can imagine a bio-chemical sequential process with several stages, on parts of which other processes piggyback, as it were. When the hitherto nonsequential parasitic processes link up and start functioning independently, the original sequence is eventually removed by natural selection because it is redundant or drains resources.

Moving from the pretend to the actual, today's Darwinians have many examples of the most complex of processes that have been put in place by selection. Take as an example the process whereby energy from food is converted into a form that can be used by the cells. This process, called the Krebs cycle, occurs in the cell's mitochondria and centers on two molecules, ATP (adenosine triphosphate) and ADP (adenosine diphosphate). The former is more energy-rich than the latter and is degraded by the body when it needs power. Not only are the molecules themselves complex but so also is the Krebs cycle that makes ATP from other sources of energy. There are almost a dozen sub-processes in the cycle, each making a new product from an earlier one. Every one of these sub-processes demands its own enzyme (these are molecular substances that prime chemical reactions). Do not think that the cycle just appeared out of thin air, complete and entire as it were. Each part of the cycle started life doing something else and then . . . was grabbed by the cells and put to a new use. Although, when they set out, the scientists who found all of this out certainly did not have Behe and his "irreducible complexity" in mind, one could imagine that they did, especially from the way in which they set up the problem: "The Krebs cycle has been frequently quoted as a key problem in the evolution of living cells, hard to explain by

Darwin's natural selection: How could natural selection explain the building of a complicated structure in toto, when the intermediate stages have no obvious fitness functionality?"[6]

A Behe-type problem, but no Behe-type answer. To the contrary, the various parts of the Krebs cycle had their original uses, and then these were taken over for the whole:

> The Krebs cycle was built through the process that Jacob (1977) called "evolution by molecular tinkering," stating that evolution does not produce novelties from scratch: It works on what already exists. The most novel result of our analysis is seeing how, with minimal new material, evolution created the most important pathway of metabolism, achieving the best chemically possible design. In this case, a chemical engineer who was looking for the best design of the process could not have found a better design than the cycle which works in living cells.[7]

Behe's position does not seem plausible, given what we know of the nature of mutation and the stability of biological systems over time. When exactly does the Intelligent Designer supposedly strike to do its work? In *Darwin's Black Box* Behe suggests that everything might have been done long ago and then left to its own devices. "The irreducibly complex biochemical systems that I have discussed . . . did not have to be produced recently. It is entirely possible, based simply on an examination of the systems themselves, that they were designed billions of years ago and that they have been passed down to the present by the normal processes of cellular reproduction."[8] Although Behe ignores the history of the preformed genes from the point between their origin (when they would not have been needed) and today (when they are in full use), we should not. According to the biochemist Kenneth Miller, "As any student of biology will tell you, because those genes are not expressed, natural selection would not be able to weed out genetic mistakes. Mutations would accumulate in these genes at breathtaking rates, rendering them hopelessly changed and inoperative hundreds of millions of years before Behe says that they will be needed."[9] There is a mass of experimental evidence showing this to be the case. Behe's idea of a designer doing everything back then and leaving matters to their natural fate is "pure and simple fantasy."

And what about malmutations? If a designer is needed and available to solve complex engineering problems, why could not the designer take some time on the simple matters, specifically those simple matters that if unfixed lead to absolutely horrendous outcomes? Some of the worst genetic diseases are caused by one little alteration in one little part of the DNA. Sickle cell anemia, for example. If the designer is able and willing to do the very complex because it is very good, why does it not do the very simple because the alternative is very bad? Behe speaks of this as being part of the problem of evil—true enough, but just labeling it is not very helpful. Given that the opportunity and ability to do good was so obvious and yet not taken, we need to know why not.

EXPLANATORY FILTERS

Here Dembski comes to the rescue. A malmutation would surely get caught by the explanatory filter half-way down. It would be siphoned off to the side as chance, if not indeed simply put down as necessity. It certainly would not pass the specification test. This would mean that sickle cell anemia would not be credited to the designer, whereas the flagellum would be. Dembski stressed that these are mutually exclusive alternatives. "To attribute an event to design is to say that it cannot plausibly be referred to either law or chance. In characterizing design as the set-theoretic complement of the disjunction law-or-chance, one therefore guarantees that these three modes of explanation will be mutually exclusive and exhaustive."[10]

To which one might respond that of course one can define things as one will, and if one stipulates that design and law and chance are mutually exclusive, then so be it. But the downside is that one now has a stipulative definition and not necessarily a lexical definition, that is, one which accords to general use. Suppose that something is put down to chance. Does this mean that law is ruled out? Surely not! If I argue that a Mendelian mutation is chance, what I mean is that with respect to that particular theory it is chance. But I may well believe (I surely will believe) that the mutation came about by normal causes and that if these were all known, then it would no longer be chance at all but necessity. As an eminent Victorian scientist once said about these sorts of things: "I have hitherto sometimes spoken as if the variations—so common and multiform in organic beings under domestication, and in a lesser degree in those in a state of nature—had been due to chance. This, of course, is a wholly incorrect expression, but it serves to acknowledge plainly our ignorance of the cause of each particular variation."[11] The point is that chance is a confession of ignorance, not (as one might well think the case in the quantum world) an assertion about the way things are. That is, claims about chance are not ontological assertions, as presumably claims about designers must be.

More than this, one might well argue that the designer always works through law. This takes us back to deism, or to the kind of position endorsed by Baden Powell. The designer may prefer to have things put in motion in such a way that its intentions unfurl and reveal themselves as time goes by. Hugh Miller's pattern in a piece of cloth made by machine is as much an object of design as the pattern of cloth produced by a hand loom. In other words, in a sense that would conform to the normal usage of the terms, one might want to say of something that it is produced by laws, is chance with respect to our knowledge or theory, and fits into an overall context of design by the great orderer or creator of things.

One finds, indeed, real people who have made precisely this kind of claim. At the time he was writing the *Origin*, this probably even applied to Darwin. Later, Ronald Fisher certainly fit the bill. He argued that natural selection made for ongoing progress in evolution. Selection worked on the multiplicity of chance mutations that occur in every natural population. And he wrapped the whole picture up and saw it as the manifestation of the actions and intentions of a good God, in fact (no surprise here) the very Anglican God that Fisher had worshipped all of his life.

NO FREE LUNCH?

Dembski's filter does not let Behe's designer off the hook. If the designer can make—and rightfully takes credit for—the very complex and good, then the designer could prevent—and by its failure is properly criticized for not preventing—the very simple and awful. The problems in theology are as grim as are those in science. But in a way, the real crux of Dembski's case rests with the third part of his argument, about the sheer impossibility of a natural process doing the job. If that part succeeds, then by a kind of neo-Paleyian argument to the best explanation, Dembski can rightly point out that there must be a solution (and why not his?) to the fact that the designer allows (or cannot prevent) the occurrence of some terrible things.

So it is here—on the possibility issue—that we must focus critical attention, and let us start by admitting that impossibility arguments (often known as *reductio ad absurdum* arguments) are well known in mathematics and logic. Take the famous assertion (attributed to Euclid) that there can be no greatest prime number. Assume that there can be, and call the number P. Then consider the number formed by multiplying P by all of the primes less than P and adding one. That is: $2 \times 3 \times 5 \times 7x \ldots P_{-1} \times P + 1$. This number is bigger than P and is either itself a prime or factors down into primes bigger than P. (Hint: Nothing prime less than or equal to P can go into the number without leaving a remainder of 1.) Hence, there can be no greatest prime, and you do not need to spend your life checking if a prime greater than (say) $10^{2876} + 37$ exists. It does.

The point here is whether you can offer some similar proof applicable to the real world, showing that selection cannot produce design. Behe offered an empirical argument which, judged on its merits, we have rejected. Dembski offered a more theoretical argument, claiming that no free lunch theorems show that you cannot get design out unless you put design in. Fortunately, it is not necessary to dig into any sophisticated mathematics here for, as Dembski himself acknowledged, the only real relevance of such theorems is that they point to the obvious—that what comes out must have been put in. After stating that "these theorems cast doubt on the power of the Darwinian mechanism to account for all of biological complexity," Dembski at once concedes: "Granted, the No Free Lunch Theorems are book-keeping results." And then he tries to cover things by adding: "But book-keeping can be very useful. It keeps us honest about the promissory notes our various enterprises—science being one of them—can and cannot make good. In the case of Darwinism we are no longer entitled to think that the Darwinian mechanism can offer biological complexity as a free lunch."[12]

To which of course the Darwinian will reply that this is all very true but beside the point. The Darwinian is not expecting to get out design. The Darwinian is expecting to get out phenomena with the *appearance* of design—the eye, the hand. And the reason why one can get out these design-like phenomena is that natural selection works on the unorganized phenomena that are put in. Reproduction, mutations, competition, and so forth bring on selection, which brings on adaptations, which are design-like phenomena. The question is not whether design demands design. All can grant that. The question is whether design-like demands design, or if selection can do the job instead. It is here that the impossibility proof, if such there be, must strike.

As it happens, such a proof hovers in the background of all discussions like Dembski's. It holds that random mutation simply cannot produce adaptation, or design-like effects. It starts with the rate of mutation, multiples that by the number of genes carried by the average animal or plant, and comes up with a timescale for the creation of organisms that is billions and billions of years beyond the scales of even the greatest projections for the age of the earth. Powers of ten explode outward uncontrollably like the monsters of science fiction movies. "Obviously . . . a million successive, successful mutational steps, each with a probability of one-half, is almost as inconceivable as the instantaneous chance assemblage of a million components into an integrated whole. The chance of success in this case becomes one out of $(2)^{1,000,000}$, or one out of $(10)^{300,000}$."[13] And so on. Natural processes producing adaptation is about as likely as a monkey randomly typing a play by Shakespeare, these antievolutionists have claimed.

Famously, Richard Dawkins has scotched this kind of argument. Selection decimates the ever-increasing randomness factors. Choosing a line from Shakespeare—METHINKS IT IS A WEASEL—Dawkins shows that one can set up a computer program that produces letters (or blanks) randomly in all twenty-eight spaces that this sentence occupies. It can produce UMMK JK CDZZ F ZD DSDSKSM, for instance, or S SS FMCV PU I DDRGLKDXRRDO. If one were working randomly, the chances of producing the target sentence in one try is about 1 in 10,000 million million million million million million against. Just impossible in fact. Now rejig the program so that it remembers a successful move, in this case getting a little closer to the target sentence. With this constraint added into a system for producing random letters, the target can be reached in less than fifty moves. So much for all of that multiplication. "There is a big difference, then, between cumulative selection (in which each improvement, however slight, is used as a basis for future building), and single-step selection (in which each new 'try' is a fresh one)."[14]

The Intelligent Design people do not give this example much weight, pointing out (correctly) that it has many dis-analogies with real-life situations, beginning with the fact that Dawkins specified the end-point, whereas in nature there is supposedly no such fixed goal. Even a progressionist like Dawkins is not going to say that the Cambrian led inevitably to Englishmen. But Dawkins himself conceded this as soon as he gave his example. He was not trying to simulate nature in every respect. He was simply showing that arguments which multiply randomness to a point beyond possibility can be countered simply by factoring in selection. The real question is whether more sophisticated computer models can show that selective forces can generate genuine complexity—the kind that we associate with real adapted organisms—without having to put such complexity into the pool in the first place. And the answer is that they can.

A beautiful example was devised by the biologist Thomas S. Ray. Tierra—an artificial world he created—lives in Ray's computer; the "organisms" who inhabit it are self-replicating programs of an initially fixed length (80 instructions long). "Having determined the address of its [the organism's] beginning and end, it subtracts the two to calculate its size, and allocates a block of memory of this size for a daughter cell. It then calls the copy procedure which copies the entire genome into the daughter-cell memory, one instruction at a time."[15] Other than being self-replicating, these creatures (as we might neutrally call them) have no functions built in. They exist in a kind of memory pool, and each creature has a chunk of this memory. They cannot write into the program of other creatures, but they can read the information from other creatures and use this information. Time is limited for each creature, and when it has a block of time, it can use it to self-replicate. It then goes to the end of the queue and has to wait its turn for more time. There is a process (the "reaper") by which creatures get eliminated, but creatures can put off extinction by performing tasks (like reproduction) more efficiently than their fellows. Mutations are introduced into the mix by making the information of the creatures, and their replication, subject to random changes.

What happens when you set things in motion?

Once the soup is full, individuals are initially short-lived, generally reproducing only once before dying; thus, individuals turn over very rapidly. More slowly, there appear new genotypes of size 80, and then new size classes. There are changes in the genetic composition of each size class, as new mutants appear, some of which increase significantly in frequency, sometimes replacing the original genotype. The size classes which dominate the community also change through time, as new size classes appear ... some of which competitively exclude sizes present earlier. Once the community becomes diverse, there is a greater variance in the longevity and fecundity of individuals.

In addition to the raw diversity of genotypes and genome sizes, there is an increase in the ecological diversity. Obligate commensurable parasites evolve, which are not capable of self-replication in isolated culture, but which can replicate when cultured with normal (self-replicating) creatures. These parasites execute some part of the code of their hosts, but cause them no direct harm, except as competitors. Some potential hosts have evolved immunity to the parasites, and some parasites have evolved to circumvent this immunity.[16]

There are even more exciting results, including the evolution of hyper-parasites that not only reproduce on their own but, when subject to para-sitism, turn around and use the parasites' own resources to augment their own well-being. One particularly remarkable new feature has an ability to measure internal length when one of the end points (templates) had gone missing. "These creatures located the address of the template marking their beginning, and then the address of a template in the middle of their genome. These two addresses were then subtracted to calculate half of their size, and this value was multiplied by two (by shifting left) to calculate their frill size."[17]

All of this leads to the conclusion that here we have the evolution of adaptations—of specified complexity—through selection, without the need to introduce design in the first place. Just what people like Dembski say cannot happen. Of course this is an artificial situation. We have not got real organisms, simplifications have been introduced, the program was set up to give results in our lifetimes, and so forth. But to object that this (or any sim-ilar program) therefore does not prove the nondesigned production of speci-fied complexity, because Ray (or whoever) had to build up the system in the first place, and this required design, is to miss the whole point of experi-mentation. The key question is whether, even in principle, blind variation acted upon by selection can produce adaptation—design-like features. And the answer is that it can and did.

You cannot get much blinder than Ray's variation. He had no control over where and when it struck. It produced parasitism. Of course it was arti-ficial parasitism. We know that. But if you asked a programmer to produce parasitism, he or she could not get it by striking the keys randomly; design would be required. We know also that an artificial situation is not a real sit-uation. Whether Ray's system tells us anything real about nature requires questions about mutation rate and so forth, and this is another matter. What we are dealing with now is Dembski's claim that blind processes cannot lead to specified complexity, and a system like Ray's Tierra shows that Dembski is just plain wrong.

THE BLIND WATCHMAKER

Suppose you decide to take up Darwinian evolution. Does this now commit you to reject natural theology—or a theology of nature? Is Darwinism positively hostile to any kind of genuine design—inexplicable, illustrative, inspirational, or whatever? Dawkins is one of several who have argued just this. Science and religion make claims, and those claims clash. One side is right and one side is wrong. Dawkins gives and expects no quarter. "A cowardly flabbiness of the intellect afflicts otherwise rational people confronted with long-established religions."[18] As a Darwinian, Dawkins was not about to deny that the Christians got the question right. It was their answer that they got wrong. Speaking of Archdeacon William Paley with respect, if not reverence, Dawkins willingly allowed that *Natural Theology* articulates the teleological argument "more clearly and convincingly than anyone had before."[19] The trouble is that "the analogy between telescope and eye, between watch and living organism, is false. All appearances to the contrary, the only watchmaker in nature is the blind forces of physics, albeit deployed in a very special way." A genuine watchmaker plans everything and puts his purposes into action. Natural selection simply acts. It has no purposes. "It has no mind and no mind's eye. It does not plan for the future. It has no vision, no foresight, no sight at all. If it can be said to play the role of watchmaker in nature, it is the *blind* watchmaker."[20] To put it in our language, Paley was spot-on about the argument to complexity, but he was dead wrong about the argument to design.

Now obviously not all Christians are going to be upset by this. Wolfhart Pannenberg's response will simply be that Paley's mistake was in thinking that God's creative powers could act only through miracle. (Frederick Temple made exactly this point more than a hundred years ago.) Darwin showed that the route to creation must lie through evolution by natural selection. But why should not God have worked this way rather than in some other fashion? Darwin himself thought this when he wrote the *Origin of Species*. It is true that, by this time, Darwin was a deist rather than a theist, but among Christians the Augustinian for one has no theological worries here. You cannot separate Becoming and Being. Although Augustine himself was certainly no evolutionist, he laid the theological groundwork for precisely such a scientific theory.

None of this will convince Dawkins, who has a number of back-up arguments ready to keep Darwinism and Christianity apart. Most powerful to him as a counter-argument against God is the traditional problem of pain and evil, which the Darwinian approach exacerbated. Natural selection presupposes a struggle for existence, and the struggle on many, many occasions is downright nasty. Using the notion of a "utility function" for the end purpose being intended, Dawkins drew attention to the interactions between cheetahs and antelopes, and asks: "What was God's utility function?" Cheetahs seem wonderfully designed to kill antelopes "The teeth, claws, eyes, nose, leg muscles, backbone and brain of a cheetah are all precisely what we should expect if God's purpose in designing cheetahs was to maximize deaths among antelopes." But conversely, "we find equally impressive evidence of design for precisely the opposite end: the survival of antelopes and starvation among cheetahs." It is almost as though two warring gods were at work, making different animals and then setting them to compete with one another. If there is only one god who made the two animals, then what kind of god could it be? "Is He a sadist who enjoys spectator blood sports? Is He trying to avoid over-population in the mammals of Africa? Is He maneuvering to maximize David Attenborough's television ratings?" The whole thing is ludicrous.[21] Truly, concludes Dawkins, there are no ultimate purposes to life, no deep religious meanings. There is nothing.

PAIN

At this point spokespersons in the science/religion community simply retreat. On their way out the door, most agree that Dawkins has a good point—Darwinism does show that life is mean and nasty, without any purpose. But the best way to avoid so unpleasant a conclusion is to abandon Darwinism, rather than give up on religion or even evolution per se. They scramble to find an evolutionism with a warmer, friendlier face. After all, there must be some way to get what you want—adaptation possibly, humans definitely—with a fairly firm guarantee of desired direction. . . . Holmes Rolston III [see last selection in this edited collection] . . . stands out only because—to his credit—he is so clear and forthright in his likes and dislikes and in his personal conviction that Darwinism is not going to speak to them.

This will not do. Whether or not Darwinism—adaptation brought about by natural selection—taken as a whole is both true and in basic outlines essentially complete, it is an active and forward-looking science. Whether we like it or not, we are stuck with it. The Darwinian revolution is over, and Darwin won.

Hence, any satisfactory response to Dawkins must be on his terms—adaptation, selection, blind variation, pain, and all. It must be on terms that recognize that Dawkins is right, that Darwinism is a major challenge to religious belief, and that you cannot simply pretend that nothing very much has happened. But once this is accepted, things start to fall into place.

Dawkins is absolutely right that total separation of religion and science is no response. Darwinism *does* talk about origins, and the theologically inclined must take note of what it teaches. Even if one goes the route of Newman by separating science and religion, one must agree that this path does not confer a license to say whatever one likes about events and phenomena in the other domain. Pure Paley is also no longer possible in light of Darwinian evolution; natural selection rules out the necessity of an appeal to an intervening God. This leaves only the third option, a theology of nature. The only possible response to Dawkins is that, Darwin or not, you feel compelled to accept that our understanding of nature, of living things, is changed and illuminated and made complete by your acceptance of the existence and creative power and sustaining nature of God.

Where stands this response in the light of Dawkins's attack? Can one still "relate all of nature to the reality that is the true theme of theology—the reality of God?"[22] What about the problem of evil? This is always the really tough one. Dawkins wants to claim that the coming of Darwin made the God hypothesis impossible. After Darwin we see that the world is simply not how it would be if an all-loving, all-powerful creator had made it (the cheetah and antelope argument). Nothing like this could possibly occur, given a loving god. But this is exactly what one would expect from blind, purposeless law. However, the appeal to blind unbroken law—things not working perfectly and pain and strife being commonplace—can be turned on its head, to yield a traditional argument protecting the possibility of the Christian God. As Darwin himself saw, one must and can properly invoke some version of the argument used by the philosopher Leibniz, namely that God's powers only extend to doing the possible. Having once committed himself to creation by law, everything else follows as a matter of course. Leibniz's argument was parodied by Voltaire in *Candide*—everything in this world happens for the best of all possible reasons—but just as that counter-argument fails in the world of religion, so also it fails in the world of science.

Think of trying to make physical processes entirely pain-free. Start with fire. It could no longer burn or produce smoke. But if this were the case would it still be hot? If so, then how could this be? There would have to be wholesale changes at the molecular level. If fire were not hot, how would we warm ourselves and cook our food? One change by God would require a knock-on compensation, and another and another. And even then, could we get a system that worked properly? "Human beings are sentient creatures of nature. As physiological beings they interact with Nature; they cause natural events and in turn are affected by natural events. Hence, insofar as humans are natural, sentient beings, constructed of the same substance as Nature and interacting with it, they will be affected in any natural system by lawful natural events."[23]

Once we start altering things to eliminate pain and suffering, there is no end to it—except that we would have changed humans so that they are no longer truly human. And even then, who would dare say we humans would be better situated? "Whether humans would have evolved but no infectious virus or bacilli, or whether there would have resulted humans with worse and more painful diseases, or whether there would have been no conscious, moral beings at all, cannot be discerned."[24] All things in the world fit into an interlocking whole. We should not assume that God could have made things in another way, avoiding instances of physical evil.

In fact, somewhat humorously, one can appeal to Dawkins's own writings to drive home this line of argument. As a good Darwinian, he insists that adaptive complexity is the mark of the living. This and this alone picks out the quick from the dead, or rather from the never quick. But how is one to get this adaptive complexity? Dawkins insists that it is through and only through natural selection. Alternative mechanisms like Lamarckism or hopeful monsters (mutationism) simply will not work. "Wherever in the universe adaptive complexity shall be found, it will have come into being gradually through a series of small alterations, never through large and sudden increments in adaptive complexity."[25] Adaptive complexity does not come through regular physical processes, immediately bringing on marks of the living. Sudden changes bring chaos and disorder. Planes crashing break up into useless pieces. Planes do not suddenly and spontaneously rise from the junkyard, pieces coming together into functioning wholes. Likewise for organisms. Dawkins has no love of Stuart Kauffman's "order for free." There is no alternative to natural selection. No other purely physical process brings about the adaptive, organized complexity of living things. "However diverse evolutionary mechanisms may be, if there is no other generalization that can be made about life all around the Universe, I am betting that it will always be recognizable as Darwinian life. The Darwinian Law . . . may be as universal as the great laws of physics."[26] You cannot get adaptive complexity without natural selection.

In other words, if God's process of creation is through unbroken law, then he had to do it as he did—natural selection, pain and agony, imperfection, and all. One might still argue that God should not have created in the first place (it is an essential part of Christian theology that the act of creation was done freely from love by God), but that is a somewhat different point. If one objects, as did the novelist Dostoevsky, that the pain in the world could never be trumped by the happy end result—no amount of bliss in heaven for Mother Teresa could ever balance the agony of a neglected, starving child—one is not necessarily implicating the coming of Darwinism. The pain would happen irrespective of natural selection. So, ultimately, effective though this line of argument may or may not be, it is irrelevant to our main line of discussion. Darwinism as such does not make irresistible the argument from natural evil. It may even make the solution easier to grasp.

TURNING BACK THE CLOCK?

Behe, Dembski, and their nemesis, Dawkins, share a desire to return to the high Victorian era, when Britain ruled the waves and science and religion could never agree. They would have made sure that the clash between Huxley and Wilberforce really was everything claimed of it. But the world has moved on. The old disjunction is gone. Evolution has been proven true, and is widely accepted as such. God did not intervene miraculously to make each species separately. Christians can and do accept this fact. Yet, in another sense, I come to praise these old-fashioned people and to argue that they have grasped something from the past that too many who write on the science/religion relationship have lost or never even seen. This is the argument to organized, adaptive complexity.

However one might criticize Behe's conclusions, when he speaks about the inner workings of the cell, his audience senses the presence of a man who truly loves the natural world. Say what you like in criticism of Dawkins, when he writes about the echolocation mechanism of the bat or about the eye and its varieties, he reveals to his readers an uncommon delight in the intricate workings of the organic world. In this Behe and Dawkins are at one with Aristotle, John Ray, Georges Cuvier, and of course Charles Darwin. And they are at one with modern-day researchers like Nicholas Davies, who spent long hours, tedious in the extreme to an outsider, standing in the dark and the rain of an early Cambridge morning with his dunnocks and cuckoos—observing, measuring, theorizing. Scrabbling around in the muck of the undergrowth to find just what it was that the female dunnock ejected when the male pecked at her backside. Patiently holding back as the cuckoo chick systematically destroys all of its foster siblings. Hauling off to Iceland with phony, plastic eggs to test a hypothesis. A man more in touch—literally as well as metaphorically—with the living world, and in love with it, we would have difficulty imagining. But he is equaled by all of the others, crouched over their microscopes, marveling at the beauty of the eyes of the fruit fly; sweating in the humid tropical heat, waist-deep in water searching for little fish; clambering around fig trees in Panama trying to find minute wasps. All of these people are simply overwhelmed by the glory of creation. They appreciate the organized complexity of the natural world.

Around 1875, natural theology took a wrong if understandable turn, and in the process lost this appreciation. Natural theology threw out the baby with the bathwater, for with the old-fashioned argument to design it rejected—or at least started significantly to ignore—the argument to complexity. It thought that when Paley's conclusion went, his premises had to go too. This, again, was understandable around 1875, when Darwinians like Huxley were stressing homology and belittling adaptation. But this rejection of the argument to complexity was simply a mistake. Adaptation reigns as never before, and it moves people as much as it ever did—more in fact, because now we can start to understand the why as well as the what. Gilbert White knew about the dunnocks and cuckoos, but how much deeper and more profound and more satisfying is the understanding of Nicholas Davies. Cope and Marsh knew about stegosaurus, but how much deeper and more profound and more satisfying is the understanding of those who have worked out the reasons for those ridiculous plates. Probably nobody knew much about fruit flies, and yet see how they have opened up the mysteries of nature to evolutionists.

What I am arguing for is a theology of nature—for let us agree that natural theology is now gone—where the focus is back on adaptation. A theology of nature that sees and appreciates the complex, adaptive glory of the living world, rejoices in it, and trembles before it. I argue for this even though the people who reveal it to us today in its fullest majesty may be people for whom Christianity evokes emotions ranging from bored indifference to outright hostility. This is irrelevant, especially to those of us who know professional Darwinian evolutionists. As Ernst Mayr once said to me: "People forget that it is possible to be intensely religious in the entire absence of theological belief."[27] Theologians working on the science/religion relationship, few of whom have actually had hands-on experience with nature, let the hostility of atheists like Dawkins, or their embarrassment with the Intelligent Design enthusiasts, blind them to the genuine love and joy with which today's professional evolutionists respond to their subjects. We should strip away the pseudo-arguments in the way of a full appreciation of the argument to complexity and start sharing what moved the natural theologians of old and what still moves the evolutionists of today.

Canon Charles Raven, although no friend to Darwinism, was a naturalist as well as a theologian. He knew whereof I speak. In his Gifford Lectures, he wrote of how much time he had spent and sheer pleasure he had derived from following and studying butterflies all over England and Scotland. "Every specimen differed from the rest, in detail from those of its own group, in total effect from those of others. Each was in itself a perfect design, satisfying in whole and parts, inviting one to concentrate one's whole attention upon it. To move from one to another, to sense the difference of impact, to work out the quality of this difference in the detailed modifications of the general pattern, this was a profoundly moving experience." For Raven, this was the real edge of the science/religion encounter. This is what makes it all meaningful to the believer. Not proof, but simply flooding, overwhelming experience that could not be denied. In Raven's words: "Here is beauty— whatever the philosophers and art critics who have never looked at a moth may say—beauty that rejoices and humbles, beauty remote from all that is meant by words like random or purposeless, utilitarian or materialistic, beauty in its impact and effects akin to the authentic encounter with God."[28]

I have nothing more to add.

NOTES

1. Michael Behe, *Darwin's Black Box: The Biochemical Challenge to Evolution* (New York: Free Press, 1996), 39.

2. Ibid., 42.

3. Ibid., 96.

4. William A. Dembski, "The Third Mode of Explanation: Detecting Evidence of Intelligent Design in the Sciences," in *Science and Evidence for Design in the*

Universe, eds. M. Behe, W. A. Dembski, and S. C. Meyer (San Francisco: Ignatius Press, 2000), 27–28.

5. William A. Dembski, *No Free Lunch: Why Specified Complexity Cannot Be Purchased without Intelligence* (Lanham, MD: Rowman and Littlefield, 2002), 212.

6. Enrique Melendez-Hevia, Thomas G. Waddell, and Marta Cascante, "The Puzzle of the Krebs Citric Acid Cycle: Assembling the Pieces of Chemically Feasible Reactions, and Opportunism in the Design of Metabolic Pathways during Evolution," *Journal of Molecular Evolution* 43 (1996): 293–303.

7. Ibid., 302.

8. Behe, *Darwin's Black Box*, 227–28.

9. Kenneth Miller, *Finding Darwin's God* (New York: Harper and Row, 1999), 162–63.

10. William A. Dembski, *The Design Inference: Eliminating Chance through Small Probabilities* (Cambridge: Cambridge University Press, 1998), 98.

11. Charles Darwin, *On the Origin of Species* (London: John Murray, 1859), 131.

12. Dembski, *No Free Lunch*, 212.

13. Henry M. Morris, ed., *Scientific Creation* (San Diego: Creation-Life, 1974), 69.

14. Richard Dawkins, *The Blind Watchmaker* (New York: Norton, 1986), 49.

15. Thomas S. Ray, "An Approach to the Synthesis of Life," in *The Philosophy of Artificial Life*, ed. M. A. Boden (Oxford: Oxford University Press, 1996), 121–23.

16. Ibid., 124.

17. Ibid., 127.

18. Richard Dawkins, "Obscurantism to the Rescue," *Quarterly Review of Biology* 72 (1997): 397–99.

19. Dawkins, *The Blind Watchmaker*, 4.

20. Ibid., 5.

21. Richard Dawkins, *A River Out of Eden* (New York: Basic Books, 1995), 105.

22. Wolfhart Pannenberg, *Towards a Theology of Nature* (Louisville, KY: Westminster/John Knox Press, 1993), 73.

23. Bruce R. Reichenbach, *Evil and a Good God* (New York: Fordham University Press, 1982), 111–12.

24. Ibid., 113.

25. Richard Dawkins, "Universal Darwinism," in *Molecules to Men*, ed. D. S. Bendall (Cambridge: Cambridge University Press, 1983), 412.

26. Ibid., 423.

27. Ernst Mayr, Emeritus Professor of Zoology, Harvard University, in conversation with the author, March 30, 1988.

28. Charles E. Raven, *Natural Religion and Christian Theology: Experience and Interpretation* (Cambridge: Cambridge University Press, 1953), 112–13.

THE EVIDENCE AGAINST
THE NEW CREATIONISM

ROBERT T. PENNOCK

Intelligent-design creationists' most carefully crafted game plan appears in the textbook *Of Pandas and People*, which was supposedly written for secondary school biology students, but which really looks like it was written to try to circumvent Supreme Court rulings against young-earth creation-science. However, almost all of the arguments that appear are exactly the same negative ones as those of the young-earth creationists: they recite the same litany of supposedly insuperable problems with evolutionary theory, with the aim of showing that it does not have the resources to account for the origin of life, the Cambrian Explosion, and biological complexity and adaptedness. Again, the most important difference involves what they leave out. They conclude that if the world looks designed and evolutionary theory cannot explain that fact with its natural mechanisms, then we must conclude that the world is designed. This is just the same failed strategy we saw before: they offer two models and try to support the one by negative arguments against the other. If this were all there

Robert T. Pennock, "Chariots of the Gods," *Tower of Babel: The Evidence Against the New Creationism* (Cambridge, MA: MIT Press, 1999), chapter 5.

was to intelligent-design theory then we could dismiss it without further ado. However, IDC does offer one important new positive argument.

THE SETI ANALOGY

The authors of *Pandas* are keen to reject the notion that IDC is necessarily religious or supernatural. There is nothing unscientific, they say, about investigating intelligent design. The reason some might think otherwise, they claim, is that many scientists have confused the notion of intelligence with the idea of the supernatural.

> [S]cientists from Western culture failed to distinguish between intelligence, which can be recognized by uniform sensory experience, and the supernatural, which cannot. Today, we recognize that appeals to intelligent design may be considered in science, as illustrated by the current NASA search for extraterrestrial intelligence (SETI).[1]

It is hard to believe that scientists really did not understand the difference between intelligence and the supernatural, but, be that as it may, it is worth examining the IDCs' claims in more detail. It is certainly an interesting idea that the creationist hypothesis could be investigated on the model of the search for extraterrestrial intelligence. To be able to evaluate their analogy, we must begin with a bit of background about the SETI project.

The modern search for extraterrestrial intelligence began with the work of Frank Drake, a radio astronomer who realized that microwave radio waves might be a way to send interstellar messages. He reasoned that if there were intelligent beings on other planets with that level of technological advancement, we might be able to pick up their transmissions. In the spring of 1960 he made the first search for such microwave signals, training an 85-foot antenna on two nearby sun-like stars. Drake's receiver operated at only one frequency and picked up no signs of life, but his project inspired others. In the early 1970s, NASA sponsored Project Cyclops, a feasibility study of SETI science and technology issues, and its positive assessment led the agency to commit further resources to the project, establishing SETI programs at Ames Research Center and at the Jet Propulsion Laboratory. Intelligent-design creationists fail to mention that the main reason scientists think there might be intelligent life elsewhere in the universe is the plausibility of cosmic evolution—that is, it is reasonable to think that evolution, as a natural process, occurs regularly throughout the cosmos where conditions are favorable. Of course, it is hard to estimate how likely it is that evolutionary mechanisms would produce intelligent beings similar enough to us for us to be able to hear and understand them. Drake devised an equation to help assess the probabilities. It begins with the rate of star formation and then progressively whittles this number by factoring in the proportion of stars that could be expected to have a planetary system, the proportion of these that have suitable conditions for life, and so on. At first, putting numbers into the Drake Equation was mostly blind guesswork, and most of the factors in the equation still have wide margins of error, but in the last few years the first observations of planets orbiting other stars and of possible microfossil evidence of bacterial life on Mars have actually increased estimates of what was admittedly a long shot. After more than a decade of preliminary design work, NASA began observations in 1992, but within a year Congress terminated funding. Part of the NASA project continued as Project Phoenix with private funding, pursuing a Targeted Search of 1,000 nearby sun-like stars. Several other SETI projects that began in the 1970s at Ohio State University, the University of California (SERENDIP), and the Planetary Society (META) continue observations. The SETI Institute has a home page on the Internet where one can keep up with the latest developments.

The one development that has yet to be reported is any sign of intelligent life, though over the decades a few candidate signals have briefly tantalized researchers. . . .

THE TALKING PULSAR

Intelligent-design theorists argue that just as the scientists of the SETI Project seek evidence of intelligence beyond the world, so too do they. In a clever rhetorical move, they frequently quote the late astronomer and SETI pioneer Carl Sagan to show that even a confirmed skeptic such as he admitted that such investigation is scientifically legitimate. But are IDCs really sincere in their protestations that theirs is not a religious hypothesis? Can they use the SETI model to ground the hypothesis of intelligent design as a truly scientific alternative to evolution? To begin to examine their claims, let us take an extended representative passage that sets out the main lines of their argument. There is one important item of information that we will want to watch for in anyone who promotes ID creationism as a scientific theory. We need to check out their ID card and determine the identity of the intelligent designer!

Intelligent-design creationist Fred Heeren is up-front about the identity of the designer in his recent book, *Show Me God: What the Message from Space Is Telling Us about God.* In it, he summarizes the key points of the IDC argument in a fictional dialogue between Margaret, a SETI project researcher, and the Sultan of Brunei, who is considering helping to fund the project. The Sultan begins with a question:

> "How will you be sure when you've received a signal from an intelligent source? How do you tell the difference between a natural, pulsating signal, as from a pulsar, and a signal from an intelligence?"
>
> "If you get a message in Morse code," explained Margaret, "you know there's intelligence behind it. Nature can't duplicate that. In the same way, if we get a signal containing encoded information, even if we can't break the code at first, we'll know it's coming from an intelligent source."
>
> "You mean like the encoded information we find in DNA."
>
> Margaret didn't hear this interruption and continued her speech: "Nature can't duplicate specified complexity. The chance of nature creating a pattern that has meaning is almost infinitely small."
>
> "Like the specified complexity of hemoglobin. . . . Are you familiar with the calculations of Hoyle and Wickramasinghe? . . . Did you know that the chance that amino acids would line up randomly to create the first hemoglobin protein is one in ten to the 850th power? Which is in the realm of infinity, considering the fact that there are only 10 to the 80th power atoms in the entire universe."
>
> Mark and Margaret could only stare at each other. This man obviously had more than a casual interest in science.
>
> The Sultan continued: "There's an even smaller chance that the DNA code could have randomly reached the required specificity: one chance in 10 to the 78,000th power even for the DNA of a simple microorganism. This must be a signal of intelligence, wouldn't you say?"[2]

As the story continues, the star Epsilon Eridani begins flashing out a signal in Morse code that turns out to be some familiar words in Hebrew: "In the beginning God created the heavens and the earth." The signal continues and, over the course of a year and a half, transmits the entire Hebrew Bible, and then it stops. Following the SETI protocol for post-contact procedure, the nations of the world meet and decide how to respond. The UN sends back a reply asking "What does this mean? What do you expect us to do with this message?" Epsilon Eridani is eleven light years away, so they expect to wait 22 years for the signal to reach there and for a response to get back, but instead the star begins immediately to transmit the New Testament in ancient Greek: "The beginning of the good news about Jesus Christ, the Son of God." Then scientists find that the message is beaming from all stars and from all parts of the sky. Margaret is finally convinced that this is a message from God, but Mark is not and asks why doesn't God just appear before him if he wants to be known. Margaret replies:

> "If God were to personally appear before you, in any form that was spec-
> tacular enough to convince you that it was really Him, then you wouldn't
> have any real choice about following Him—you'd know you had to. And
> when there's no choice, there's no opportunity for love. That's what He
> wants, He doesn't want to make you follow Him."
> Mark looked for holes in the argument but found none.[3]

Of course, no Bible-quoting pulsars have yet been observed, so the last part of the story is not meant to provide any positive evidence, but it is important in that it lets us know how intelligent-design creationists want us to interpret the first part. Because it serves so well to connect the ideas of information, divine intelligence, and the SETI project, the talking pulsar has become a regular character in IDC arguments. The first talking-pulsar story I heard was in a presentation by William Dembski at an IDC conference in Dallas. In his version, the pulsar says, again in Morse code, that it is the "mouthpiece of Yahweh" and proceeds to prove it by answering any question that is deposited in an ark on Mount Zion, predicting future events, giving cures for diseases, and providing answers to provably hard math problems.[4] After a discussion in which he argued that this science-fiction case would be an indi-cation of a super-intelligence because of the extreme improbability that the correct answers could have been found, Dembski then moved on to the improbability of the specific sequences of nucleotides in the genome of bio-logical organisms. In discussion and in other papers Dembski also makes the connection to the SETI project. We are supposed to think that the informa-tion in DNA molecules is a sign from God in the same way as would be a transmission of the Bible in Morse code beamed from a pulsar. The SETI project looks for intelligent life in the universe by searching for a signal with information, and IDCs claim that we find such an information signal in the DNA of every cell, which therefore indicates the existence of an intelligent designer who put it there. The *Pandas* text substitutes a love note scrawled in the sand for the talking pulsar and speaks only of a generic intelligent designer instead of specifying that it is God, but the argument is otherwise the same. The lessons we are asked to take from the SETI analogy are two-fold. First, we are supposed to agree that intelligent-design creationism is not religion but good science. Second, we are supposed to conclude that intelligent design is the best scientific conclusion to draw from the DNA data.

As we will see, the intelligent-design creationists' SETI analogy is a space-age version of the classic philosophical argument from design for the existence of God. To evaluate it we will therefore not only have to look a bit at scientific work on information theory and probability and their applications in evolutionary biology, but also return to deeper philosophical questions about the nature of evidence, to help us differentiate science from religion and from pseudoscience. We will also have to consider a bit of theology to understand the importance of Heeren's concluding remarks about why God doesn't just make a spectacular appearance. . . . [I]t will be useful to first investigate these issues in a context that allows us to consider them afresh and without prejudice. Moreover, for philosophical analysis of an issue, it is often very helpful to have a contrasting case that can highlight conceptual features that we might otherwise be blind to. For these reasons I now want to introduce one further sort of anti-evolutionary viewpoint.

EXTRATERRESTRIAL INTELLIGENT DESIGN

Suppose we adopt, for the sake of argument, the intelligent-design creationists' claim that the evidence supports their hypothesis that life is the result of intelligent creation. Let us also take them at their word that they mean to provide scientific support on the SETI model. If so, then it looks as though the conclusion we should draw is that we were designed and created by intelligent extraterrestrials. Interestingly, Heeren writes that when the first edition of his book was published he was "barraged with calls from UFO watchers and skimming readers who wanted to know more facts about this reported contact with extraterrestrials," and he says that he "felt like Orson Welles must have felt after his radio broadcast of War of the Worlds in 1939."[5] My original intention at this point was to devise an alternative extraterrestrial intelligent design (ET-ID) view of this kind and to show how ID creationism's arguments compared to those of the UFO enthusiasts whom we would expect to believe such a story. As it turns out, I did not need to concoct such a tale, for once again truth is stranger than fiction. A large international group—the Raëlian Movement—advocates just this ET-ID view. Like creationism, this is a religiously based movement that rejects evolution. Unlike creationism, Raëlianism denies supernatural divine creation. Raëlians promote a third view—that intelligent aliens landed here millennia ago in spaceships and formed all of life on earth, including human beings, using highly advanced genetic engineering. I think that if we investigate the question of intelligent design in this context it will be easier to see why the IDC conclusion is not scientific.

The Raëlian Movement originated in the early 1970s in France and now claims over 35,000 members in over eighty-five countries around the world. Outsiders think of it as a New Age religion, and in many ways that is a fair characterization, but Raëlians think of their religion as being directly linked to Christianity and the other great world religions, and moreover, as the final religious form now that the world has entered the time of the Apocalypse. The beliefs of Raëlians are based upon messages our extraterrestrial creators conveyed to the world through the "Guide of Guides," Claude Vorilhon, a French journalist and race-car enthusiast. Vorilhon, who later adopted the name "Raël," claims to have been twice contacted by an alien in a flying saucer who revealed to him the true story of the creation of life on earth. Here, in brief, is the story, as described in *The Book That Tells The Truth*.

Eons ago, on a distant planet, these aliens—the Elohim—had reached an advanced level of scientific understanding and technical ability that enabled them to create primitive living cells in the laboratory. Some of them were fearful, however, of creating some new life form that might prove dangerous to life on their own planet, so they sought a lifeless planet where they might pursue their experiments safely. That planet was the earth. They began with simple cells but as research progressed they soon were able to engineer seeds, grasses, and a wide variety of vegetation. As their technical abilities developed, the scientists collaborated with artists to produce beautifully decorative and scented plants. Plankton, small fish, and then bigger fish came next, and as the scientists created new species they worked to see that each fit well into the ecology of the whole system. Eventually, they began to create animals—dinosaurs, sea and land creatures, herbivores and carnivores. The artists had a big hand in the creation of birds, going to such wild aesthetic extremes in some cases in their design of plumage that the creatures could hardly fly. Finally, the scientists were ready for their greatest technical challenge, creating beings like themselves. Several teams set to work. After producing a series of prototypes (some of the skulls and bones of which we have found), the scientists successfully created *Homo sapiens*. Their final forms were all slightly different—the various human races—but all were alike in being made in the image of their creators.

Evolution is a myth, according to Raëlianism. Biologists are correct that life forms of increasing complexity appeared over time, but that is because the alien scientists began with simple cells and then progressively modified these to produce more complex life forms as their techniques improved. Biologists are also partially correct in saying that humans descended from earlier primates; according to the Elohim scientist who contacted Raël, "Human beings . . . are only an improved model of the monkey, to which we added that which makes us people."[6] However, do not think that this happened by chance with purely natural mechanisms! No natural need could produce the beautiful curled horns of certain wild goats or the wild exotic colors of tropical fish. It is incredibly improbable that accidental evolution could produce the wide array of life forms. No, the complex biological world is all the result of the intentional design work of the Elohim scientists and artists.

It is important to understand that Raëlianism fulfills all the elements that intelligent-design creationists set out to characterize their view, at least in the minimal version they propose for public consumption. The only difference is that Raëlianism specifies that the intelligent designers were not supernatural spirits or gods, but alien beings from another planet. We thus have a real example of an ET-ID view. In all other respects, Raëlianism is very similar to standard Creationism. They have been far less organized and productive than creationists in arguing against evolution, because they are more interested in proselytizing their positive message, but when they do talk about it they tend to follow the same negative argumentation strategy.

Raëlians make many of the same bad arguments against evolutionary theory as creationists. The Raëlian who explained their view at an introductory meeting I attended began by noting that evolution is "simply a theory," and she suggested that radiometric dating of fossils is inaccurate because radiation decay is not constant. Raëlians follow creationists in proclaiming that evolution "lies in direct contradiction" to the second law of thermodynamics.[7] We also hear an echo of Phillip Johnson's allegation that evolution is akin to religious dogma; Marcel Terrusse, Raëlian Bishop Guide for France, writes that scientists "indoctrinate" us with the evolutionary view, and that people would need "the courage to be seen as heretics"[8] to question openly these professors. Raëlians also question how random mutations could ever be advantageous and improve survival or increase organized complexity. . . .

Raëlians speak of whacking a computer with a wrench in the same way that creationists speak of a tornado whipping through a junkyard. Could such random processes improve the programming of a computer or create a working automobile? they ask rhetorically. What evolutionists want you to believe is absurd, they conclude. But, as we saw before, such analogies are highly misleading. They misrepresent evolutionary processes, which are not random in this way at all. In fact it is not only theoretically possible to improve a computer's programming using Darwinian mechanisms, it has already been done. Nathan Myrhvold, director of the Advance Technology Group at Microsoft, developed a "software breeder" in the late 1980s using genetic algorithms. . . . Discussing this work, Stuart Brand explains, "A human programmer comes at a problem with a mind-set that causes him or her to solve it one way; in fact, there's a large space of other solutions—and evolution can find them. . . ."[9] For instance, Myrhvold's software breeder found an efficient way to translate files from binary into ASCII form.

Another interesting point about the Raëlian creation story is that it seems it might be only partially antievolutionary. The passage that describes the process that the Elohim scientists used to form increasingly complex life forms is ambiguous, but one reasonable interpretation is that they produced new life forms by modifying earlier ones. Raël writes, "In reality the first living organism created on earth was unicellular, and afterwards it produced more complex life. But not by chance!"[10] Together with the previously quoted passage of how humans were made by modifying monkeys, this suggests that Raëlians could accept a form of Darwin's view of descent with modification, namely, that organisms form an interconnected ancestor-descendant tree of life. If so, it looks like they might agree with the basic fact of evolution, though they would no doubt disagree about the pathways and pace of the diversification. Their major disagreement, however, is the same one that Johnson and the intelligent-design creationists have, namely, over the "blind watchmaker" mechanisms: They reject evolution by natural selection and insist upon intelligent design. Of course the bio-engineering process used by the Elohim is no doubt not standard biological reproduction, but if it involved manipulating genetic material taken from each species of organisms to produce the next in sequence, then there is an important sense in which Raëlians accept the fact that evolution occurred. Even if the Elohim did not directly manipulate genetic material from each species to create the next, but instead used a process that was more indirect, this still fits with a form of the common descent thesis.

Suppose they started with the "genetic recipe" for individual cells, say, in the form of a digital computer program that specified the organism's genome, and had a machine to churn out DNA molecules like pasta noodles once they added the chemical ingredients and entered the recipe for the desired sequences. (This may not be so far-fetched a possibility; already microbiologists have machines that allow them to build short DNA strands with the exact sequence of nucleotides they choose just by pressing the buttons A, T, G, and C in the desired order.) And suppose they designed subsequent cells by using this recipe as a model and simply adding to it and changing bits here and there, the way a cook modifies a recipe to produce a variation of an old favorite. They could continue in this way to produce, in turn, more complex organisms. For each new species they would have their machine crank out the prototypes to be released into the wild. This would certainly be a nonstandard method of reproduction, but it would maintain the basic idea that organisms are connected in a relationship of descent with modification at just a slightly higher level of abstraction.

This is probably just one of those odd hypothetical science-fiction scenarios that only a philosopher could love, but it does lead to a very interesting conceptual possibility when we connect it back to the view of *Genesis* creationists. Perhaps God created the biological world in such a manner. As we noted, some of the creationists with whom Darwin argued held that God created biological organisms following "ideal plans," and who is to say these were not master genetic recipes? A creationist who thought that special creation worked in this way would thereby accept the basic fact of evolution (though in a nonscientific form). Indeed, it would even be open for such a creationist to accept the more direct method—after all, perhaps God was extracting genetic information when he created Eve from Adam's rib![11] I mention this odd scenario because it leads to a further ironic twist in our comparison. Let us return a moment to the Raëlian creation story. Didn't that line about the Elohim creating humans in their image sound rather familiar? Isn't this just a corrupt retelling of *Genesis*? Almost, but not quite, explains the Raëlian, and here is where the story really begins to get interesting. Actually, it is the other way around; the Bible contains a partial and somewhat corrupted version of the true story. Now that the truth has been revealed to

Raël, we can correctly interpret the Bible at last. According to Raëlians, evolution is a myth but so is creationism.

The Bible was written by the created beings on earth, but they did not know the complete truth about their creation, and what they did know they were unable to fully comprehend. Arthur C. Clarke, dean of science-fiction writers, who predicted the use of telecommunication satellites, wrote that any sufficiently advanced technology would be indistinguishable from magic. Think of what primitive peoples would have thought had they encountered modern people with our technology—they would have viewed us as sorcerers and magicians. According to Raëlians, the Elohim, with their even greater scientific technologies, were thought of as supernatural beings—as gods. Indeed, we translate the Hebrew term "Elohim" in the Bible as "God," but it is not a singular form but a plural term, which Raëlians claim means "those who came from the sky." There are no divine beings and there was nothing supernatural about the creation of life. We should respect and be thankful to the Elohim who are our creators but they are natural beings as we are, and everything that is supposedly miraculous in the Bible can be explained scientifically. With the new knowledge given to Raël, they say, mysterious passages in the Bible suddenly make sense.

Who were the "sons of God" who married many of the "daughters of men" after human beings once again spread over the world after the Flood, causing Yahweh to feel disgrace (Genesis 6:1–4)? Raëlians claim they were aliens who had been exiled to earth because they had loved their creations too much and violated the home planet's ruling that they be kept in ignorance of scientific knowledge. (Compare that to ICR's Henry Morris's explanation that they were Satan's evil angels coming down to earth to violate human women.) What was the fire and brimstone that rained from the sky, destroying Sodom and Gomorrah and the surrounding plains (Genesis 19:23–28)? Atomic bombs dropped on those cities, say the Raëlians. The pillar of cloud and fire that led Moses and the Israelites out of Egypt? A rocket ship with repellent beams that parted the Red Sea. Indeed, Moses had many encounters with UFOs including the one that descended upon Mount Sinai to deliver the tablets of the Decalogue.

The mountain of Sinai was wrapped in smoke, because Yahweh had descended on it in fire. Like smoke from a furnace the smoke went up, and the whole mountain shook violently. And the voice of the trumpet sounded long and waxed louder and louder. (Exodus 19:18–19)

Purported references to UFOs and alien encounters are not confined to Genesis but occur throughout the Bible. Some are not at all obvious (Raëlians believe that the Tower of Babel was not a ziggurat, but a spaceship that would literally allow them to reach heaven—the home planet of the Elohim), but others are startlingly realistic. Think of those most striking and bizarre passages in which Ezekiel gives extended descriptions of when he saw the chariot of Yahweh, that begin "I looked; a stormy wind blew from the north, a great cloud with light around it, a fire from which flashes of lightning darted, and in the center a sheen like molten bronze," and speak of strangely garbed and helmeted beings that moved in vehicles of wheels within wheels that glittered like crystal (Ezekiel 1:4–28). Raëlians outdo even literalist creationists in their interpretation of such passages, insisting that they are factual descriptions rather than symbolic mystical "visions."

In talking with Raëlians and reading their literature, one is struck not only by their similarity to creationists but also to UFO enthusiasts. Raëlian books typically appear in bookstores on the same shelf as books on UFOs. A classic of the UFO genre is Erich von Däniken's aptly titled *Chariots of the Gods*. Von Däniken was the first to point out several passages in the Bible that could be interpreted as referring to extraterrestrial visitation. Indeed, he cites the Ezekiel passage in a chapter titled "Was God an Astronaut?" and rhetorically inquires why an omnipotent God who can be anywhere he pleases would "come hurtling up from a particular direction" with such "noise and fuss."[12] Who were the four living beings with the likenesses of men who emerged from the fiery landing of Yahweh's chariot to speak to Ezekiel? Von Däniken concludes that:

> They were certainly not "gods" in the traditional sense of the word, or they would not have needed a vehicle to move from one place to another. This kind of locomotion seems to me to be quite incompatible with the idea of an almighty God.[13]

Von Däniken notes similar references in the mythological literature of other cultures as well. He discusses ancient carvings, illustrations, monoliths, and other physical artifacts that he believes support the idea that the earth was visited by ancient astronauts. He also looked for physical evidence and, lending new credence to the aphorism about birds of a feather, sent a cameraman in 1975 to Glen Rose, Texas, to film the Paluxy river prints, which he supposed not to be "manprints" but footprints of giant extraterrestrials.

Raëlians point to similar facts as well as eye-witness sightings of UFOs as evidence of the truth of their view. The Raëlian who gave the introductory talk I heard explained that she had written to von Däniken about the Raëlian Movement, and she showed me the letter she had received from him expressing interest but polite skepticism about some of Raël's claims. Raëlians are used to having their views dismissed out of hand and mocked, so this lukewarm response from someone who might be thought to be naturally sympathetic was accepted with equanimity. *The Book That Tells the Truth* ends with a plea for open-mindedness. Raël writes:

> Now that you have read this book . . . in which I have tried to reproduce as clearly as possible all that was said to me [by the extraterrestrial], if you will think perhaps that I have a great imagination and that these writings were simply to amuse you, I shall be profoundly disappointed. Perhaps these revelations will give you confidence in the future and allow you to understand the mystery of the creation and the destiny of humanity, thus answering the many questions that ever since childhood we pose during the night, asking why we exist and what is our purpose on this earth.[14]

According to Raëlians, the evidence that this story of creation is true exists before our eyes. Others can bear witness to the reality of their encounters with aliens and flying saucers, and you might have the chance to observe one yourself, Raël tells his readers. He concludes:

> If you still have doubts, read the newspapers and look to the sky where you will see that the appearances of the mysterious crafts will be more and more numerous. . . .[15]

Raëlianism offers the possibility of a meeting with the extraterrestrials when they arrive in their spaceships as the ultimate potential observational evidence of its truth. The Raëlian I spoke with, however, admitted that she herself had never seen a UFO, let alone had a close encounter with any extraterrestrial. Like most Raëlians, she bases her belief in the return of the Elohim upon faith in Raël's account of his transformational encounter, in much the same way that early Christians had to take the word of the Apostles that they had encountered the risen Jesus. (Actually, the parallel is particularly strong on this point, for Raël claims to have met Jesus as well when he was transported for a brief visit to the Elohim homeworld.) Also like the early Christians, she says she fully expects that the hoped-for return will occur within her lifetime. Of course, the history of religion is filled with Christian sects who believed that the Second Coming was imminent and some even hazarded a guess about when it would happen, but these invariably saw the predicted dates come and go without the expected rapture. Recent history has seen groups of UFO believers who have been similarly disappointed when the Mother Ship failed to land at the time of an anticipated arrival. Supposing that Elohim in either the Christian or Raëlian form do eventually return in a convincing fashion, we would then have reason to consider seriously the respective creation account. But given that such an appearance remains but a hope, the pertinent question is whether we currently have scientific evidence of the existence of an intelligent designer of the world or whether that belief is religious.

NOTES

1. Percival Davis and Dean H. Kenyon, *Of People and Pandas: The Central Question of Biological Origins* (Richardson, TX: Foundation for Thought and Ethics, 1993), 126.

2. Fred Heeren, *Show Me God: What the Message from Space Is Telling Us about God*, vol. 1, *Wonders that Witness to God's Truth* (Wheeling, IL: Searchlight Publications, 1995), 36–37.

3. Ibid., 54.

4. William A. Dembski, "The Incompleteness of Scientific Naturalism," in *Darwinism: Science or Philosophy*, ed. Jon Buell and Virginia Hearn (Richardson, TX: Foundation for Thought and Ethics, 1994), 83.

5. Heeren, *Show Me God*, 27.

6. Claude Vorilhon Raël, "The Book Which Tells the Truth," in *The Message Given to Me by Extra-Terrestrials* (Tokyo: AOM Corporation, 1986), 103.

7. Marcel Terrusse, "Obscurantism and the Neo-Darwinian Myth," http://www.rael.org/broch01.html#50, 1996.

8. Ibid.

9. Nathan Myrhvold, interview by Stewart Brand, *Wired* 3 (September 1995): 152–55.

10. Raël, "The Incompleteness of Scientific Naturalism," 103.

11. A year after writing this, I learned from Tom McIver that at least one creationist holds a very similar sort of view. A. E. Wilder-Smith claims in *The Reliability of the Bible* (San Diego: Master Books, 1983), that God literally "cloned" Eve

from Adam. He writes that "The entire report [in Genesis] reads exactly like a historical description of surgery under normal physiological conditions for surgery" (Wilder-Smith, 55) and that in the operation God removed a cell from Adam's rib, deleted the Y chromosome and doubled the remaining X to produce a female. When it comes to creationism, "Truth" is indeed stranger than fiction.

12. Erich von Däniken, *Chariots of the Gods: Unsolved Mysteries of the Past* (New York: G. P. Putnam's Sons, 1968), 55.

13. Ibid., 57.

14. Raël, "The Incompleteness of Scientific Naturalism," 134–35.

15. Ibid., 136.

TESTING DARWIN

CARL ZIMMER

If you want to find alien life-forms, hold off on booking that trip to the moons of Saturn. You may only need to catch a plane to East Lansing, Michigan.

The aliens of East Lansing are not made of carbon and water. They have no DNA. Billions of them are quietly colonizing a cluster of 200 computers in the basement of the Plant and Soil Sciences building at Michigan State University. To peer into their world, however, you have to walk a few blocks west on Wilson Road to the engineering department and visit the Digital Evolution Laboratory. Here you'll find a crew of computer scientists, biologists, and even a philosopher or two gazing at computer monitors, watching the evolution of bizarre new life-forms.

These are digital organisms—strings of commands—akin to computer viruses. Each organism can produce tens of thousands of copies of itself within a matter of minutes. Unlike computer viruses, however, they are made

Carl Zimmer, "Testing Darwin," *Discover* (February 2005): 29–35.

up of digital bits that can mutate in much the same way DNA mutates. A software program called Avida allows researchers to track the birth, life, and death of generation after generation of the digital organisms by scanning columns of numbers that pour down a computer screen like waterfalls.

After more than a decade of development, Avida's digital organisms are now getting close to fulfilling the definition of biological life. "More and more of the features that biologists have said were necessary for life we can check off," says Robert Pennock, a philosopher at Michigan State and a member of the Avida team. "Does this, does that, does this. Metabolism? Maybe not quite yet, but getting pretty close."

One thing the digital organisms do particularly well is evolve. "Avida is not a simulation of evolution; it is an instance of it," Pennock says. "All the core parts of the Darwinian process are there. These things replicate, they mutate, they are competing with one another. The very process of natural selection is happening there. If that's central to the definition of life, then these things count."

It may seem strange to talk about a chunk of computer code in the same way you talk about a cherry tree or a dolphin. But the more biologists think about life, the more compelling the equation becomes. Computer programs and DNA are both sets of instructions. Computer programs tell a computer how to process information, while DNA instructs a cell how to assemble proteins.

The ultimate goal of the instructions in DNA is to make new organisms that contain the same genetic instructions. "You could consider a living organism as nothing more than an information channel, where it's transmitting its genome to its offspring," says Charles Ofria, director of the Digital Evolution Laboratory. "And the information stored in the channel is how to build a new channel." So a computer program that contains instructions for making new copies of itself has taken a significant step toward life.

A cherry tree absorbs raw materials and turns them into useful things. In goes carbon dioxide, water, and nutrients. Out comes wood, cherries, and toxins to ward off insects. A computer program works the same way. Consider a program that adds two numbers. The numbers go in like carbon dioxide and water, and the sum comes out like a cherry tree.

In the late 1990s Ofria's former adviser, physicist Chris Adami of Caltech, set out to create the conditions in which a computer program could evolve the ability to do addition. He created some primitive digital organisms and at regular intervals presented numbers to them. At first they could do nothing. But each time a digital organism replicated, there was a small chance that one of its command lines might mutate. On a rare occasion, these mutations allowed an organism to process one of the numbers in a simple way. An organism might acquire the ability simply to read a number, for example, and then produce an identical output.

Adami rewarded the digital organisms by speeding up the time it took them to reproduce. If an organism could read two numbers at once, he would speed up its reproduction even more. And if they could add the numbers, he would give them an even bigger reward. Within six months, Adami's organisms were addition whizzes. "We were able to get them to evolve without fail," he says. But when he stopped to look at exactly how the organisms were adding numbers, he was more surprised. "Some of the ways were obvious, but with others I'd say, 'What the hell is happening?' It seemed completely insane."

On a trip to Michigan State, Adami met microbiologist Richard Lenski, who studies the evolution of bacteria. Adami later sent Lenski a copy of the Avida software so he could try it out for himself. On a Friday, Lenski loaded the program into his computer and began to create digital worlds. By Monday he was tempted to shut down his lab and dedicate himself to Avida. "It just had the smell of life," says Lenski.

It also mirrored Lenski's own research. Since 1988 he has been running the longest continuous experiment in evolution. He began with a single bacterium—Escherichia coli—and used its offspring to found 12 separate colonies of bacteria that he nurtured on a meager diet of glucose, which creates a strong incentive for the evolution of new ways to survive. Over the past 17 years, the colonies have passed through 35,000 generations. In the process, they've become one of the clearest demonstrations that natural selection is real. All 12 colonies have evolved to the point at which the bacteria can replicate almost twice as fast as their ancestors. At the same time, the bacterial cells have gotten twice as big. Surprisingly, these changes didn't unfold in a smooth, linear process. Instead, each colony evolved in sudden jerks, followed by hundreds of generations of little change, followed by more jerks.

Similar patterns occur in the evolution of digital organisms in Avida. So Lenski set up digital versions of his bacterial colonies and has been studying them ever since. He still marvels at the flexibility and speed of Avida, which not only allow him to alter experimental conditions with a few keystrokes but also to automatically record every mutation in every organism. "In an hour I can gather more information than we had been able to gather in years of working on bacteria," Lenski says. "Avida just spits data at you."

With this newfound power, the Avida team is putting Darwin to the test in a way that was previously unimaginable. Modern evolutionary biologists have a wealth of fossils to study, and they can compare the biochemistry and genes of living species. But they can't look at every single generation and every single gene that separates a bird, for example, from its two-legged dinosaur ancestors. By contrast, Avida makes it possible to watch the random mutation and natural selection of digital organisms unfold over millions of generations. In the process, it is beginning to shed light on some of the biggest questions of evolution.

QUESTION #1: WHAT GOOD IS HALF AN EYE?

If life today is the result of evolution by natural selection, Darwin realized, then even the most complex systems in biology must have emerged gradually from simple precursors, like someone crossing a river using stepping-stones. But consider the human eye, which is made of many different parts—lens, iris, jelly, retina, optic nerve—and will not work if even one part is missing. If the eye evolved in a piecemeal fashion, how was it of any use to our ancestors? Darwin argued that even a simpler version of today's eyes could have helped animals survive. Early eyes might have been nothing more than a patch of photosensitive cells that could tell an animal if it was in light or shadow. If that patch then evolved into a pit, it might also have been able to detect the direction of the light. Gradually, the eye could have taken on new functions, until at last it could produce full-blown images. Even today, you can find these sorts of proto-eyes in flatworms and other animals. Darwin declared that the belief that natural selection cannot produce a complex organ "can hardly be considered real."

Digital organisms don't have complex organs such as eyes, but they can process information in complex ways. In order to add two numbers together, for example, a digital organism needs to carry out a lot of simpler operations, such as reading the numbers and holding pieces of those numbers in its memory. Knock out the commands that let a digital organism do one of these simple operations and it may not be able to add. The Avida team realized that by watching a complex organism evolve, they might learn some lessons about how complexity evolves in general.

The researchers set up an experiment to document how one particularly complex operation evolved. The operation, known as equals, consists of comparing pairs of binary numbers, bit by bit, and recording whether each pair of digits is the same. It's a standard operation found in software, but it's not a simple one. The shortest equals program Ofria could write is 19 lines long. The chances that random mutations alone could produce it are about one in a thousand trillion trillion.

To test Darwin's idea that complex systems evolve from simpler precursors, the Avida team set up rewards for simpler operations and bigger rewards for more complex ones. The researchers set up an experiment in which organisms replicate for 16,000 generations. They then repeated the experiment 50 times.

Avida beat the odds. In 23 of the 50 trials, evolution produced organisms that could carry out the equals operation. And when the researchers took away rewards for simpler operations, the organisms never evolved an equals program. "When we looked at the 23 tests, they were all done in completely different ways," adds Ofria. He was reminded of how Darwin pointed out that many evolutionary paths can produce the same complex organ. A fly and an octopus can both produce an image with their eyes, but their eyes are dramatically different from ours. "Darwin was right on that—there are many different ways of evolving the same function," says Ofria.

The Avida team then traced the genealogy leading from the first organism to each one that had evolved the equals routine. "The beauty of digital life is that you can watch it happen step by step," says Adami. "In every step you would ordinarily never see there is a goal you're going toward." Indeed, the ancestors of the successful organisms sometimes suffered harmful mutations that made them reproduce at a slower rate. But mutations a few generations later sped them up again.

When the Avida team published their first results on the evolution of complexity in 2003, they were inundated with e-mails from creationists. Their work hit a nerve in the antievolution movement and hit it hard. A popular claim of creationists is that life shows signs of intelligent design, especially in its complexity. They argue that complex things could never have evolved, because they don't work unless all their parts are in place. But as Adami points out, if creationists were right, then Avida wouldn't be able to produce complex digital organisms. A digital organism may use 19 or more simple routines in order to carry out the equals operation. If you delete any of the routines, it can't do the job. "What we show is that there are irreducibly complex things and they can evolve," says Adami.

The Avida team makes their software freely available on the Internet, and creationists have downloaded it over and over again in hopes of finding a fatal flaw. While they've uncovered a few minor glitches, Ofria says they have yet to find anything serious. "We literally have an army of thousands of unpaid bug testers," he says. "What more could you want?"

QUESTION #2: WHY DOES A FOREST
HAVE MORE THAN ONE KIND OF PLANT?

When you walk into a forest, the first thing you see is diversity. Trees tower high overhead, ferns lurk down below, vines wander here and there like tangled snakes. Yet these trees, ferns, and vines are all plants, and as such, they all make a living in the same way, by catching sunlight. If one species was better than all the rest at catching sunlight, then you might expect it to outcompete the other plants and take over the forest. But it's clear that evolution has taken a different course.

Figuring out why is a full-time job for a small army of biologists. A number of them seek enlightenment by comparing places that are rich and poor in species and trying to figure out the other things that make them different. One intriguing pattern has to do with food. Ecologists have found that the more energy a habitat can provide organisms, the more species it can support. But a habitat can get too productive. Then it supports fewer species. This pattern has emerged time and again in studies on ecosystems ranging from grasslands to Arctic tundra.

Until recently, a typical Avida experiment would end up with a single dominant organism. The Avida researchers suspected that was the result of providing an endless supply of food—in this case, numbers. Perhaps, they reasoned, if they put their digital organisms on a diet, they might evolve into different forms—just as it happens in nature. So the Avida team retooled their software to limit the supply of numbers flowing into their digital worlds. Then they made the numbers even more scarce by splitting them up into smaller supplies, each of which could be used only for a particular operation, such as adding two numbers. As the organisms used the numbers at a faster rate, they got a smaller benefit. And if too many organisms gorged themselves on one supply of numbers, they would stop replicating altogether.

The Avida team subsequently flooded some digital worlds with numbers and limited others to a scant supply, and the same pattern of diversity found in global ecosystems emerged. When the number supply was low, only one type of organism could survive. At intermediate levels, three or four different types emerged and coexisted. Each type evolved into a specialist at one or a few kinds of operations. But when the number supply got too abundant, diversity dropped to a single species again.

Bringing diversity into Avida has brought more bad news for those who think complexity cannot evolve. Ofria decided to run the complexity experiment over again, this time with a limit on the supply of numbers. "It just floored me," he says. "I went back and checked this so many ways." In the original experiment, the organisms evolved the equals routine in 23 out of 50 trials. But when the experiment was run with a limited supply of numbers, all the trials produced organisms that could carry out the equals routine. What's more, they needed only a fifth of the time to do it.

Ofria suspects that the difference comes from the fact that several species are now evolving in the experiment rather than just one. More species mean more opportunities for success.

QUESTION #3: WHY BE NICE?

Human society depends on countless acts of cooperation and personal sacrifice. But that doesn't make us unique. Consider Myxococcus xanthus, a species of bacteria that Lenski and his colleagues study. Myxococcus travels in giant swarms 100,000 strong, hunting down E. coli and other bacteria like wolves chasing moose. They kill their prey by spitting out antibiotics, then spit out digestive enzymes that make the E. coli burst open. The swarm then feasts together on the remains. If the Myxococcus swarm senses that they've run out of prey to hunt, they gather together to form a stalk. The bacteria at the very top of the stalk turn into spores, which can be carried away by wind or water to another spot where they can start a new pack. Meanwhile, the individuals that formed the stalk die.

This sort of cooperation poses a major puzzle because it could be undermined by the evolution of cheaters. Some bacteria might feast on the prey killed by their swarm mates and avoid wasting their own energy making antibiotics or enzymes. Others might evolve ways of ensuring that they always end up becoming spores and never get left behind in the dead stalk. Such cheaters are not theoretical: Lenski and his colleagues have evolved them in their lab.

The Avida team is now trying to address the mystery of cooperation by creating new commands that will let organisms exchange packages of information. "Once we get them to communicate, can we get them to work together to solve a problem?" asks Ofria. "You can set up an information economy, where one organism can pay another one to do a computation for it."

If digital organisms cooperate, Ofria thinks it may be possible to get them working together to solve real-world computing problems in the same way Myxococcus swarms attack their prey. "I think we'll be able to solve much more complex problems, because we won't have to know how to break them down. The organisms will have to figure it out for themselves," says Ofria. "We could really change the face of a lot of computing."

QUESTION #4: WHY SEX?

Birds do it, bees do it, and even fleas do it—but why they all do it is another matter. Reproduction is possible without sex. Bacteria and protozoa simply split in two. Some trees send shoots into the ground that sprout up as new trees. There are even lizard species that are all female. Their eggs don't need sperm to start developing into healthy baby female lizards.

"One of the biggest questions in evolution is, why aren't all organisms asexual?" says Adami. Given the obvious inefficiency of sex, evolutionary biologists suspect that it must confer some powerful advantage that makes it so common. But they have yet to come to a consensus about what that advantage is.

So Dusan Misevic, a biologist at Michigan State, has spent the past couple of years introducing sex into Avida. While digital sex may lack romance, it features the most important element from an evolutionary point of view: the genetic material from two parents gets mixed together in a child. When a digital organism makes a copy of itself, the copy doesn't immediately take its own place in Avida and start reproducing. Instead, chunks of its code are swapped with the copy of another new organism. Only after this exchange do the two creatures start to reproduce.

In 1964 the German biologist H. J. Muller proposed that sex allows organisms to mix their genomes together in combinations that can overcome the effects of harmful mutations. Asexual organisms, on the other hand, are stuck with all the mutations their ancestors pass down to them. Over time, Muller argued, they can't reproduce as quickly as their sexual competitors. Misevic designed an experiment to put Muller's hypothesis to the test." It's a classic explanation, so it seemed like a good place to start," he says.

Misevic created two kinds of worlds: one full of sexual digital organisms and the other full of asexuals. After they had evolved for tens of thousands of generations, he measured how fast they could replicate. "The overall conclusion we got was that, yes, there are some situations where sex is beneficial," says Misevic. But there were surprises. Sex is good mainly as a way to escape annihilation from lethal mutations. But in Avida, sexual organisms had to pay a price for that insurance—they carried more nonlethal yet harmful mutations than the asexual organisms.

"We must look to other explanations to help explain sex in general," says Misevic.

QUESTION #5: WHAT DOES LIFE ON OTHER PLANETS LOOK LIKE?

Life on Earth is based on DNA. But we can't exclude the possibility that life could evolve from a completely different system of molecules. And that raises some worrying questions about the work going on these days to find signs of extraterrestrial life. NASA is funding a wide range of life-detecting instruments, from rovers that prowl across Mars to telescopes that will gaze at distant solar systems. They are looking for the signs of life that are produced on Earth. Some are looking for high levels of oxygen in the atmospheres of other planets. Others are looking for bits of DNA or fragments of cell walls. But if there's non-DNA-based life out there, we might overlook it because it doesn't fit our preconceptions.

"We can look at how known life-forms leave marks on their environment," says Evan Dorn, a member of Chris Adami's lab at Caltech, "but we can never make universal statements about them because we have only one example."

Dorn says Avida is example number two. By finding patterns that are shared by life on Earth and life in Avida, he thinks he will be able to offer some ideas about how to look for life that the universe might be harboring.

Some researchers have suggested the best way to look for signs of life is to look for weird chemistry. Take the building blocks of proteins—amino acids—which are found on meteorites and can also be created in the lab simply by running an electric current through ammonia and other compounds. In a lifeless setting, the most common amino acid that results is the simplest: glycine. Some slightly less simple amino acids are also common, but all the larger ones make up only a trace or are missing altogether. That's because it takes a lot of energy to make those big amino acids. "There's a limited repertoire of chemistry in the absence of life," says Dorn.

If you analyze a scoop of soil or pond water, however, you'll find a completely different profile of amino acids. Life has evolved ways of building certain big amino acids, and when organisms die, those big amino acids float around in the environment.

What if life on another planet made compounds that were radically different from amino acids? Would it alter its planet's chemistry in some similar way?

To test this idea, Dorn created a world devoid of life. Instead of containing a self-replicating program, each cell contained a random assortment of commands. All of the commands in the Avida language were present at equal levels. Here was the signature of a lifeless planet.

Then Dorn began dropping organisms into this world, like spores falling to Earth. At the beginning of the experiment, he set the mutation rate so high that no spore could replicate very long on the planet. (Think of Mars, where ultraviolet rays pelt the surface.) Gradually, he lowered the mutation rate until life could survive. "As soon as the environment was habitable, the organism took over and dominated the environment," Dorn says.

As the digital organisms evolved to adapt to the world, Dorn found that some commands became rare and others became far more common. This distinctive signature stayed stable as long as life could survive on the planet. And no matter how many times Dorn repeated the experiment, the same signature of life appeared. Whether manipulating amino acids or computer commands, life does seem to leave the same mark. "It gives us a pretty strong indication that this process is universal," says Dorn.

If Dorn is right, discovery of non-DNA life would become a little less spectacular because it would mean that we have already stumbled across it here on Earth—in East Lansing, Michigan.

QUESTION #6: WHAT WILL LIFE ON EARTH LOOK LIKE IN THE FUTURE?

One of the hallmarks of life is its ability to evolve around our best efforts to control it. Antibiotics, for example, were once considered a magic bullet that would eradicate infectious diseases. In just a few decades, bacteria have evolved an arsenal of defenses that make many antibiotics useless.

Ofria has been finding that digital organisms have a way of outwitting him as well. Not long ago, he decided to see what would happen if he stopped digital organisms from adapting. Whenever an organism mutated, he would run it through a special test to see whether the mutation was beneficial. If it was, he killed the organism off. "You'd think that would turn off any further adaptation," he says. Instead, the digital organisms kept evolving. They learned to process information in new ways and were able to replicate faster. It took a while for Ofria to realize that they had tricked him. They had evolved a way to tell when Ofria was testing them by looking at the numbers he fed them. As soon as they recognized they were being tested, they stopped processing numbers. "If it was a test environment, they said, 'Let's play dead,'" says Ofria. "There's this thing coming to kill them, and so they avoid it and go on with their lives."

When Ofria describes these evolutionary surprises, admiration and ruefulness mix in is voice. "Here I am touting Avida as a wonderful system where you have full knowledge of everything and can control anything you want—except I can't get them to stop adapting. Life will always find a way."

Thinking about such adaptable creatures lurking on the Michigan State campus, furiously feeding on data, can be unsettling. Should the Avida team be working in quarantine? Lenski argues that Avida itself acts as a quarantine, because its organisms can exist only in its computer language. "They're living in an alien world," Lenski says. "They may be nasty predators from Mars, but they'd drop dead here."

Still, Ofria acknowledges that harmful computer viruses may eventually evolve like his caged digital organisms. "Some day it's going to happen, and it's going to be scary," Ofria says. "Better to study them now so we know how to deal with them."

PHILLIP JOHNSON ON TRIAL

A Critique of His Critique of Darwin
NANCEY MURPHY

INTRODUCTION

Phillip E. Johnson's recent book, *Darwin on Trial*[1] has attracted a fair amount of attention among conservative Christians. Yet it may create an inaccurate impression of the status of evolutionary biology—an impression that I hope to correct in this article. On the book's dust jacket it is said that Johnson, a professor of law at the University of California at Berkeley, took up the study of Darwinism because he judged the books defending it to be dogmatic and unconvincing. I, at least, find Johnson's own arguments dogmatic and unconvincing. The main reason is that he does not adequately understand scientific reasoning.

Many readers will be impressed, even overawed, by Professor Johnson's credentials. He is not a scientist but a lawyer, who claims that his law career, with "a specialty in analyzing the logic of arguments and identifying the

Nancey Murphy, "Phillip Johnson on Trial: A Critique of His Critique of Darwin," *Perspectives on Science and Faith* 45, no. 1 (March 1993): 26–36.

assumptions that lie behind those arguments" well qualifies him for the task (p. 13). The fact that he is a professor at U.C. Berkeley certainly adds to his credibility in the eyes of many. But I wish you would bear with me in a little foolishness (cf. 2 Cor. 11:1). Is he from Berkeley? So am I. One of my doctorates was earned in the philosophy department at U.C. Berkeley, where I specialized in philosophy of science. Is he an expert in critical reasoning? So am I. I teach critical reasoning to seminary students (now at Fuller Theological Seminary) and have just completed a textbook on the subject. Most of my other research and writing deals with methodological issues in theology, science, and the relations between the two.[2]

My plan is to describe some of the basic moves in scientific reasoning, and then examine in detail an important (and typical) passage in Johnson's book, explaining why it appears fallacious to one trained in scientific reasoning. Next, I shall describe some recent refinements in philosophers' understanding of scientific reasoning, and use them to describe the sort of study that would be required to make a fair assessment of the scientific standing of evolutionary biology.

Another issue that needs to be addressed is the very nature of science, and how it relates to religion. A bit of history will help us understand some of the positions taken by evolutionary biologists and excuse them from some of Johnson's criticisms.

I shall end with a few remarks on what I take to be the proper attitude for Christians toward evolutionary biology.

Before I proceed to the attack, however, I must say that Johnson's book has many good features. Johnson describes some of the failures and problems faced by evolutionary biology, and provides a valuable critique of popular writings that turn the science of evolutionary biology into an atheistic metaphysical system with many of the trappings of religion.

BASIC SCIENTIFIC REASONING

Francis Bacon's description of scientific reasoning has been influential for many years. In brief, he claimed that scientists must first rid their minds of all prejudice and preconceptions, then collect all the facts relevant to the issue at hand, and finally draw inductive inferences from the facts.[3] This view of scientific reasoning is inadequate, however, since it only accounts for our knowledge of observed regularities. An important advance in the philosophy of science of this century was the recognition of what has been called "hypothetico-deductive" reasoning.[4] This kind of reasoning frees science from dependence on direct observation, and accounts for all of our theoretical knowledge. It is called "hypothetical" because it relies on the formation of hypotheses to explain a given set of data or observations. It is called "deductive" because hypotheses must be tested by drawing conclusions from them and seeing if they are corroborated by further observation or experiment. So the test of a hypothesis is not by direct observation (most scientific hypotheses postulate unobservable entities or processes), but by asking what observable consequences follow from the hypothesis, and by testing these instead. Another way of putting the matter: a hypothesis is accepted on the basis of its ability to explain observations and results of experiments.

Consider the following analogy drawn from everyday experience. You come home from work and find the front door ajar and muddy tracks leading into the kitchen. You form a hypothesis: the kids were here. But of course, there could be other explanations, such as a prowler. To test the hypothesis, you make predictions based on your knowledge of the children's behavior. For example, you check to see if anyone has been into the cookies, or if their school clothes are on the floor upstairs. If your predictions are confirmed you do not need to see the children to know that your original hypothesis was correct.

So the form of hypothetico-deductive reasoning is as follows:

- We observe O_1.
- We formulate a hypothesis (H), which, if true, would explain O_1.
- Then we ask, if H is true, what additional observations $(O_2 \ldots O_n)$ ought we be able to make?
- Finally, if O_2 through O_n are observed, H is confirmed.

It is important to note that O_2 through O_n are not equivalent to H; they are observable consequences that we deduce from H with the aid of additional assumptions—nibbled cookies and strewn clothing are not children.

Because the hypothesized entities or processes are unobservable, scientists often make use of *models*—observable entities or processes that are similar in important respects to the theoretical entities. A famous example is the billiard-ball model used to understand and account for the behavior of gasses in a closed container. Models are often helpful in deriving testable predictions from hypotheses (theories).

It is also important to note that hypothetical reasoning (like all reasoning about matters of fact) can never amount to proof. The best that can be hoped for is a high degree of confirmation. Much of what philosophy of science is about is examination of the conditions under which a scientific theory can be said to be well-confirmed. So objecting that *any* scientific theory is "not proved" is empty—none can be.

The foregoing provides enough terminology to analyze some of Johnson's arguments, so we turn now to these.

JOHNSON ON NATURAL SELECTION

Chapter Two of *Darwin on Trial* is an examination of the thesis that natural selection, or survival of the fittest, (when combined with natural variation) provides an adequate account of macroevolution—that is, the evolution of all known species of living things from one or a few primitive ancestors. A crucial step in Johnson's overall criticism of evolutionary biology is his assessment of evidence for the efficacy of natural selection, so we must examine this short passage (pp. 17–20) with care. Johnson begins by noting that Darwin could not point to examples of natural selection in action, and so he had to rely heavily on an argument by analogy with artificial selection by breeders of domestic plants and animals.

However, Johnson replies to Darwin's argument as follows:

> Artificial selection is not basically the same sort of thing as natural selection, but rather is something fundamentally different. Human breeders produce variations among sheep or pigeons for purposes absent in nature, including sheer delight in seeing how much variation can be achieved. If the breeders were interested only in having animals capable of surviving in the wild, the extremes of variation would not exist. . . .
>
> What artificial selection actually shows is that there are definite limits to the amount of variation that even the most highly skilled breeders can achieve. Breeding of domestic animals has produced no new species, in the commonly accepted sense of new breeding communities that are infertile when crossed with the parent group. . . .
>
> In other words, the reason dogs don't become as big as elephants, much less change into elephants, is not that we just haven't been breeding them long enough. Dogs do not have the genetic capacity for that degree of change, and they stop getting bigger when the genetic limit is reached (p. 18).

Next, Johnson turns to evidence cited by contemporary evolutionists:

> Darwinists disagree with that judgment, and they have some points to make. They point with pride to experiments with laboratory fruitflies. These have not produced anything but fruitflies, but they have produced changes in a multitude of characteristics. Plant hybrids have been developed which can breed with each other, but not with the parent species, and which therefore meet the accepted standard for new species. With respect to animals, Darwinists attribute the inability to produce new species to a lack of sufficient time. . . . In some cases, convincing circumstantial evidence exists of evolution that has produced new species in nature. Familiar examples include the hundreds of fruitfly species in Hawaii and the famous variations among "Darwin's Finches" on the Galapagos Islands. . . .
>
> Lack of time would be a reasonable excuse if there were no other known factor limiting the change that can be produced by selection, but in fact selective change is limited by the inherent variability in the gene pool. After a number of generations the capacity for variation runs out. It might conceivably be renewed by mutation, but whether (and how often) this happens is not known (p. 19).

And now Johnson's conclusion, drawn from the above considerations:

> Whether selection has ever accomplished speciation (i.e., the production of a new species) is not the point. A biological species is simply a group capable of interbreeding. Success in dividing a fruitfly population into two or more separate populations that cannot interbreed would not constitute evidence that a similar process could in time produce a fruitfly from a bacterium. If breeders one day did succeed in producing a group of dogs that can reproduce with each other but not with other dogs, they would still have made only the tiniest step towards proving Darwinism's important claims.
>
> That the analogy to artificial selection is defective does not necessarily mean that Darwin's theory is wrong, but it does mean that we will have to look for more direct evidence to see if natural selection really does have a creative effect (pp. 19–20).

ANALYSIS

What are we to make of this set of arguments? Before I begin a serious analysis, permit me another bit of foolishness: The series of steps in Johnson's argument recalls an old lawyer's joke about a defendant in a murder trial: "Your honor, I didn't kill him, and besides, it was an accident, and on top of that he really had it coming!" Similarly: artificial selection is not analogous to natural selection, and besides, selective breeders have not produced any new species, and on top of that they have only produced new plant species, but no new animal species.

More seriously, we must ask what observations or results are required to confirm (not prove) the scientific hypothesis that natural selection is capable of producing *radically different new species*.[5] Since we cannot directly observe natural selection at work, we need an observable model. Selective breeding has been proposed. (We will come back to the issue of the suitability of this model below.) What is at stake in testing the power of natural selection, then, is that our analogue to natural selection be shown to accomplish two things: First, we need to see that selection can produce *radical differences* within a population. Second, we need to see that selection can result in *speciation*—the development of one species out of another. The criterion here is incapacity to breed with the parent species.

Johnson seems to believe that both of these effects need to be observed in the same instance. He would have a point if there were something about one effect that precluded the other or made it less likely; for example, from the fact that you can pat your head and can also rub your stomach, I cannot infer with much confidence that you can do both at once. However, this does not appear to be such a case. The splitting of a population into two species isolates the gene pools, allowing them to diverge, and ultimately to manifest different physical characteristics. We can also imagine that a wide enough physical variation within a species would tend to isolate two or more gene pools and provide a necessary though not sufficient condition for speciation. Johnson notes, for example, that while dogs are all theoretically capable of interbreeding, size differences make it practically impossible.

Now, Johnson admits that we have examples of both of these changes as a result of intentional selective breeding. Regarding the first, he would like to see dogs as big as elephants, but the difference between a toy poodle and a great dane seems adequate to me. Regarding the second, there are instances from plant breeding and, he says, circumstantial evidence that many species of fruitflies have developed from one or a few species originally introduced to Hawaii. Yet his conclusion is that none of this is adequate evidence for the Darwinian thesis. In effect, he is claiming that because plant speciation and intra-species variation *are not equivalent to* macroevolution they provide no evidence for the power of natural selection. But recall that we never hoped to *observe* a case of macroevolution by means of natural selection. We were about the more modest task (and the only realistic task) of providing confirmatory evidence by means of a model—an analogous process—that macroevolution by means of natural selection is possible (given sufficient time and enough environmental pressure).

The form of the Darwinian reasoning is as follows:

- O_1 is observed (here, the patterns of speciation in existence today).
- A hypothesis (H) is formulated which, if true, would explain O_1 (here, the correlative hypotheses of variation, natural selection, and geographical isolation).
- If H is true, what additional observations $(O_2 \ldots O_n)$ ought we be able to make? (here, O_2: radical change within a population, and O_3: speciation).
- Finally, O_2 and O_3 have been observed, so H is confirmed.

Again, O_2 and O_3 are not equivalent to H; they are observable consequences that can be deduced from H with the aid of additional assumptions.

One of the crucial assumptions here is that selective breeding is like natural selection in relevant respects. It *is* like natural selection in that it operates by means of differential reproduction rates and within the variation that nature supplies. These seem to me to be the relevant factors. Johnson's claim that the characteristics breeders look for are different from the ones for which "Nature" selects seems to me beside the point. The issue is whether selective breeding can produce radical changes, including speciation; not the particular nature of those changes.

I believe it could be shown by examining other arguments that Johnson *consistently* fails to distinguish between evidence confirmatory of a hypothesis and a set of observations that together are equivalent to the hypothesis. For example, on pp. 25–27 he first lists six pieces of evidence that have been offered in support of the power of natural selection, then concludes *without explanation* that "none of these 'proofs' provides *any* persuasive reason for believing that natural selection can produce new species..." (p. 27, emphasis mine). In Chapter 8, discussing theories about the origin of life, he concludes that because the synthesis of some of the components of living organisms does not actually amount to the production of life in the laboratory there is "*no reason* to believe that life has a tendency to emerge when the right chemicals are sloshing about in a soup" (p. 103, emphasis mine).

RECENT PHILOSOPHY OF SCIENCE

I shall introduce in this section some of the refinements contributed by recent philosophers of science by commenting on further aspects of Johnson's arguments.

In the section quoted above, Johnson has said that there are definite limits to the amount of variation that even the most highly skilled breeders can achieve; that dogs do not get as big as elephants because they do not have the genetic capacity for that degree of change (p. 18); and that after a number of generations the capacity for variation runs out (p. 19). He then admits that *mutation* might renew the capacity for change, but claims that whether and how often this happens is not known (p. 19).

When Darwin proposed his theory of evolution, he speculated that there must be a mechanism that works predominantly to maintain the characteristics of a population from one generation to another, but that also allowed for some degree of fluctuation and for genuine novelty. At that time, of course, he did not know what that mechanism was. A great triumph for evolutionary theory, but one Johnson does not mention, came from the discovery of the role of genes in reproduction. The gene pool provides for variation within overall stability in most instances, but mutations allow for genuine novelty.

Johnson mentions mutation as though it is scarcely important at all, but in fact it is an essential "auxiliary hypothesis" for the evolutionary program, and it is simply not possible to draw Johnson's strong conclusions about the limits of variation without considering the frequency and kinds of mutations, and their potential contribution to viable changes in a population.[6]

This fact illustrates an important point stressed by philosophers of science. Theories (hypotheses) rarely or never face the test of experience standing alone. We are (almost) always faced with the testing of whole networks of theories and auxiliary hypotheses. This makes the falsification of a major theory very difficult—when negative evidence comes along, it can often be reconciled with the central theory by adding or changing lower-level (auxiliary) theories. If positive evidence is lacking, its absence can often be explained by the same strategy.

Johnson's book is full of examples of changes of this sort to make evolutionary theory consistent with the evidence (or the absence of evidence). For example, Darwin expected that the fossil record would soon provide evidence of species intermediate between known species and their ancestors (the "missing links"). When few such intermediates were found, later theorists proposed auxiliary hypotheses to explain their absence: for example, the fossil record is still only a small sample of all of the creatures that have existed, and it is to be expected that the intermediate species, being in between well-adapted forms, would not last long and would therefore leave little evidence behind in the form of fossils.

Theorizing of this sort is extremely common in science. Since major theories come along only rarely, most of scientific advance consists in the careful elaboration and qualification of major theories, fine-tuning them to fit the evidence. Several philosophers of science have noted, though, that there is a kind of fine-tuning that represents genuine improvement and growth in scientific knowledge, and another kind that is a mere face-saving device—linguistic tricks to protect a theory from falsification. So the important question is how to tell the difference.

Imre Lakatos (d. 1974) made a major contribution to philosophy of science by providing a criterion for distinguishing "progressive" from "degenerative" or "*ad hoc*" refinements of a network of theories.[7] The essence of his criterion is this: if a hypothesis that is added to the network not only explains the problems for which it was designed, but also leads to the prediction and corroboration of new facts of a different sort, then the modification is progressive. On the other hand, if it only takes care of the problem and is not independently confirmed by the successful prediction of novel facts, then it is a degenerative move. Lakatos made a double claim about this criterion. First, he claimed that it could account for the history of science better than other views,[8] in that history would show that scientists generally abandon research programs that are making mostly degenerative moves in favor of a more progressive rival. His second claim is that scientists *should* accept progressive programs and abandon degenerative ones—that this is what scientific rationality consists in.

APPLICATION TO DARWINISM

Now, what consequences does this criterion of "progressiveness" have for evaluating evolutionary theory? It shows, first of all, that the only fair way to assess the program is by examining the auxiliary hypotheses that have been added to it to see whether each is a progressive or degenerative modification.

It is clear that Johnson is aware of the problem of *ad hoc* developments of a theory, as the following passage indicates:

Darwinists have evolved an array of subsidiary concepts capable of furnishing a plausible explanation for just about any conceivable eventuality. For example, the living fossils, which have remained basically unchanged for millions of years while their cousins were supposedly evolving into more advanced creatures like human beings, are no embarrassment to Darwinists. They failed to evolve because the necessary mutations didn't arrive, or because of "developmental constraints," or because they were already adequately adapted to their environment. In short, they didn't evolve because they didn't evolve.

Some animals give warning signals at the approach of predators, apparently reducing their own safety for the benefit of others in the herd. How does natural selection encourage the evolution of a trait for self-sacrifice? Some Darwinists attribute the apparent anomaly to "group selection." Human nations benefit if they contain individuals willing to die in battle for their country, and likewise animal groups containing self-sacrificing individuals may have an advantage over groups composed exclusively of selfish individuals.

Other Darwinists are scornful of group selection and prefer to explain altruism on the basis of "kinship selection." By sacrificing itself to preserve its offspring or near relations an individual promotes the survival of its genes. Selection may thus operate at the genetic level to encourage the perpetuation of genetic combinations that produce individuals capable of altruistic behavior. By moving the focus of selection either up (to the group level) or down (to the genetic level), Darwinists can easily account for traits that seem to contradict the selection hypothesis at the level of individual organisms.

Potentially the most powerful explanatory tool in the entire Darwinist armory is *pleiotropy*, the fact that a single gene has multiple effects. This means that any mutation which affects one functional characteristic is likely to change other features as well, and whether or not it is advantageous depends upon the net effect. Characteristics which on their face appear to be maladaptive may therefore be presumed to be linked genetically to more favorable characteristics, and natural selection can be credited with preserving the package.

I am not implying that there is anything inherently unreasonable in invoking pleiotropy, or kinship selection, or developmental constraints to explain why apparent anomalies are not necessarily inconsistent with Darwinism. If we assume that Darwinism is basically true than it is perfectly reasonable to adjust the theory as necessary to make it conform to the observed facts. The problem is that the adjusting devices are so flexible that in combination they make it difficult to conceive of a way to test the claims of Darwinism empirically (pp. 29–30).

However, this passage also indicates that Johnson sees no difference between auxiliary hypotheses that are testable and those that are not. It is difficult to conceive a test for the hypothesis that the living fossils failed to evolve because they were already adapted to their environment—or to be more precise, it is hard to conceive of a way of showing this claim *false*. This seems to be an instance of a "linguistic trick" to protect the theory from falsification. But not so with all of the examples Johnson has cited here. For example, kinship selection is testable: if it is true, then there should be a direct relationship between the percentage of genes shared with another individual and the degree of "altruism" exhibited toward that individual—a prediction that has in fact been confirmed. In addition, genetic mapping makes the concept of pleiotropy empirically testable.

So it is clear that Johnson has failed to see the import of such cases. He does not understand their role in demonstrating that there are in fact ways "to test the claims of Darwinism empirically" (p. 30).

In general Johnson has given too little attention to the role genetic theory has played in the history of evolutionary biology. Genetics arose as a major new theory in complete independence of evolutionary biology. Initially there was strong antagonism between workers in the two fields. However, with the advent of population genetics under Fisher, Wright, and Haldane, the two fields were reconciled. In Lakatos's terms, the entire genetic program came to function as an "auxiliary hypothesis" within the evolutionary program, providing a tremendous amount of fresh empirical evidence—evidence of exactly the sort that Lakatos has led us to expect from a progressive program. Another instance is "neutral allele" theory, with its associated phenomenon of molecular clocks.

Much remains to be done to provide an adequate assessment of the evolutionary program. There are a number of problems with the theory, but whether there are more than with other major theories, such as Big-Bang cosmology, remains to be seen. It must be emphasized, though, that the mere existence of problems does not disqualify a theory—good theories are always in process, and the question is whether they are progressing, overall, or degenerating. So the important question is *how* the evolutionary program deals with its problems; whether the auxiliary hypotheses needed to account for anomalies—for the absence of certain kinds of expected confirmatory evidence—can be independently tested and confirmed. Johnson does not pursue this question; nor can I do so here. Adequate treatment would require another book. But this is where the battle must be joined if we are to have a fair assessment of the evolutionary program.

It has been noted[9] that the kind of "novel facts" needed to provide independent confirmation of auxiliary hypotheses are usually rare, and get harder rather than easier to find as a program progresses. This suggests that the crucial evidence for evolutionary theory, if it can be produced, will not be massive. It will consist in a few confirmed predictions here and there. In this way, evolutionary biology will be entirely in line with many well-respected programs such as Big-Bang cosmology.

A major problem for anyone undertaking an assessment of the evolutionary program is that philosophy of science provides criteria for relative rather than absolute assessment. That is, the criteria we have been discussing are only capable of telling us which of two or more competing programs is the most acceptable. While there is competition within the evolutionary program, between punctuated equilibrium and gradualist theories of change, for instance, there is no major scientific competitor for the program as a whole. This being the case, there are limits to what critics of Darwinism can hope to accomplish. When a theory is the only one available, the burden of proof falls on those who wish to do away with it. It is simply a fact of the history of science that a theory is seldom—perhaps never—abandoned when there is no competitor to take its place. If criteria for rational choice are necessarily comparative, then this is a rational way to proceed. Beyond that, there is the practical question: what would evolutionary biologists *do* if there is no other conception of the field to guide their research?

THE NATURE OF SCIENCE

In this section I shall take up three issues raised by Johnson:

1. Evolutionary biology is not scientific because (according to Karl Popper) science is characterized by falsifiability, and the central ideas of Darwinism are held dogmatically.
2. Evolutionary theory is held dogmatically because it is the only account of life that fits with a naturalistic philosophy.
3. Evolutionary biologists ought to consider the possibility that life is the product of creative intelligence.

SCIENCE AND FALSIFIABILITY

In his final chapter Johnson adopts Karl Popper's criterion for distinguishing science from pseudoscience. Popper argued that what made science scientific was not its subject matter but the willingness of its proponents to allow their theories to be falsified.[10] In Johnson's words: "Progress is made not by searching the world for confirming examples, which can always be found, but by searching out the falsifying evidence that reveals the need for a new and better explanation" (p. 147).

Imre Lakatos was a colleague of Popper's at the London School of Economics. Lakatos treated Popper's claims about the nature of science as an empirical theory and argued that, as such, the history of science *falsified* Popper's account. His own theory, introduced above, was proposed as a "new and better explanation" of the course of the history of science. We have already seen his proposed criterion for distinguishing between acceptable and unacceptable (progressive and degenerating) research programs. Here it is relevant to introduce another feature of his account of science.

All scientific research programs, he concluded, include a central idea, called the hard core, which is usually too vague to be tested directly. In addition, there are the auxiliary hypotheses that mediate between the core theory and empirical data. Lakatos's study of the history of science convinced him that a certain amount of dogmatism with respect to the core of a program was both a regular feature of good science and a necessary strategy to allow for the development of scientific thought. His new version of falsificationism allows researchers to protect their core theory "dogmatically" so long as the program is progressive overall.[11]

From what has just been reported,[12] it follows that Johnson's criticism in the following quotation shows *not* the unscientific character of evolutionary biology, but rather that Johnson approaches it with an inadequate understanding of the philosophy of science:

> The central Darwinist concept that later came to be called the "fact of evolution"—descent with modification—was thus from the start protected from empirical testing. Darwin did leave some important questions open, including the relative importance of natural selection as a mechanism of change. The resulting arguments about the process, which continue to this day, distracted attention from the fact that the all-important central concept had become a dogma (p. 149).

That is, the usual strategy in science is to hold on to a central idea—hold it "dogmatically," if you will—so long as the theoretical elaborations and additions that are necessary to reconcile it with the evidence lead to new discoveries rather than to blind alleys.

EVOLUTION AND NATURALISM

Johnson explains the evolutionists' dogmatism by attributing it, not to the usual processes of scientific development, but to an atheistic philosophical naturalism. Johnson is quite right about this in some cases, and perhaps in most of the cases of *popular* books written in defense of evolution.

However, a subtle distinction needs to be made here. On the one hand there are the proponents of "a religion of scientific naturalism, with its own ethical agenda and plan for salvation through social and genetic engineering" (Johnson, p. 150). This religion is fair game for criticism by proponents of other religions, and ought not be allowed *establishment* in the curriculum of the public schools. On the other hand, there is what we might call *methodological atheism*, which is by definition common to all natural science. This is simply the principle that scientific explanations are to be in terms of natural (not supernatural) entities and processes.

Johnson is critical of biologists and philosophers who define science in this way. However, it is a fact of history (perhaps an accident of history) that this is how the institution of *natural* science is understood in our era. It is ironic, perhaps, that Isaac Newton and Robert Boyle, two of the scientists who led the move to exclude all natural theology from science (then called "natural philosophy") did so for *theological* reasons. Their Calvinist doctrine of God's transcendence led them to make a radical distinction between God the Creator and the operation of the created universe, and hence to seek to protect *theology* from contamination *by science*. The metaphysical mixing of science and religion, Boyle and Newton believed, corrupted true religion.[13]

So, for better or for worse, we have inherited a view of science as *methodologically* atheistic—meaning that science *qua* science, seeks naturalistic explanations for all natural processes. Christians and atheists alike must pursue scientific questions in our era without invoking a creator. The conflict between Christianity and evolutionary thought only arises when scientists conclude that if the only *scientific* explanation that can be given is a chance happening, then there is no other explanation at all. Such a conclusion constitutes an invalid inference from a statement expressing the limits of scientific knowledge to a metaphysical (or a-religious or anti-religious) claim about the ultimate nature of reality.

This is a subtle difference—one beyond the grasp of a fourth-grade science class (and perhaps beyond the grasp of some outspoken scientific naturalists as well?). For this reason I am sympathetic with Christians who object to the teaching of evolution in the public schools. But the answer is to help educators make the distinction, not to cooperate in blurring it as Johnson has done.[14]

CREATIVE INTELLIGENCE AS A SCIENTIFIC HYPOTHESIS

Johnson writes:

> Why not consider the possibility that life is what it so evidently seems to be, the product of creative intelligence? Science would not come to an end, because the task would remain of deciphering the languages in which genetic information is communicated, and in general finding out how the whole system *works*. What scientists would lose is not an inspiring research program, but the illusion of total mastery of nature. They would have to face the possibility that beyond the natural world there is a further reality which transcends science (p. 110).

The answer to Johnson's question is that anyone who attributes the characteristics of living things to creative intelligence has by definition stepped into the arena of either metaphysics or theology. Some might reply that the definition of science, then, needs to be changed. And perhaps it would be better if science had not taken this particular turn in its history. Could the nature of science change again in the near future to admit theistic explanations of natural events? There are a number of reasons for thinking this unlikely. A practical reason is the fact that much of the funding for scientific research in this country comes from the federal government. The mixing of science and religion would raise issues of the separation of church and state.

A second reason for thinking such a change unlikely is that many Christians in science, philosophy, and theology are still haunted by the idea of a "God of the gaps." Newton postulated divine intervention to adjust the orbits of the planets. When Laplace provided better calculations, God was no longer needed. Many Christians are wary of invoking divine action in any way in science, especially in biology, fearing that science will advance, providing the naturalistic explanations that will make God appear once again to have been an unnecessary hypothesis.

CONCLUDING REMARKS

What, then, of the relation between Christianity and Darwinism? I hope I have made it clear that this question is ambiguous. One question is: How ought Christianity be related to evolutionary biology—the pure science? The other is: How ought Christianity be related to evolutionary metaphysics? The latter system of thought involves the use of scientific theory to legitimate a metaphysical-religious point of view, and it has been so successful that many cannot imagine Christian thought making its own, different use of biology. Nonetheless it can be done, and it has been done by the likes of biochemist-theologian Arthur Peacocke.[15]

Peacocke notes that the sciences can be organized in a hierarchy, with higher sciences studying more complex levels of organization in reality. For example, chemistry studies more complex organizations of matter than does physics; biochemistry more so than inorganic chemistry; within biology alone there is a hierarchy as we move from biochemistry to the study of cells, to tissues, organs, and finally to the functioning of entire organisms within their environments.

Each science has its recognized domain, and concepts and theories appropriate to its own level of interest. Yet each science is conditioned by the levels above and below. Lower levels set limits on the behavior of entities at higher levels—for example, chemical processes in nerves and muscles set limits on how high or fast an animal can jump. However, lower levels do not uniquely determine the behavior of entities at higher levels—here one also has to take account of the environment. Thus, the animal's particular movements within the range permitted by chemistry and physics will be to some extent conditioned by ecological factors as well.

So any science alone provides an incomplete account of reality; it finds limits above and below, beyond which its explanatory concepts cannot reach. But what about the limits of the highest (or lowest) science in the hierarchy? Peacocke proposes that at the top of the hierarchy of the sciences we reach theology, the science that studies the most complex system of all—the interaction of God and the whole of creation.[16]

Peacocke's suggestion provides the groundwork for an exciting account of the relations between the sciences and theology. We can examine the kinds of relations that hold between two hierarchically ordered sciences, and then look for analogous relations between theology and one or more sciences. One relation we may expect to find is that when a science reaches an inherent limit, there may be a role for theology to play at that point. For example, it *may* be inherently impossible for science to describe what happened "before" the Big Bang.

Peacocke's understanding of the relation between science and theology means that we need not turn biology into theology, but we may and must bear in mind that there is a discipline "above" biology that answers questions that biology alone cannot answer. Is this discipline to be an atheistic metaphysic that elevates "Chance" to the role of ultimate explanation, or is it to be a theology of benevolent Design? The question calls for a careful comparison of the explanatory force of these two competing accounts of reality. The former has to explain (or explain away) all appearances of order and purpose; the latter has to explain a number of features of the world that (as biologists correctly point out) appear inconsistent with intelligent design.[17]

It looks to many as though these two explanatory systems are at a standoff. For every feature that appears to be the product of design, there is another that appears to be the product of chance. However, I suspect that the design hypothesis, as the core of the theological research program, could be shown to be *more progressive* (in Lakatos's sense) than a research program based on chance. My guess is that while the atheistic program could explain (or explain away) all the evidence for design, it will have to do so by means of an assortment of *ad hoc* hypotheses. Besides this, the Christian program has at its disposal additional supporting evidence from a variety of domains: religious experience, history, the human sciences.

So there are two issues before us, both of which cry out for much more extensive and careful treatment than I have given them here: First, what is the true standing of evolutionary biology *as a science* and measured against the best criteria that have so far been proposed for evaluating scientific acceptability (truth). I make two claims with regard to Johnson's book: first, that he has allowed the Evolutionary Naturalists to confuse evolutionary science with something else and, second, that he has used too primitive a view of scientific methodology for his evaluation. I do not claim to have definitively refuted his claims against evolutionary science, but I hope to have undermined them, and to have shown the direction a definitive evaluation of evolutionary biology would have to take.

The second big issue is the clash of world views: evolutionary naturalism versus Christianity; Chance with a capital "C" versus Design. Settling this controversy is well beyond the capability of any single scholar on either side, but we do educators, school children, and perhaps even evolutionary biologists a great favor by carefully distinguishing this issue from the first.

An important effect of separating the theological-metaphysical issue from the scientific one may be to lessen the anxiety and heat of controversy that surrounds the latter. We want scientists to stop their attacks on Christianity, but all Bible-readers should know that the cessation of hostilities is not to be left to our opponents. Better to turn away wrath with a gentle word.[18]

NOTES

1. Phillip E. Johnson, *Darwin on Trial* (Downers Grove, IL: InterVarsity, 1991).

2. This sort of credential swapping is quite out of place in academic writing, but nonetheless it deserves a name. In practical reasoning, some arguments are called *ad hominem* (to or against the man); this argument I shall dub an *ab femina* argument (from the woman).

3. This view of science has been particularly influential in conservative American Christian circles. John Witherspoon promoted Bacon's views among the Princeton theologians, such as Charles Hodge, who have influenced American Fundamentalism. It is described and criticized at somewhat greater length by Johnson, pp. 146–47.

4. This term was coined by Carl Hempel. See his *Philosophy of Natural Science* (Englewood Cliffs, NJ: Prentice-Hall, 1966).

5. Actually, we are asking more of natural selection here than is required by the theory. Darwinian theory does not require that natural selection be directly responsible for reproductive isolation. The classical theory is that geographical isolation, followed by differential adaptation to different conditions, is the principal agent of speciation.

6. Johnson does take up this issue in the following chapter. My point is that the conclusions he draws in this chapter regarding the limits of variation are quite unwarranted because they cannot be made *independently* of the assessment of the possibilities for mutations.

7. See "Falsification and the Methodology of Scientific Research Programmes," in J. Worrall and G. Currie, eds., *The Methodology of Scientific Research Programmes: Philosophical Papers, Volume 1* (Cambridge: Cambridge University Press, 1978), 8–101.

8. Such as Karl Popper's falsificationism.

9. By Alan Musgrave, "Logical vs. Historical Theories of Confirmation," *British Journal for the Philosophy of Science* 25 (1974): 1–23.

10. Popper first elaborated this thesis in *Logik der Forschung* (Vienna: J. Springer, 1935); English translation, *The Logic of Scientific Discovery* (New York: Harper, 1965).

11. There is insufficient space here to show that Lakatos's understanding of science is superior to Popper's. See my *Theology in the Age of Scientific Reasoning* (Ithaca, NY: Cornell University Press, 1990), chapter 3; as well as Lakatos's "Falsification and the Methodology of Scientific Research Programmes," op. cit.; and especially his "History of Science and Its Rational Reconstructions," also in *The Methodology of Scientific Research Programmes*, 102–38.

12. The same point is made by Thomas Kuhn in *The Structure of Scientific Revolutions* (Chicago: University of Chicago, 1970); Paul Feyerabend in *Against Method* (London: New Left Books, 1975); and Larry Laudan in *Progress and Its Problems* (Berkeley: University of California Press, 1977).

13. See Eugene Klaaren, *Religious Origins of Modern Science* (Grand Rapids, MI: Eerdmans, 1977); and Frank Manuel, *A Portrait of Isaac Newton* (Cambridge, MA: Harvard University Press, 1968).

14. For an excellent discussion of this and other issues, see Howard Van Till, Robert Snow, John Stek, and Davis Young, eds., *Portraits of Creation* (Grand Rapids, MI: Eerdmans, 1990).

15. See *Creation and the World of Science* (Oxford: Clarendon, 1979); *Intimations of Reality* (Notre Dame, IN: University of Notre Dame Press, 1985); or *Theology for a Scientific Age* (Cambridge, MA: Basil Blackwell, 1990).

16. I elaborate and apply this view of the hierarchy of the sciences and their relation to theology in "Evidence of Design in the Fine-Tuning of the Universe," in Robert Russell, Nancey Murphy, and Chris Isham, eds., *Quantum Cosmology and the Laws of Nature: Scientific Perspectives on Divine Action* (Vatican City State: The Vatican Observatory; Berkeley: Center for Theology and Natural Sciences, 1993).

17. Peacocke's view is that God creates through exploration of the possibilities provided by chance as well as through law-governed design.

18. I wish to thank Philip Spieth at the University of California, Berkeley, for helpful comments on an earlier draft of this paper.

BOARD RESOLUTION ON INTELLIGENT DESIGN THEORY

AMERICAN ASSOCIATION FOR THE ADVANCEMENT OF SCIENCE

Approved October 18, 2002

T he contemporary theory of biological evolution is one of the most robust products of scientific inquiry. It is the foundation for research in many areas of biology as well as an essential element of science education. To become informed and responsible citizens in our contemporary technological world, students need to study the theories and empirical evidence central to current scientific understanding.

Over the past several years proponents of so-called "intelligent design theory," also known as ID, have challenged the accepted scientific theory of biological evolution. As part of this effort they have sought to introduce the teaching of "intelligent design theory" into the science curricula of the public schools. The movement presents "intelligent design theory" to the public as a theoretical innovation, supported by scientific evidence, that offers a more adequate explanation for the origin of the diversity of living organisms than the current scientifically accepted theory of evolution. In response to this

"Board Resolution on Intelligent Design Theory," *American Association for the Advancement of Science,*" October 18, 2002.

effort, individual scientists and philosophers of science have provided substantive critiques of "intelligent design," demonstrating significant conceptual flaws in its formulation, a lack of credible scientific evidence, and misrepresentations of scientific facts.

Recognizing that the "intelligent design theory" represents a challenge to the quality of science education, the Board of Directors of the AAAS unanimously adopts the following resolution:

Whereas, ID proponents claim that contemporary evolutionary theory is incapable of explaining the origin of the diversity of living organisms;

Whereas, to date, the ID movement has failed to offer credible scientific evidence to support their claim that ID undermines the current scientifically accepted theory of evolution;

Whereas, the ID movement has not proposed a scientific means of testing its claims;

Therefore Be It Resolved, that the lack of scientific warrant for so-called "intelligent design theory" makes it improper to include as a part of science education;

Therefore Be It Further Resolved, that AAAS urges citizens across the nation to oppose the establishment of policies that would permit the teaching of "intelligent design theory" as a part of the science curricula of the public schools;

Therefore Be It Further Resolved, that AAAS calls upon its members to assist those engaged in overseeing science education policy to understand the nature of science, the content of contemporary evolutionary theory, and the inappropriateness of "intelligent design theory" as subject matter for science education;

Therefore Be It Further Resolved, that AAAS encourages its affiliated societies to endorse this resolution and to communicate their support to appropriate parties at the federal, state and local levels of the government.

NATIONAL SCIENCE TEACHERS ASSOCIATION STATEMENT ON EVOLUTION

ADOPTED BY THE NSTA BOARD OF DIRECTORS

July 2003

INTRODUCTION

The National Science Teachers Association (NSTA) strongly supports the position that evolution is a major unifying concept in science and should be included in the K-12 science education frameworks and curricula. Furthermore, if evolution is not taught, students will not achieve the level of scientific literacy they need. This position is consistent with that of the National Academies, the American Association for the Advancement of Science (AAAS), and many other scientific and educational organizations.

NSTA also recognizes that evolution has not been emphasized in science curricula in a manner commensurate to its importance because of official policies, intimidation of science teachers, the general public's misunderstanding of evolutionary theory, and a century of controversy. In addition, teachers are being pressured to introduce creationism, "creation science,"

"Statement on Evolution," *National Science Teachers Association*, July 2003.

and other nonscientific views, which are intended to weaken or eliminate the teaching of evolution.

DECLARATIONS

Within this context, NSTA recommends that

Science curricula, state science standards, and teachers should emphasize evolution in a manner commensurate with its importance as a unifying concept in science and its overall explanatory power.

Science teachers should not advocate any religious interpretations of nature and should be nonjudgmental about the personal beliefs of students.

Policy makers and administrators should not mandate policies requiring the teaching of "creation science" or related concepts, such as so-called "intelligent design," "abrupt appearance," and "arguments against evolution." Administrators also should support teachers against pressure to promote nonscientific views or to diminish or eliminate the study of evolution.

Administrators and school boards should provide support to teachers as they review, adopt, and implement curricula that emphasize evolution. This should include professional development to assist teachers in teaching evolution in a comprehensive and professional manner.

Parental and community involvement in establishing the goals of science education and the curriculum development process should be encouraged and nurtured in our democratic society. However, the professional responsibility of science teachers and curriculum specialists to provide students with quality science education should not be compromised by censorship, pseudoscience, inconsistencies, faulty scholarship, or unconstitutional mandates.

Science textbooks shall emphasize evolution as a unifying concept. Publishers should not be required or volunteer to include disclaimers in textbooks that distort or misrepresent the methodology of science and the current body of knowledge concerning the nature and study of evolution.

STATEMENT OF THE POSITION OF THE ASSOCIATION OF SOUTHEASTERN BIOLOGISTS REGARDING THE TEACHING OF EVOLUTION IN THE CLASSROOM

Adopted April 16, 2004

The Association of Southeastern Biologists is a regional association devoted to the promulgation of biology in all its myriad forms to scientists, students, and the general public. As part of its duties, the Association represents biological scientists from throughout the southeastern region of the United States on various issues of concern. This statement contains the Association's recommendations concerning the teaching of evolution in the classroom.

Evolution is the only currently acceptable *scientific* theory for the development of life on earth, and is supported by an enormous body of evidence from a wide variety of disciplines, including, but not limited to, biology, chemistry, geology, and physics. Across all of these scientific disciplines, the data are in congruence with regards to the theory of evolution, and there are no data that contradict the fundamental truth of evolution. Such consilience gives credence and support to the concept that all life is related and that it has evolved over time primarily through the process of natural selection. The

"Statement of the Position Regarding the Teaching of Evolution in the Classroom," Association of Southeastern Biologists, April 16, 2004.

Association believes that the study of evolution is crucial if students are to gain a proper understanding of life on earth.

In recent years, the public schools have been pressured to teach "alternative" theories to evolution, most notably, creationism and intelligent design. However, both creationism and intelligent design are based in faith and do not follow acceptable scientific principles. Both movements are rooted in preconceived notions about the development of life and its origins, yet fail to present any credible scientific evidence to support those claims. In contrast, the evidence in support for evolution is being added to on a daily basis, and is now so overwhelmingly strong that we can state with certainty that evolution occurs.

Because creationism and intelligent design do not operate within the definitional limits of science, they cannot and should not be treated as such. Neither movement can satisfy the aims of science, which are to make observations and develop questions to explain natural phenomena, to design tests of those hypotheses, and then to either accept or reject those hypotheses, based on a fair and objective evaluation of the evidence accumulated. Creationism and intelligent design offer a mixture of empirically untestable and empirically non-scientific hypotheses, which their proponents fail to retract or modify in the light of contrary evidence. Thus, they do not conform to accepted scientific protocols.

Therefore, since neither creationism nor intelligent design is a scientific endeavor, we oppose any attempts to insert them into the science curricula of any public schools. While religion has played and continues to play a significant role in many people's lives, and in schools' curricula, we object to any attempts to insert religious dogma, such as creationism or intelligent design, into science classes.

Furthermore, we strongly oppose attempts to undermine or compromise the teaching of evolution, whether by eliminating the word 'evolution' from state science standards, requiring textbook disclaimers that misleadingly describe evolution as "merely" a theory, or by encouraging scientifically unwarranted criticism of evolution under the guise of "analysis," "objectivity," "balance," or "teaching the controversy." Such tactics are clearly intended to leave the false impression that evolution is scientifically precarious and will thus deprive students of a sound scientific education.

In conclusion, the Association of Southeastern Biologists strongly opposes the teaching of any alternative non-scientific theories to evolution that are not based on established scientific concepts, endorses the meaningful teaching of evolution in science classrooms, and opposes any attempts to water down the teaching of evolution by singling out the subject for special treatment not given any other sciences.

PART FIVE

RELIGION AND EVOLUTION

Compatibility Issue

TRUTH CANNOT CONTRADICT TRUTH

ADDRESS OF POPE JOHN PAUL II TO THE
PONTIFICAL ACADEMY OF SCIENCES

October 22, 1996

W ith great pleasure I address cordial greeting to you, Mr. President, and to all of you who constitute the Pontifical Academy of Sciences, on the occasion of your plenary assembly. I offer my best wishes in particular to the new academicians, who have come to take part in your work for the first time. I would also like to remember the academicians who died during the past year, whom I commend to the Lord of life.

1. In celebrating the 60th anniversary of the academy's refoundation, I would like to recall the intentions of my predecessor Pius XI, who wished to surround himself with a select group of scholars, relying on them to inform the Holy See in complete freedom about developments in scientific research, and thereby to assist him in his reflections.

He asked those whom he called the Church's "senatus scientificus" to serve the truth. I again extend this same invitation to you today, certain that

Pope John Paul II, "Truth Cannot Contradict Truth," Address to the Pontifical Academy of Sciences, October 22, 1996.

we will be able to profit from the fruitfulness of a trustful dialogue between the Church and science.[1]

2. I am pleased with the first theme you have chosen, that of the origins of life and evolution, an essential subject which deeply interests the Church, since revelation, for its part, contains teaching concerning the nature and origins of man. How do the conclusions reached by the various scientific disciplines coincide with those contained in the message of revelation? And if, at first sight, there are apparent contradictions, in what direction do we look for their solution? We know, in fact, that truth cannot contradict truth.[2] Moreover, to shed greater light on historical truth, your research on the Church's relations with science between the 16th and 18th centuries is of great importance. During this plenary session, you are undertaking a "reflection on science at the dawn of the third millennium," starting with the identification of the principal problems created by the sciences and which affect humanity's future. With this step you point the way to solutions which will be beneficial to the whole human community. In the domain of inanimate and animate nature, the evolution of science and its applications give rise to new questions. The better the Church's knowledge is of their essential aspects, the more she will understand their impact. Consequently, in accordance with her specific mission she will be able to offer criteria for discerning the moral conduct required of all human beings in view of their integral salvation.

3. Before offering you several reflections that more specifically concern the subject of the origin of life and its evolution, I would like to remind you that the magisterium of the Church has already made pronouncements on these matters within the framework of her own competence. I will cite here two interventions.

In his encyclical *Humani Generis*,[3] my predecessor Pius XII had already stated that there was no opposition between evolution and the doctrine of the faith about man and his vocation, on condition that one did not lose sight of several indisputable points.

For my part, when I received those taking part in your academy's plenary assembly on October 31, 1992, I had the opportunity with regard to Galileo to draw attention to the need of a rigorous hermeneutic for the correct interpretation of the inspired word. It is necessary to determine the proper sense of Scripture, while avoiding any unwarranted interpretations that make it say what it does not intend to say. In order to delineate the field of their own study, the exegete and the theologian must keep informed about the results achieved by the natural sciences.[4]

4. Taking into account the state of scientific research at the time as well as of the requirements of theology, the encyclical *Humani Generis* considered the doctrine of "evolutionism" a serious hypothesis, worthy of investigation and in-depth study equal to that of the opposing hypothesis. Pius XII added two methodological conditions: that this opinion should not be adopted as though it were a certain, proven doctrine and as though one could totally prescind from revelation with regard to the questions it raises. He also spelled out the condition on which this opinion would be compatible with the Christian faith, a point to which I will return. Today, almost half a century after the publication of the encyclical, new knowledge has led to the recognition of the theory of evolution as more than a hypothesis. [*Aujourdhui, près dun demi-siècle après la parution de l'encyclique, de nouvelles connaissances conduisent à reconnaitre dans la théorie de l'évolution plus qu'une hypothèse.*] It is indeed remarkable that this theory has been progressively accepted by researchers, following a series of discoveries in various fields of knowledge. The convergence, neither sought nor fabricated, of the results of work that was conducted independently is in itself a significant argument in favor of this theory.

What is the significance of such a theory? To address this question is to enter the field of epistemology. A theory is a metascientific elaboration, distinct from the results of observation but consistent with them. By means of it a series of independent data and facts can be related and interpreted in a unified explanation. A theory's validity depends on whether or not it can be verified; it is constantly tested against the facts; wherever it can no longer explain the latter, it shows its limitations and unsuitability. It must then be rethought.

Furthermore, while the formulation of a theory like that of evolution complies with the need for consistency with the observed data, it borrows certain notions from natural philosophy.

And, to tell the truth, rather than the theory of evolution, we should speak of several theories of evolution. On the one hand, this plurality has to do with the different explanations advanced for the mechanism of evolution, and on the other, with the various philosophies on which it is based. Hence the existence of materialist, reductionist and spiritualist interpretations. What is to be decided here is the true role of philosophy and, beyond it, of theology.

5. The Church's magisterium is directly concerned with the question of evolution, for it involves the conception of man: Revelation teaches us that he was created in the image and likeness of God.[5] The conciliar constitution

Gaudium et Spes has magnificently explained this doctrine, which is pivotal to Christian thought. It recalled that man is "the only creature on earth that God has wanted for its own sake."[6] In other terms, the human individual cannot be subordinated as a pure means or a pure instrument, either to the species or to society; he has value *per se*. He is a person. With his intellect and his will, he is capable of forming a relationship of communion, solidarity and self-giving with his peers. St. Thomas observes that man's likeness to God resides especially in his speculative intellect, for his relationship with the object of his knowledge resembles God's relationship with what he has created.[7] But even more, man is called to enter into a relationship of knowledge and love with God himself, a relationship which will find its complete fulfillment beyond time, in eternity. All the depth and grandeur of this vocation are revealed to us in the mystery of the risen Christ.[8] It is by virtue of his spiritual soul that the whole person possesses such a dignity even in his body. Pius XII stressed this essential point: If the human body take its origin from preexistent living matter, the spiritual soul is immediately created by God ("animas enim a Deo immediate creari catholica fides nos retinere iubei").[9] Consequently, theories of evolution which, in accordance with the philosophies inspiring them, consider the spirit as emerging from the forces of living matter or as a mere *epiphenomenon* of this matter, are incompatible with the truth about man. Nor are they able to ground the dignity of the person.

6. With man, then, we find ourselves in the presence of an ontological difference, an ontological leap, one could say. However, does not the posing of such ontological discontinuity run counter to that physical continuity which seems to be the main thread of research into evolution in the field of physics and chemistry? Consideration of the method used in the various branches of knowledge makes it possible to reconcile two points of view which would seem irreconcilable. The sciences of observation describe and measure the multiple manifestations of life with increasing precision and correlate them with the time line. The moment of transition to the spiritual cannot be the object of this kind of observation, which nevertheless can discover at the experimental level a series of very valuable signs indicating what is specific to the human being. But the experience of metaphysical knowledge, of self-awareness and self-reflection, of moral conscience, freedom, or again of aesthetic and religious experience, falls within the competence of philosophical analysis and reflection, while theology brings out its ultimate meaning according to the Creator's plans.

7. In conclusion, I would like to call to mind a Gospel truth which can

shed a higher light on the horizon of your research into the origins and unfolding of living matter. The Bible in fact bears an extraordinary message of life. It gives us a wise vision of life inasmuch as it describes the loftiest forms of existence. This vision guided me in the encyclical which I dedicated to respect for human life, and which I called precisely "Evangelium Vitae."

It is significant that in St. John's Gospel *life* refers to the divine light which Christ communicates to us. We are called to enter into eternal life, that is to say, into the eternity of divine beatitude. To warn us against the serious temptations threatening us, our Lord quotes the great saying of Deuteronomy: "Man shall not live by bread alone, but by every word that proceeds from the mouth of God."[10] Even more, "life" is one of the most beautiful titles which the Bible attributes to God. He is the living God.

NOTES

1. Pope John Paul II, "Address to the Academy of Sciences" (Vatican City, October 28, 1986) and "L'Osservatore Romano," English edition (Vatican City, November 24, 1986), 22.

2. Pope Leo XIII, Encyclical "Providentissimus Deus" *[On the Study of Holy Scripture]*, November 18, 1893.

3. Pope Pius XII, Encyical "Humani Generis" *[On Human Origin]*, August 12, 1950.

4. Pope John Paul II, "Address to the Pontifical Biblical Commission," *AAS* 85 (January 8, 1993): 764–72, and Pope John Paul II, "The Interpretation of the Bible in the Church," *AAS* 86 (January 8, 1994): 232–43.

5. Gen. 1:27–29.

6. Pope Paul VI, *"Gaudium et Spes,"* Pastoral Constitution on the Church in the Modern World Second Vatican Council, December 7, 1965, no. 24.

7. St. Thomas Aquinas, *Summa Theologica,* I-II:3:5, ad 1.

8. Pope Paul VI, *"Gaudium et Spes,"* no. 22.

9. Pope Pius XII, "Humani Generis." 36.

10. Deut. 8:3 and Matt. 4:4.

NONOVERLAPPING MAGISTERIA

STEPHEN JAY GOULD

Incongruous places often inspire anomalous stories. In early 1984, I spent several nights at the Vatican housed in a hotel built for itinerant priests. While pondering over such puzzling issues as the intended function of the bidets in each bathroom, and hungering for something other than plum jam on my breakfast rolls (why did the basket only contain hundreds of identical plum packets and not a one of, say, strawberry?), I encountered yet another among the innumerable issues of contrasting cultures that can make life so interesting. Our crowd (present in Rome for a meeting on nuclear winter sponsored by the Pontifical Academy of Sciences) shared the hotel with a group of French and Italian Jesuit priests who were also professional scientists.

At lunch, the priests called me over to their table to pose a problem that had been troubling them. What, they wanted to know, was going on in America with all this talk about "scientific creationism"? One asked me: "Is evolution really in some kind of trouble; and if so, what could such trouble be? I have always been taught that no doctrinal conflict exists between evo-

Stephen Jay Gould, "Nonoverlapping Magisteria," *Natural History* 106 (March 1997): 16–22, 60–62.

lution and Catholic faith, and the evidence for evolution seems both entirely satisfactory and utterly overwhelming. Have I missed something?"

A lively pastiche of French, Italian, and English conversation then ensued for half an hour or so, but the priests all seemed reassured by my general answer: Evolution has encountered no intellectual trouble; no new arguments have been offered. Creationism is a homegrown phenomenon of American sociocultural history—a splinter movement (unfortunately rather more of a beam these days) of Protestant fundamentalists who believe that every word of the Bible must be literally true, whatever such a claim might mean. We all left satisfied, but I certainly felt bemused by the anomaly of my role as a Jewish agnostic, trying to reassure a group of Catholic priests that evolution remained both true and entirely consistent with religious belief.

Another story in the same mold: I am often asked whether I ever encounter creationism as a live issue among my Harvard undergraduate students. I reply that only once, in nearly thirty years of teaching, did I experience such an incident. A very sincere and serious freshman student came to my office hours with the following question that had clearly been troubling him deeply: "I am a devout Christian and have never had any reason to doubt evolution, an idea that seems both exciting and particularly well documented. But my roommate, a proselytizing Evangelical, has been insisting with enormous vigor that I cannot be both a real Christian and an evolutionist. So tell me, can a person believe both in God and evolution?" Again, I gulped hard, did my intellectual duty, and reassured him that evolution was both true and entirely compatible with Christian belief—a position I hold sincerely, but still an odd situation for a Jewish agnostic.

These two stories illustrate a cardinal point, frequently unrecognized but absolutely central to any understanding of the status and impact of the politically potent, fundamentalist doctrine known by its self-proclaimed oxymoron as "scientific creationism"—the claim that the Bible is literally true, that all organisms were created during six days of twenty-four hours, that the earth is only a few thousand years old, and that evolution must therefore be false. Creationism does not pit science against religion (as my opening stories indicate), for no such conflict exists. Creationism does not raise any unsettled intellectual issues about the nature of biology or the history of life. Creationism is a local and parochial movement, powerful only in the United States among Western nations, and prevalent only among the few sectors of American Protestantism that choose to read the Bible as an inerrant document, literally true in every jot and tittle.

I do not doubt that one could find an occasional nun who would prefer to teach creationism in her parochial school biology class or an occasional orthodox rabbi who does the same in his yeshiva, but creationism based on biblical literalism makes little sense in either Catholicism or Judaism for neither religion maintains any extensive tradition for reading the Bible as literal truth rather than illuminating literature, based partly on metaphor and allegory (essential components of all good writing) and demanding interpretation for proper understanding. Most Protestant groups, of course, take the same position—the fundamentalist fringe notwithstanding.

The position that I have just outlined by personal stories and general statements represents the standard attitude of all major Western religions (and of Western science) today. (I cannot, through ignorance, speak of Eastern religions, although I suspect that the same position would prevail in most cases.) The lack of conflict between science and religion arises from a lack of overlap between their respective domains of professional expertise—science in the empirical constitution of the universe, and religion in the search for proper ethical values and the spiritual meaning of our lives. The attainment of wisdom in a full life requires extensive attention to both domains—for a great book tells us that the truth can make us free and that we will live in optimal harmony with our fellows when we learn to do justly, love mercy, and walk humbly.

In the context of this standard position, I was enormously puzzled by a statement issued by Pope John Paul II on October 22, 1996, to the Pontifical Academy of Sciences, the same body that had sponsored my earlier trip to the Vatican. In this document, entitled "Truth Cannot Contradict Truth," the pope defended both the evidence for evolution and the consistency of the theory with Catholic religious doctrine. Newspapers throughout the world responded with front-page headlines, as in the *New York Times* for October 25: "Pope Bolsters Church's Support for Scientific View of Evolution."

Now I know about "slow news days" and I do admit that nothing else was strongly competing for headlines at that particular moment. (The *Times* could muster nothing more exciting for a lead story than Ross Perot's refusal to take Bob Dole's advice and quit the presidential race.) Still, I couldn't help feeling immensely puzzled by all the attention paid to the pope's statement (while being wryly pleased, of course, for we need all the good press we can get, especially from respected outside sources). The Catholic Church had never opposed evolution and had no reason to do so. Why had the pope issued such a statement at all? And why had the press responded with an orgy of worldwide, front-page coverage?

I could only conclude at first, and wrongly as I soon learned, that journalists throughout the world must deeply misunderstand the relationship between science and religion, and must therefore be elevating a minor papal comment to unwarranted notice. Perhaps most people really do think that a war exists between science and religion, and that (to cite a particularly newsworthy case) evolution must be intrinsically opposed to Christianity. In such a context, a papal admission of evolution's legitimate status might be regarded as major news indeed—a sort of modern equivalent for a story that never happened, but would have made the biggest journalistic splash of 1640: Pope Urban VIII releases his most famous prisoner from house arrest and humbly apologizes, "Sorry, Signor Galileo . . . the sun, er, is central."

But I then discovered that the prominent coverage of papal satisfaction with evolution had not been an error of non-Catholic Anglophone journalists. The Vatican itself had issued the statement as a major news release. And Italian newspapers had featured, if anything, even bigger headlines and longer stories. The conservative *Il Giornale*, for example, shouted from its masthead: "Pope Says We May Descend from Monkeys."

Clearly, I was out to lunch. Something novel or surprising must lurk within the papal statement but what could it be?—especially given the accuracy of my primary impression (as I later verified) that the Catholic Church values scientific study, views science as no threat to religion in general or Catholic doctrine in particular, and has long accepted both the legitimacy of evolution as a field of study and the potential harmony of evolutionary conclusions with Catholic faith.

As a former constituent of Tip O'Neill's, I certainly know that "all politics is local"—and that the Vatican undoubtedly has its own internal reasons, quite opaque to me, for announcing papal support of evolution in a major statement. Still, I knew that I was missing some important key, and I felt frustrated. I then remembered the primary rule of intellectual life: when puzzled, it never hurts to read the primary documents—a rather simple and self-evident principle that has, nonetheless, completely disappeared from large sectors of the American experience.

I knew that Pope Pius XII (not one of my favorite figures in twentieth-century history, to say the least) had made the primary statement in a 1950 encyclical entitled *Humani Generis*. I knew the main thrust of his message: Catholics could believe whatever science determined about the evolution of the human body, so long as they accepted that, at some time of his choosing, God had infused the soul into such a creature. I also knew that I had no problem with this statement, for whatever my private beliefs about souls, science cannot touch such a subject and therefore cannot be threatened by any theological position on such a legitimately and intrinsically religious issue. Pope Pius XII, in other words, had properly acknowledged and respected the separate domains of science and theology. Thus, I found myself in total agreement with *Humani Generis*—but I had never read the document in full (not much of an impediment to stating an opinion these days).

I quickly got the relevant writings from, of all places, the Internet. (The pope is prominently on-line, but a Luddite like me is not. So I got a computer-literate associate to dredge up the documents. I do love the fracture of stereotypes implied by finding religion so hep and a scientist so square.) Having now read in full both Pope Pius's *Humani Generis* of 1950 and Pope John Paul's proclamation of October 1996, I finally understand why the recent statement seems so new, revealing, and worthy of all those headlines. And the message could not be more welcome for evolutionists and friends of both science and religion.

The text of *Humani Generis* focuses on the magisterium (or teaching authority) of the Church—a word derived not from any concept of majesty or awe but from the different notion of teaching, for *magister* is Latin for "teacher." We may, I think, adopt this word and concept to express the central point of this essay and the principled resolution of supposed "conflict" or "warfare" between science and religion. No such conflict should exist because each subject has a legitimate magisterium, or domain of teaching authority—and these magisteria do not overlap (the principle that I would like to designate as NOMA, or "nonoverlapping magisteria").

The net of science covers the empirical universe: what is it made of (fact) and why does it work this way (theory). The net of religion extends over questions of moral meaning and value. These two magisteria do not overlap, nor do they encompass all inquiry (consider, for starters, the magisterium of art and the meaning of beauty). To cite the arch clichés, we get the age of rocks, and religion retains the rock of ages; we study how the heavens go, and they determine how to go to heaven.

This resolution might remain all neat and clean if the nonoverlapping magisteria (NOMA) of science and religion were separated by an extensive no man's land. But, in fact, the two magisteria bump right up against each other, interdigitating in wondrously complex ways along their joint border. Many of our deepest questions call upon aspects of both for different parts of a full answer—and the sorting of legitimate domains can become quite complex and difficult. To cite just two broad questions involving both evolutionary facts and moral arguments: Since evolution made us the only earthly creatures with advanced consciousness, what responsibilities are so entailed for our relations with other species? What do our genealogical ties with other organisms imply about the meaning of human life?

Pius XII's *Humani Generis* is a highly traditionalist document by a deeply conservative man forced to face all the "isms" and cynicisms that rode the wake of World War II and informed the struggle to rebuild human decency from the ashes of the Holocaust. The encyclical, subtitled "Concerning some false opinions which threaten to undermine the foundations of Catholic doctrine" begins with a statement of embattlement:

> Disagreement and error among men on moral and religious matters have always been a cause of profound sorrow to all good men, but above all to the true and loyal sons of the Church, especially today, when we see the principles of Christian culture being attacked on all sides.

Pius lashes out, in turn, at various external enemies of the Church: pantheism, existentialism, dialectical materialism, historicism, and of course and preeminently, communism. He then notes with sadness that some well-meaning folks within the Church have fallen into a dangerous relativism— "a theological pacifism and egalitarianism, in which all points of view become equally valid"—in order to include people of wavering faith who yearn for the embrace of Christian religion but do not wish to accept the particularly Catholic magisterium.

What is this world coming to when these noxious novelties can so discombobulate a revealed and established order? Speaking as a conservative's conservative, Pius laments:

> Novelties of this kind have already borne their deadly fruit in almost all branches of theology. . . . Some question whether angels are personal beings, and whether matter and spirit differ essentially. . . . Some even say that the doctrine of Transubstantiation, based on an antiquated philosophic notion of substance, should be so modified that the Real Presence of Christ in the Holy Eucharist be reduced to a kind of symbolism.

Pius first mentions evolution to decry a misuse by overextension often promulgated by zealous supporters of the anathematized "isms":

Some imprudently and indiscreetly hold that evolution . . . explains the origin of all things. . . . Communists gladly subscribe to this opinion so that, when the souls of men have been deprived of every idea of a personal God, they may the more efficaciously defend and propagate their dialectical materialism.

Pius's major statement on evolution occurs near the end of the encyclical in paragraphs 35 through 37. He accepts the standard model of NOMA and begins by acknowledging that evolution lies in a difficult area where the domains press hard against each other. "It remains for Us now to speak about those questions which, although they pertain to the positive sciences, are nevertheless more or less connected with the truths of the Christian faith."[1]

Pius then writes the well-known words that permit Catholics to entertain the evolution of the human body (a factual issue under the magisterium of science), so long as they accept the divine Creation and infusion of the soul (a theological notion under the magisterium of religion):

The Teaching Authority of the Church does not forbid that, in conformity with the present state of human sciences and sacred theology, research and discussions, on the part of men experienced in both fields, take place with regard to the doctrine of evolution, in as far as it inquires into the origin of the human body as coming from pre-existent and living matter—for the Catholic faith obliges us to hold that souls are immediately created by God.

I had, up to here, found nothing surprising in *Humani Generis*, and nothing to relieve my puzzlement about the novelty of Pope John Paul's recent statement. But I read further and realized that Pope Pius had said more about evolution, something I had never seen quoted, and that made John Paul's statement most interesting indeed. In short, Pius forcefully proclaimed that while evolution may be legitimate in principle, the theory, in fact, had not been proven and might well be entirely wrong. One gets the strong impression, moreover, that Pius was rooting pretty hard for a verdict of falsity.

Continuing directly from the last quotation, Pius advises us about the proper study of evolution:

However, this must be done in such a way that the reasons for both opinions, that is, those favorable and those unfavorable to evolution, be weighed and judged with the necessary seriousness, moderation and measure. . . .

Some, however, rashly transgress this liberty of discussion, when they act as if the origin of the human body from pre-existing and living matter were already completely certain and proved by the facts which have been discovered up to now and by reasoning on those facts, and as if there were nothing in the sources of divine revelation which demands the greatest moderation and caution in this question.

To summarize, Pius generally accepts the NOMA principle of nonoverlapping magisteria in permitting Catholics to entertain the hypothesis of evolution for the human body so long as they accept the divine infusion of the soul. But he then offers some (holy) fatherly advice to scientists about the status of evolution as a scientific concept: the idea is not yet proven, and you all need to be especially cautious because evolution raises many troubling issues right on the border of my magisterium. One may read this second theme in two different ways: either as a gratuitous incursion into a different magisterium or as a helpful perspective from an intelligent and concerned outsider. As a man of good will, and in the interest of conciliation, I am happy to embrace the latter reading.

In any case, this rarely quoted second claim (that evolution remains both unproven and a bit dangerous)—and not the familiar first argument for the NOMA principle (that Catholics may accept the evolution of the body so long as they embrace the creation of the soul)—defines the novelty and the interest of John Paul's recent statement.

John Paul begins by summarizing Pius's older encyclical of 1950, and particularly by reaffirming the NOMA principle—nothing new here, and no cause for extended publicity:

In his encyclical "Humani Generis" (1950), my predecessor Pius XII had already stated that there was no opposition between evolution and the doctrine of the faith about man and his vocation.

To emphasize the power of NOMA, John Paul poses a potential problem and a sound resolution: How can we reconcile science's claim for physical continuity in human evolution with Catholicism's insistence that the soul must enter at a moment of divine infusion:

With man, then, we find ourselves in the presence of an ontological difference, an ontological leap, one could say. However, does not the point of such ontological discontinuity run counter to that physical continuity which seems to be the main thread of research into evolution the fields of physics and chemistry? Consideration of the methods used in the various branches of knowledge makes it possible to reconcile two points of view which would seem irreconcilable. The sciences of observation describe and measure the multiple manifestations of life with increasing precision and correlate them with the time line. The moment of transition to the spiritual cannot be the object of this kind of observation.

The novelty and news value of John Paul's statement lies, rather, in his profound revision of Pius's second and rarely quoted claim that evolution, while conceivable in principle and reconcilable with religion, can cite little persuasive evidence, and may well be false. John Paul states—and I can only say amen, and thanks for noticing—that the half century between Pius's surveying the ruins of World War II and his own pontificate heralding the dawn of a new millennium has witnessed such growth of data, and such a refinement of theory, that evolution can no longer be doubted by people of good will:

> Pius XII added . . . that this opinion [evolution] should not be adopted as though it were a certain, proven doctrine. . . . Today, almost half a century after the publication of the encyclical, new knowledge has led to the recognition of more than one hypothesis in the theory of evolution. It is indeed remarkable that this theory has been progressively accepted by researchers, following a series of discoveries in various fields of knowledge. The convergence, neither sought nor fabricated, of the results of work that was conducted independently is in itself a significant argument in favor of the theory.

In conclusion, Pius had grudgingly admitted evolution as a legitimate hypothesis that he regarded as only tentatively supported and potentially (as I suspect he hoped) untrue. John Paul, nearly fifty years later, reaffirms the legitimacy of evolution under the NOMA principle—no news here—but then adds that additional data and theory have placed the factuality of evolution beyond reasonable doubt. Sincere Christians must now accept evolution not merely as a plausible possibility but also as an effectively proven fact. In other words, official Catholic opinion on evolution has moved from "say it ain't so, but we can deal with it if we have to" (Pius's grudging view of 1950) to John Paul's entirely welcoming "it has been proven true; we always celebrate nature's factuality, and we look forward to interesting discussions of theological implications." I happily endorse this turn of events as gospel—literally "good news." I may represent the magisterium of science, but I welcome the support of a primary leader from the other major magisterium of our complex lives. And I recall the wisdom of King Solomon: "As cold waters to a thirsty soul, so is good news from a far country."[2]

Just as religion must bear the cross of its hard-liners, I have some scientific colleagues, including a few prominent enough to wield influence by their writings, who view this rapprochement of the separate magisteria with dismay. To colleagues like me—agnostic scientists who welcome and celebrate the rapprochement, especially the pope's latest statement—they say: "C'mon, be honest; you know that religion is addle-pated, superstitious, old-fashioned b.s.; you're only making those welcoming noises because religion is so powerful, and we need to be diplomatic in order to assure public support and funding for science." I do not think that this attitude is common among scientists, but such a position fills me with dismay—and I therefore end this essay with a personal statement about religion, as a testimony to what I regard as a virtual consensus among thoughtful scientists (who support the NOMA principle as firmly as the pope does).

I am not, personally, a believer or a religious man in any sense of institutional commitment or practice. But I have enormous respect for religion, and the subject has always fascinated me, beyond almost all others (with a few exceptions, like evolution, paleontology, and baseball). Much of this fascination lies in the historical paradox that throughout Western history organized religion has fostered both the most unspeakable horrors and the most heart-rending examples of human goodness in the face of personal danger. (The evil, I believe, lies in the occasional confluence of religion with secular power. The Catholic Church has sponsored its share of horrors, from Inquisitions to liquidations—but only because this institution held such secular power during so much of Western history. When my folks held similar power more briefly in Old Testament times, they committed just as many atrocities with many of the same rationales.)

I believe, with all my heart, in a respectful, even loving concordat between our magisteria—the NOMA solution. NOMA represents a principled position on moral and intellectual grounds, not a mere diplomatic stance. NOMA also cuts both ways. If religion can no longer dictate the nature of factual conclusions properly under the magisterium of science, then scientists cannot claim higher insight into moral truth from any superior knowledge of the world's empirical constitution. This mutual humility has important practical consequences in a world of such diverse passions.

Religion is too important to too many people for any dismissal or denigration of the comfort still sought by many folks from theology. I may, for example, privately suspect that papal insistence on divine infusion of the soul represents a sop to our fears, a device for maintaining a belief in human superiority within an evolutionary world offering no privileged position to any creature. But I also know that souls represent a subject outside the magisterium of science. My world cannot prove or disprove such a notion, and the concept of souls cannot threaten or impact my domain. Moreover, while I cannot personally accept the Catholic view of souls, I surely honor the metaphorical value of such a concept both for grounding moral discussion and for expressing what we most value about human potentiality: our decency, care, and all the ethical and intellectual struggles that the evolution of consciousness imposed upon us.

As a moral position (and therefore not as a deduction from my knowledge of nature's factuality), I prefer the "cold bath" theory that nature can be truly "cruel" and "indifferent"—in the utterly inappropriate terms of our ethical discourse—because nature was not constructed as our eventual abode, didn't know we were coming (we are, after all, interlopers of the latest geological microsecond), and doesn't give a damn about us (speaking metaphorically). I regard such a position as liberating, not depressing, because we then become free to conduct moral discourse—and nothing could be more important—in our own terms, spared from the delusion that we might read moral truth passively from nature's factuality.

But I recognize that such a position frightens many people, and that a more spiritual view of nature retains broad appeal (acknowledging the factuality of evolution and other phenomena, but still seeking some intrinsic meaning in human terms, and from the magisterium of religion). I do appreciate, for example, the struggles of a man who wrote to the *New York Times* on November 3, 1996, to state both his pain and his endorsement of John Paul's statement:

> Pope John Paul II's acceptance of evolution touches the doubt in my heart. The problem of pain and suffering in a world created by a God who is all love and light is hard enough to bear, even if one is a creationist. But at least a creationist can say that the original creation, coming from the hand of God was good, harmonious, innocent and gentle. What can one say about evolution, even a spiritual theory of evolution? Pain and suffering, mindless cruelty and terror are its means of creation. Evolution's engine is the grinding of predatory teeth upon the screaming, living flesh and bones of prey. . . . If evolution be true, my faith has rougher seas to sail.

I don't agree with this man, but we could have a wonderful argument. I would push the "cold bath" theory: he would (presumably) advocate the theme of inherent spiritual meaning in nature, however opaque the signal. But we would both be enlightened and filled with better understanding of these deep and ultimately unanswerable issues. Here, I believe, lies the greatest strength and necessity of NOMA, the nonoverlapping magisteria of science and religion. NOMA permits—indeed enjoins—the prospect of respectful discourse, of constant input from both magisteria toward the common goal of wisdom. If human beings are anything special, we are the creatures that must ponder and talk. Pope John Paul II would surely point out to me that his magisterium has always recognized this distinction, for *"in principio, erat verbum"*—"In the beginning was the Word."

POSTSCRIPT

Carl Sagan organized and attended the Vatican meeting that introduces this essay; he also shared my concern for fruitful cooperation between the different but vital realms of science and religion. Carl was also one of my dearest friends. I learned of his untimely death on the same day that I read the proofs for this essay. I could only recall Nehru's observations on Gandhi's death—that the light had gone out, and darkness reigned everywhere. But I then contemplated what Carl had done in his short sixty-two years and remembered John Dryden's ode for Henry Purcell, a great musician who died even younger: "He long ere this had tuned the jarring spheres, and left no hell below."

The days I spent with Carl in Rome were the best of our friendship. We delighted in walking around the Eternal City, feasting on its history and architecture—and its food! Carl took special delight in the anonymity that he still enjoyed in a nation that had not yet aired *Cosmos*, the greatest media work in popular science of all time.

I dedicate this essay to his memory. Carl also shared my personal suspicion about the nonexistence of souls—but I cannot think of a better reason for hoping we are wrong than the prospect of spending eternity roaming the cosmos in friendship and conversation with this wonderful soul.

NOTES

1. Interestingly, the main thrust of these paragraphs does not address evolution in general but lies in refuting a doctrine that Pius calls "polygenism," or the notion of human ancestry from multiple parents—for he regards such an idea as incompatible with the doctrine of original sin, "which proceeds from a sin actually committed by an individual Adam and which, through generation, is passed on to all and is in everyone as his own." In this one instance, Pius may be transgressing the NOMA principle—but I cannot judge, for I do not understand the details of Catholic theology and therefore do not know how symbolically such a statement may be read. If Pius is arguing that we cannot entertain a theory about derivation of all modern humans from an ancestral population rather than through an ancestral individual (a potential fact) because such an idea would question the doctrine of original sin (a theological construct), then I would declare him out of line for letting the magisterium of religion dictate a conclusion within the magisterium of science.

2. Prov. 25:25.

OPPRESSED BY EVOLUTION

MATT CARTMILL

A s far as we can tell, all of earth's living things are descended from
a distant common ancestor that lived more than 3 billion years ago.
This is an important discovery, but it's not exactly news. Biologists started
putting forward the idea of evolution back in the 1700s, and thanks to
Darwin's unifying theory of natural selection, it's been the accepted wisdom
in biology for more than a hundred years. So you might think that by now
everyone would have gotten used to the idea that we are blood kin to all other
organisms, and closer kin to great apes than to spiders. On the face of it, the
idea makes a certain amount of plain common sense. We all know that we
share more features with apes than we do with spiders or snails or cypress
trees. The theory of evolution simply reads those shared features as family
resemblances. It doesn't deny that people are unique in important ways. Our
kinship with apes doesn't mean we're only apes under the skin, any more
than the kinship of cats with dogs means that your cat is repressing a secret
urge to bark and bury bones.

Matt Cartmill, "Oppressed by Evolution," *Discovery* (March 1998): 78–83.

Yet many people don't accept the idea of evolution, and even feel downright threatened by it. Conservative Christians, in particular, have opposed it; to them, science ran off track in 1859 when Darwin's *Origin of Species* first hit the bookstores. Over the decades, we biologists have become accustomed to this opposition, but in recent years there has been a change in the antievolution camp. Now we find ourselves defending Darwin against attacks not only from the religious right but from the academic left as well.

In the United States the religious opposition to Darwin is chiefly made up of evangelical Protestants. Some of them are smart, savvy, angry, and well organized, and they have been working here for almost a hundred years to stop biologists from telling people about the history of life. In the early part of this century they persuaded the legislatures of several states to pass laws against teaching evolution. When the courts threw out those laws, the antievolutionists tried a different strategy: fighting for laws giving equal classroom time to "creation science"—that is, Bible-based biology. That didn't work, either. Now they're trying to compel teachers to present evolution as a mere theory rather than a fact. So far they haven't succeeded, but they're still working at it.

It seems clear that these religious antievolutionists aren't going to go away in the foreseeable future; biologists will have to fight them for another century or two to keep them from outlawing Darwin. But if we are to succeed, I think we'll need to give serious thought to our opponents' motives. I suspect they are deeper and subtler than most scientists like to think—or than most crusaders against evolution themselves believe.

One reason I believe this is that the motives publicly claimed by Christian antievolutionists don't make sense. Many will tell you that the evolution issue is a religious struggle between a godless scientific establishment and so-called creationists—that is, themselves. But a lot of evolutionary biologists are creationists, too—devout Christians, Jews, and Muslims, who believe in an eternal God who created the world. They just don't see any reason to think that he created it as recently as 4000 BCE.

Many opponents of the idea of evolution say they reject it because it contradicts the Bible. They claim to believe that every word in the Bible is literally true. But no one really believes that. We all know that when, in John 7:38, Jesus said, "He that believeth on me . . . out of his belly shall flow rivers of living water," he didn't mean it literally. It's a figure of speech. Practically every book of the Bible contains some such passages, which have to be read as either figures of speech or errors of fact. Consider Biblical astronomy. The Old Testament depicts the "firmament" as a strong dome or tent spread out above the Earth. It has the sun, moon, and stars set in it—and water up above it, and windows in it to let the water out when it rains.[1] This is a lovely picture. If you read it as poetry, it's gorgeous. But taken literally, it's just plain wrong. There isn't any firmament or any water above the firmament, and the sun, moon, and stars aren't attached to anything. And if we can all agree that there isn't any firmament, then we can all agree that the literal truth of the Bible can't be the real issue here.

Some religious people say they reject the idea of evolution because it lowers human beings to the level of the beasts and blinds us to the nobility of man. In his closing speech for the prosecution in the 1925 Scopes monkey trial, William Jennings Bryan pointed angrily to a high-school textbook that classed *Homo sapiens* as a mammal. "No circle is reserved for man alone," Bryan protested. "He is, according to the diagram, shut up in the lime circle entitled 'Mammals,' with thirty-four hundred and ninety-nine other species of mammals. . . . What shall we say of the intelligence, not to say religion, of those who are so particular to distinguish between fishes and reptiles and birds, but put a man with an immortal soul in the same circle with the wolf, the hyena, and the skunk? What must be the impression made upon children by such a degradation of man?"

What, indeed? But if you are going to classify living things at all, you have to group people and wolves together in some category, since they are both living things. Actually, the classification that Bryan railed against was in place a century before Darwin published his ideas on evolution. It was the pious creationist Carl von Linne, not some atheistic evolutionist, who named the Mammalia and classed *Homo sapiens* among them, back in 1758. And even then, in the mid-eighteenth century, classifying people as animals was an ancient idea. The Old Testament itself says bluntly that human beings are beasts, and no nobler than any of the others.[2] Yes, of course we are mammals: hairy, warmblooded vertebrates with milk glands and big forebrains, like wolves and hyenas and skunks. What's so awful about that? What else could we possibly be? Insects? Plants? Seraphim?

Most religious antievolutionists recognize that people resemble animals, but they refuse to believe it's a literal family resemblance. They think it insults human dignity to describe people as modified apes. But the Bible says that God made man from the dust of the ground.[3] Why is being a made-over ape more humiliating than being made-over dirt?

Given such patent contradictions, it seems apparent that there must be something else about Darwinian evolution that bothers antievolutionists.

And I think we can get some idea of what it is by studying the strange alliance against Darwin that's emerged in recent years between the forces of the religious right and the academic left.

The academic left is a diverse group. It includes all shades of opinion from the palest pink liberals to old-fashioned bright red Marxists. Probably no two of them have the same opinions about everything. But a lot of them have bought into some notions that are deeply hostile to the scientific enterprise in general and the study of evolution in particular. Although these notions are often expressed in a mind-numbing "postmodern" jargon, at bottom they're pretty simple. We can sum them up in one sentence: Anybody who claims to have objective knowledge about anything is trying to control and dominate the rest of us.

The postmodern critique of science runs something like this: There are no objective facts. All supposed "facts" are contaminated with theories, and all theories are infested with moral and political doctrines. Because different theories express different perceptions of the world, there's no neutral yardstick for measuring one against another. The choice between competing theories is always a political choice. Therefore, when some guy in a lab coat tells you that such and such is an objective fact—say, that there isn't any firmament, or that people are related to wolves and hyenas—he must have a political agenda up his starched white sleeve.

"Science is politics," writes Robert Young, editor of the journal *Science as Culture*. "Recent work has made it clear to those with eyes to see that there is no place in science, technology, medicine, or other forms of expertise where you cannot find ideology acting as a constitutive determinant."

To those who see it through a postmodernist lens, science as currently practiced is pretty bad stuff. Science is oppressive: by demanding that everyone talk and argue in certain approved ways, it tries to control our minds and limit our freedom to question authority. Science is sexist: designed by males and driven by domineering male egos, it prefers facts to values, control to nurturance, and logic to feelings—all typical patriarchal male hang-ups. Science is imperialist: it brushes aside the truths and insights of other times and cultures. ("Claims about the universality of science," insists historian Mario Biagioli, "should be understood as a form of cognitive colonialism.") And of course, science is capitalist (and therefore wicked): it serves the interests of big corporations and the military-industrial complex.

The scholar Ania Grobicki summed it up this way: "Western science is only one way of describing reality, nature, and the way things work—a very effective way, certainly, for the production of goods and profits, but unsatis-factory in most other respects. It is an imperialist arrogance which ignores the sciences and insights of most other cultures and times. . . . It is important for the people most oppressed by Western science to make use of what resources there are, to acquire skills and confidence, and to keep challenging the orthodox pretensions of 'scientific' hierarchies of power."

In this view, science is really aiming at a totalitarian control over our lives and thoughts. And though all fields of science are suspect, what most left-wing anxiety centers on is biology. You can get an idea of the fear that pervades this literature—and a taste of the convoluted prose some of these people write—by reading what the philosopher Jean Baudrillard has to say about biochemistry. "That which is hypostatized in biochemistry," he writes, "is the ideal of a social order ruled by a sort of genetic code of macromolecular calculation . . . irradi-ating the social body with its operational circuits. . . . Schemes of control have become fantastically perfected . . . to a neocapitalist cybernetic order that aims now at total control. This is the mutation for which the biological theorization of the code prepares the ground. . . . It remains to be seen if this operationality is not itself a myth, if DNA is not also a myth."

I don't know exactly what it means to have a genetic code irradiating things with its operational circuits, but it sounds pretty nasty. And Bau-drillard isn't the only one who has it in for nucleic acids. Last year in the *Nation*, author Barbara Ehrenreich and anthropologist Janet McIntosh recounted the story of a psychologist who spoke at an interdisciplinary con-ference on the emotions. When several audience members rose to criticize her use of the oppressive, sexist, imperialist, and capitalist scientific method, the psychologist tried to defend science by pointing to its great discoveries—for example, DNA. The retort came back: "You believe in DNA?"

Why this suspicion of genetics? One reason is its political history. Defenders of privilege have always argued that the people below them on the social ladder deserve their lowly status because they're innately inferior; and scientists who believe this sort of thing haven't been shy about invoking biology to prove it. From the social Darwinists of the nineteenth century, the eugenics movement of the 1920s, and the race-hygiene savants of the Third Reich, down to the psychologists who today insist that social status is deter-mined by our genes, there has always been an abundant supply of rich white male professors gathering data to demonstrate that rich people, white people, and men are biologically superior to everyone else. No wonder genetics is greeted with raised eyebrows and snickers on the left.

But more fundamentally, many people see the biological worldview as a threat to the ideal of human freedom. If people are animals, and animals are machines driven by instinct and conditioning controlled by genes, then the way things are is pretty much the way they have to be. Consequently, trying to transform the world by human action is likely to be a futile undertaking. Those who don't much like the world the way it is—a group that includes most left-wing academics—naturally find this view abhorrent.

As a result, in academic circles outside the natural sciences today, any mention of human genetics is likely to arouse protests and angry accusations of "biological determinism," especially if you mention genes in the same breath as human psychology or behavior. In its extreme form, this left-wing hostility to biology amounts to what Ehrenreich and McIntosh call "secular creationism"—a creed that denies our biological heritage has anything to do with what people want or how they act. "Like their fundamentalist Christian counterparts," they write, "the most extreme antibiologists suggest that humans occupy a status utterly different from and clearly `above' that of all other living beings."

In North Carolina, where I live, we recently saw how this attitude can cause the academic left to line up with the religious right. Last spring the lower house of the state legislature passed a bill requiring that "evolution shall be taught as a scientific theory, not as a proven fact" in the state's public schools. The bill eventually died in the senate. But while it was still on the table, conservative evangelicals lobbied hard for it, local evolutionists lobbied hard against it, and the newspapers were flooded with outraged letters from both sides. At the height of this dustup, Warren Nord, head of the program in Humanities and Human Values at the state university in Chapel Hill, suddenly jumped into the fight on the creationists' side—in the name of multiculturalism.

Darwin's theory, Nord complained, "undermines religious conceptions of design or purpose in nature. As we teach it, modern science is not religiously neutral. . . . [It] conflicts not just with Protestant fundamentalism . . . but with many traditional Native American, African, and Eastern religions." Nord's conclusion: "If we teach neo-Darwinian evolution and secular accounts of nature in science classes, we must also teach religious accounts of nature. . . . The only constitutional way to teach students about origins— that is, the only way to be truly neutral—is to let the contending parties (all of them) have their say."

In one sense, there's nothing wrong with Nord's argument. Of course evolution is a theory. We can imagine findings that would cause us to reject the whole idea. But that's just as true for every other big idea in science—and nobody is demanding an equal-time approach to any of the others. There are no bills cooking in America's state legislatures that will order the schools to teach the germ theory of disease and the atomic theory of matter as open questions. That might be an interesting and stimulating approach, but given that, for decades, the evidence that has come in consistently supports these two theories, the schools don't have time for it.

And nobody really wants to see science taught that way. Trying to present all ideas impartially without judging them would mean the end of science education. Like it or not, science is judgmental. It undertakes to weigh all the conflicting stories and find tests that will tell us which one is the least unlikely. If no such tests can be found, then science has nothing to say on the issue.

The idea that people evolved from apes millions of years ago is a testable scientific hypothesis. The idea that humankind was specially created in 4000 BCE is also a testable hypothesis, and it happens to be wrong. But the idea that Nord and his evangelical allies want to introduce into biology classes—that nature expresses God's purposes—isn't a scientific issue at all, because there's no way to test it. People have been arguing about it for millennia and getting nowhere. The creationists point to all the things in nature that look beautiful, orderly, and efficient. The skeptics respond by pointing to other things that look ugly, messy, cruel, and wasteful. The creationists retort that they only seem that way to the finite human mind. Maybe so. But since no tests are possible, all that science can do is shrug.

That shrug is really what distresses the crusaders against science, on both the left and the right. Both camps believe passionately that the big truths about the world are moral truths. They view the universe in terms of good and evil, not truth and falsehood. The first question they ask about any supposed fact is whether it serves the cause of righteousness. Their notions of good and evil are different, but both see the commonplace surface of the world as a veil of illusion, obscuring the deeper moral truths behind everything that give life its meaning. "Commonsense reality," insists the left-wing anthropologist Nancy Sheper-Hughes, "may be false, illusory, and oppressive. . . . [We must] work at the essential task of stripping away the surface forms of reality in order to expose concealed and buried truths."

For many people on the academic left, the facts reported by science are just the surface layer that has to be scraped off to expose the underlying moral and political reality. This postmodern approach to facts is a lot like that of the premodern St. Augustine, who wrote in the fifth century CE that we should concern ourselves with what Bible stories signify "and not worry about whether they are true."

Science, however, worries only about whether things are true and has no opinion about what they signify. In so doing, it offends both the religious right and the academic left. Both camps reject its claim to being objective and morally neutral. Because they don't think such a thing is possible, they see the pretended objectivity of science as a cover for ulterior motives. The idea of evolution is especially offensive in this regard because it implies that the universe has been value free through 99.9 percent of its history, and that people and their values were brought into being by the mechanical operations of an inhuman reality. Both the religious and the secular creationists see human life as defined by the moral choices we make. Naturally, they shrink from the biologists' vision of people as animals (since animals don't make moral choices). The right-wingers think Darwinism promotes atheism, while the left-wingers think it promotes capitalism; but both agree it's just another competing ideology, which deserves to be cast down from its high seat of intellectual privilege.

Well, is it? Having offended both the fundamentalists and the postmodernists, I am going to annoy my scientific colleagues by admitting that the antievolutionists of left and right have a point nestled deep in their rhetoric.

Science has nothing to tell us about moral values or the purpose of existence or the realm of the supernatural. That doesn't mean there is nothing to be said about these things. It just means that scientists don't have any expert opinions. Science looks exclusively at the finite facts of nature, and unfortunately, logical reasoning can't carry you from facts to values, or from the finite to the infinite. As the philosopher David Hume pointed out 250 years ago, you can't infer an infinite cause from a finite effect. But science's necessary silence on these questions doesn't prove that there isn't any infinite cause—or that right and wrong are arbitrary conventions, or that there is no plan or purpose behind the world.

And I'm afraid that a lot of scientists go around saying that science proves these things. Many scientists are atheists or agnostics who want to believe that the natural world they study is all there is, and being only human, they try to persuade themselves that science gives them grounds for that belief. It's an honorable belief, but it isn't a research finding.

Evolutionists seem to be especially prone to this mistake. The claim that evolution is purposeless and undirected has become almost an article of faith among evolutionary biologists. For example, the official "Statement on Teaching Evolution" from the National Association of Biology Teachers describes evolution as "an unsupervised, impersonal, unpredictable, and natural process." That pretty much rules God out of the picture. One popular book on evolution, Richard Dawkins's *Blind Watch Maker*, is subtitled *Why the Evidence of Evolution Reveals a Universe Without Design*. In his book *Wonderful Life*, Stephen Jay Gould argues that the evolution of human beings was fantastically improbable and that a host of unlikely events had to fall out in just the right way for intelligent life to emerge on this planet. One might well take this as a sign of God's hand at work in the evolutionary process. Gould, however, bends his argument to the opposite conclusion—that the universe is indifferent to our existence and that humans would never evolve a second time if we rewound time's videotape and started over.

But to reach this conclusion, you have to assume the very thing that you are trying to prove: namely, that history isn't directed by God. If there is a God, whatever he wills happens by necessity. Because we can't really replay the same stretch of time to see if it always comes out the same way, science has no tests for the presence of God's will in history. Gould's conclusion is a profession of his religious beliefs, not a finding of science.

The broad outlines of the story of human evolution are known beyond a reasonable doubt. However, science hasn't yet found satisfying, law-based natural explanations for most of the details of that story. All that we scientists can do is admit to our ignorance and keep looking. Our ignorance doesn't prove anything one way or the other about divine plans or purposes behind the flow of history. Anybody who says it does is pushing a religious doctrine. Both the religious creationists of the right and the secular creationists of the left object and say that a lot of evolutionists are doing just that in the name of science—and to this extent they are unfortunately right.

Fortunately, evolutionary biologists are starting to realize this. Last October, after considering several such objections, the National Association of Biology Teachers deleted the words *unsupervised* and *impersonal* from its description of the evolutionary process. To me, this seems like a step in the right direction. If biologists don't want to see the theory of evolution evicted from public schools because of its religious content, they need to accept the limitations of science and stop trying to draw vast, cosmic conclusions from the plain facts of evolution. Humility isn't just a cardinal virtue in Christian doctrine; it's also a virtue in the practice of science.

NOTES

1. See Gen. 1:6–8, 1:14–17, 7:11, 8:2; Job 37:18; Ps. 104:2; Isa. 24:18; and Mal. 3:10.

2. Eccles. 3:18–21.

3. Gen., 2:7.

TAKING THE ID DEBATE
OUT OF PUNDITS' PLAYBOOKS

OWEN GINGERICH

Along with the vast majority of members of the Abrahamic faith traditions, I believe in a created cosmos.

Thus, I believe in an intelligent Creator and Designer of the universe. I have said that I therefore believe in intelligent design, lowercase "i" and "d." But I have trouble with Intelligent Design—uppercase "I" and "D"—a movement widely seen as anti-evolutionist.

I have come to appreciate that there is immense incomprehension from both the friends and foes of Intelligent Design. There seems to be a knee-jerk reaction among the critics that ID is simply creationism in disguise. It is unfortunate that our language is so easily hijacked that a perfectly reasonable word—creationism—now almost universally refers to belief in a 6,000-year-old young-earth sculpted by a worldwide Noachian flood. Even a passionate anti-evolutionist, Phillip Johnson, objected when I referred to him as a cre-

Owen Gingerich, "Taking the ID Debate Out of Pundits' Playbooks," *Science & Theology News*, November 8, 2005.

ationist. Intelligent Design is *not* young-earth creationism, and it is not necessarily opposed to many of the ideas of evolution.

I am sure that many friends of Intelligent Design would be dismayed and alarmed to hear this. They presume that ID is a bulwark against evolution, which they assume is atheistic to the core. They do not want to hear that *Homo sapiens* could have been on the family tree with an ape-like ancestor, despite the fossil record and the DNA lineages. Many of the supporters of the teaching of ID in public schools naturally expect that this would give credence to the literal story of Adam and Eve being directly created out of the dust—please, no story of intervening generations of single cells to amphibians, reptiles and mammals.

In a panel discussion at a meeting of the American Scientific Affiliation, Michael Behe, one of the architects of ID, declared that Intelligent Design is essentially theistic evolution. For many foes of evolution—and quite possibly for many advocates of evolution as well—theistic evolution seems like a contradiction of terms. Richard Dawkins, a triumphalist atheist, lauds materialistic evolution as making atheism intellectually respectable.

On the other hand, many eminent scientists, ranging from Theodosius Dobzhansky, one of the founders of the modern synthesis of evolution, to Francis Collins, the director of the Human Genome Project, have accepted evolution as the operational means by which the Creator brought the panoply of living forms into existence.

Essential to the theory of evolution is the hypothesis of common descent, the powerful idea that every creature had a parent. As a hypothesis, it is as reasonable as the notion that the Earth goes around the sun. But children are not clones of the parents, and perhaps not always even the same species, for there is the matter of mutations. Most mutations are disasters, but perhaps some inspired few are not. Can mutations be inspired? Here is the ideological watershed, the division between atheistic evolution and theistic evolution, and frankly it lies beyond science to prove the matter one way or the other. Science will not collapse if some practitioners are convinced that occasionally there has been creative input in the long chain of being.

The leading theorists of ID argue that the mechanisms of random mutations and natural selection are inadequate to account for the intricate and astonishing variety of life the world offers. Some would argue that the evidence for intelligent input is overwhelming. In terms of final causes, they make a good case for a coherent understanding of the nature of cosmos. But they fall short in providing any mechanisms for the efficient causes that primarily engage scientists in our age. ID does not explain the temporal or geographical distribution of species, or the intricate relationships of the DNA coding.

ID is interesting as a philosophical idea, but it does not replace the scientific explanations that evolution offers. But evolution presented as a materialistic philosophy is ideology, and that is something that can be legitimately resisted. Unfortunately, the battle as it is being fought is a battle of misunderstandings on both sides of the terrain.

PLANTINGA'S DEFENSE OF SPECIAL CREATION

ERNAN McMULLEN

My colleague, Alvin Plantinga, bids the reader of his essay, "When Faith and Reason Clash: Evolution and the Bible," (appearing in *Christian Scholar's Review* 21, no. 1 [September 1991], 8–33) to take his spirited defense of special creation "with a grain of salt." Perhaps he will forgive me if I take it seriously, because I think that this is how many readers *would* take it, in the context of the continuing controversies about "creation science."

I. THEISTIC SCIENCE

His thesis in regard to evolution is that, for the Christian, the claim that God created mankind, as well as many kinds of plants and animals, separately and specially, is more probable than the claim of common ancestry that is central to the theory of evolution. And his larger context is that of an exhortation to

Ernan McMullen, "Plantinga's Defense of Special Creation," *Christian Scholar's Review* 21, no. 1 (September 1991): 55–79.

Christian intellectuals to join battle against "the forces of unbelief," particularly in academia, instead of always yielding to "the word of the experts." These intellectuals must be brought to "discern the religious and ideological connections . . . [they must not] automatically take the word of the experts, because their word might be dead wrong from a Christian standpoint." The implication that worries me is that Christian intellectuals should ally themselves with the critics of evolution, despite the almost universal support it has among experts in the relevant fields of natural science.

The "science" these Christian intellectuals profess will not be of the usual naturalist sort. Their account of the origin of species, for instance, will be at odds with that given by Darwin, on grounds that are distinctively Christian in content. Despite the fact that claims such as these on the part of the Christian depend on what he or she knows "by faith, by way of revelation," Plantinga believes that they can appropriately be called science, and he suggests as labels for them "theistic science" or "Christian science." An important function of this broader knowledge would be revisionary. He reminds us that "Scripture can correct current science," in regard to whether or not, for example, the universe originated at a particular moment in the past.

Plantinga's "theistic science" bears some similarity to the "creation science" that has commanded the headlines in the U.S. so often in recent decades. Like creation scientists, he maintains that the best explanation of the origin of "many kinds of plants and animals" is an interruption in the ordinary course of natural process, a moment when God treats "what he has created in a way different from the way in which he ordinarily treats it." Like them, he relies on a critique of the theory of evolution, pointing to what he regards as fundamental shortcomings in the Darwinian project of explaining new species by means of natural selection, and emphasizing recent criticisms of one or other facet of the synthetic theory from within the scientific community itself. Like them, he calls for a struggle against prevailing scientific orthodoxy, one which may pit the teachers of Christian youth against the "experts."

But the differences between them are obvious.[1] Most creation-scientists believe in a "young earth" dating back only a few thousand years, and attempt to undermine the many arguments that can be brought against this view. Plantinga allows "the evidence for an old earth to be strong and the warrant for the view that the Lord teaches that the earth is young to be relatively weak." The creation scientists argue for a whole series of related cosmological theses (that stars and galaxies do not change, that the history of the earth is dominated by the occurrence of catastrophe, and so forth);

Plantinga focuses on the single issue of the origins of the kinds of living things, and especially of humankind. And he is in the end more concerned to combat the claims of certainty made by the evolutionists than he is to argue that the Christian is irrevocably committed against a full evolutionary account of origins. He allows (which the creation-scientists, I suspect, would not) that as evolutionary science advances, his own present estimate that special creation is more likely might have to give way.

The creation-scientists attempt to detach their arguments from any sort of reliance on Scripture, or more generally, from theological considerations, whereas Plantinga appeals explicitly to the Scriptural understanding of the manner of God's action in the world. The former make a heroic attempt to qualify their creationism as "scientific," in what they take to be the conventional sense of that term. Their effort, I think it is fair to say, was hopeless right from the start. But it may have been prompted as much by political necessity as by strength of conviction regarding the purely scientific merits of their arguments. The creationists would undoubtedly have preferred to defend a view more explicitly based on the Bible, but the exigencies of the constitutional restrictions on what may be taught in the public schools of the U.S. prevented this. The scientists among them would have wanted to shore up their case with various consonances between the catastrophism of their young-earth account and the geological record. But the inspiration for their account lay, and clearly *had* to lie, in the Bible. Trying to fudge this, though understandable in the circumstances, proved a disastrous strategy.

Plantinga offers a far more consistent theme. True, his "theistic science" will not pass constitutional muster, so it will not serve the purposes for which creation-science was originally advanced. But that is not an argument against it; it is merely a consequence of the unique situation of public education in the U.S., a situation that imposes losses as well as gains. I do not think, however, that "theistic science" should be described as science. It lacks the universality of science, as that term has been understood in the Western tradition. It also lacks the sort of warrant that has gradually come to characterize natural science, one that points to systematic observation, generalization, and the testing of explanatory hypothesis. It appeals to a specifically Christian belief, one that lays no claim to assent from a Hindu or an agnostic. It requires faith, and faith (we are told) is a gift, a grace, from God. To use the term "science" in this context seems dangerously misleading; it encourages expectations that cannot be fulfilled, in the interests of adopting a label generally regarded as honorific.

Plantinga objects to the sort of "methodological naturalism" that would deny the label "science" to any explanation of natural process that invokes the special action of God; indeed, he characterizes it, in Basil Willey's phrase, as "provisional atheism." "Is there really any compelling or even decent reason for thus restricting our study of nature?" he asks. But, of course, methodological naturalism does *not* restrict our study of nature; it just lays down which sort of study qualifies as *scientific*. If someone wants to pursue another approach to nature—and there are *many* others—the methodological naturalist has no reason to object. Scientists *have* to proceed in this way; the methodology of natural science gives no purchase on the claim that a particular event or type of event is to be explained by invoking God's creative action directly. Calling this *methodological* naturalism is simply a way of drawing attention to the fact that it is a way of characterizing a particular *methodology*, no more. In particular, it is not an ontological claim about what sort of agency is or is not possible. Dubbing it "provisional atheism" seems to me objectionable; the scientist who does not include God's direct action among the alternatives he or she should test scientifically when attempting to explain some phenomenon is surely not to be accused of atheism!

Let me make myself clear. I do not object (as the concluding section of this essay will make clear) to the use of theological considerations in the service of a larger and more comprehensive world-view in which natural science is only one factor. I would be willing to use the term "knowledge" in an extended sense here (though I am well aware of some old and intricate issues about how faith and knowledge are to be related).[2] But I would *not* be willing to use the term "science," in this context. Nor do I think it necessary to do so in order to convey the respectability of the claim being made: that theology may appropriately modulate other parts of a person's belief-system, including those deriving from science. I would be much more restrictive than Plantinga is, however, in allowing for the situation he describes as "Scripture correcting current science." But before we come to our differences, it may be worth laying out first the large areas where he and I agree.

2. POINTS OF AGREEMENT

What really galls Plantinga are the views of people like Dawkins and Provine who not only insist that evolution is a proven "fact," but suppose that this somehow undercuts the reasonableness of any sort of belief in a Creator. Their argument hinges on the notion of design. The role of the Creator in traditional religious belief was that of Designer; the success of the theory of evolution has shown that design is unnecessary. Hence, there is no longer any valid reason to be a theist. In a recent review of a history of the creationist debate in the U.S., Provine lays out this case, and concludes that Christian belief can be made compatible with evolutionary biology only by supposing that God "works through the laws of nature" instead of actively steering biological process by way of miraculous intervention. But this view of God, he says, is "worthless," and "equivalent to atheism."[3] (On this last point, Plantinga and he might not be so far apart!) He chides scientists for publicly denying, presumably on pragmatic grounds, that evolution and Christian belief are incompatible; they *must*, he says, know this to be nonsense.

Plantinga puts his finger on an important point when he notes that for someone who does not believe in God, evolution in some form or other is the only *possible* answer to the question of origins. Prior to the publication of *The Origin of Species* in 1859, the argument from design was part of biological science itself. The founders of physico-theology two centuries earlier, naturalists like John Ray and William Derham, had shown the pervasive presence in Nature of means-end relationships, the apparently purposive adjusting of structure and instinctive behavior to the welfare of each kind of organism. Someone who rejected the idea of God had, therefore, to face some awkward problems in explaining some of the most obvious features of the living world; it seemed as though science itself testified to the existence of God.[4]

Darwin changed all this. He made it possible to reconcile atheism with biological science; from then onwards, the fortunes of atheism as a form of intellectual belief would depend upon the fortunes of the theory of evolution. No wonder, then, that evolution became a crucial "myth" (as Plantinga puts it) of our secular culture, replacing for many the Christian myth as "a shared way of understanding ourselves at the deep level of religion."[5] No wonder also that an attack on the credentials of evolutionary theory would so often evoke from its defenders a reaction reminiscent in its ferocity of the response to heresy in other days.

Is evolution fact or theory? No other question has divided the two sides in the creation-science controversy more sharply. Plantinga notes that someone who denies the existence of a Creator is left with no other option for explaining the origin of living things than an evolutionary-type account. It thus, equivalently, becomes "fact" not just because of the strength of the scientific evidence in its favor but because for the atheist no other explanation is open. On the other side, the believer in God is going to resent this use of the word, "fact," because it seems to exclude in principle the possibility of a Divine intervention, and hence by implication, the possibility of the existence of a Creator. "Fact" seems to convey not just the assurance of a well-supported theory, but the certainty that no other explanation is open.

The debate may often, therefore, be something other than it seems. Instead of being just a disagreement about the weight to be accorded to a particularly complex scientific theory in the light of the evidence available, the debate may conceal a far more fundamental religious difference, each side appearing to the other to call into question an article of faith. To religious believers, calling the assertion of common ancestry a "fact" appears to violate good scientific usage; no matter how well-supported a theory may be (they argue), it remains a theory. To non-believers, the phrase "merely a theory" comes as a provocation, because it suggests a substantial doubt about a claim that appears to them as being beyond question, a doubt prompted furthermore in their view by an illegitimate intrusion of religious belief.

At one level, then, Plantinga's essay can be read as a plea for a more informed understanding of the real nature of the creation-science debate, and a more sympathetic appreciation of what led the proponents of creation-science to take the stand they did. Even their defense of a "young" earth (the major point of disagreement between his view and theirs) ought not (he says) be regarded as "silly or irrational." One need not be "a fanatic, or a Flat Earther, or an ignorant Fundamentalist" to hold such a view. The claim that the earth is ancient is neither obvious nor inevitable; it has to be argued for, and disagreement may, therefore, easily occur.

Plantinga is right, to my mind, to see more in the creation-science debate than evolutionary scientists (or the media) have been wont to allow. And the sort of challenge he offers to the defenders of evolution, though it is not new, could serve the purposes of science in the long run if it forced a clarification and strengthening of argument on the other side, or if it punctured the sometimes troubling smugness that experts tend to display when dealing with outsiders. Plantinga leans too far in the other direction, however. The charitable reading of creation-science that he urges could easily mislead. A claim does not have to be obvious or inevitable for its rejection to connote fanaticism or ignorance. If the indirect evidence for the great age of the earth is overwhelming (Plantinga himself allows that it is "strong"), if its denial would call into question some of the best-supported theoretical findings of an array of natural sciences (cosmology, astrophysics, geology, biology), then one is entitled to issue a severe judgment on the challenger. Perusal of works like that of Morris would lead one to suspect that no matter *how* strong the scientific case were in favor of an ancient earth, it would make no difference to their authors. Their implicit commitment to a literalist interpretation of Genesis is such that it blocks a genuinely rational assessment of the alternative. The term, "fanatic," is a notoriously difficult one to apply fairly, because it conveys moral, as well as epistemic, disapprobation. But I would be willing to defend its appropriateness to such expositions of creation-science as that of Morris.

What bothers Plantinga, I suspect, about the use of the term here, is that from *his* point of view the creation-scientist's heart is in the right place, even if perhaps his head isn't. Anyone who stands up for "*sola Scriptura*" in the modern world, even in contexts as unpromising as the debate about the age of the earth, ought not (he seems to suggest) simply be dismissed. Creation-scientists may be wrong in holding that the earth is only a few thousand years old, but their *motivation* for making this claim ought to be regarded with sympathy by their fellow-Christians. I would disagree, but it is because of a deeper disagreement about the merits of the "*sola Scriptura*" premise and of the remaining major theses of creation-science. Though I would not be as harsh on the creation-scientist as leading evolutionists have been, I would, as a Christian, want to register disapproval of creation-science at least as strong as theirs, though for reasons that go beyond theirs. These reasons will become clear, I hope, in what I have to say about Plantinga's analysis of what happens when "faith and reason clash."

3. GALILEO AND GENESIS

In his *Letter to the Grand Duchess Christina* (1615), Galileo gave the most extended account that anyone perhaps had written up to that time of how the Christian should proceed when an apparent conflict between science and Scripture arises. Aided, doubtless, by some of his theologian-friends, he drew upon Augustine, Jerome, Aquinas, and an impressive array of other authorities, in order to show that the use made of Scripture by those who opposed the Copernican theory was illegitimate.[6] There may be some lessons to be drawn from this historic document in the context of the Darwinian debate, apart from the obvious one of the embarrassment that the Church would later suffer because of its ill-advised attempt to make the geocentric cosmology of the Old Testament authors a matter, equivalently, of Christian faith.

What, then, did Galileo hold about the bearing of the Scriptures on our knowledge of the natural world? It does not take long for the reader to discover that two radically different principles are proposed in different parts of the *Letter*, and to realize that Galileo almost certainly was not aware of the resulting incoherence.[7] On the one hand, he cites Augustine in support of the traditional view that in cases of apparent conflict, the literal interpretation of Scripture is to be maintained, unless the opposing scientific claim can be *demonstrated*. In that case, theologians must look for an alternative reading of the Scriptural passage(s), since it is a first principle that faith and natural reason cannot really be in conflict. However, the straightforward interpretation of Scripture is to be preferred in cases where the scientific claim has something less than "necessary demonstration" in its support, because of the inherently greater authority to be attached to the word of God.[8]

On the other hand, Galileo also argues that one should not look to Scripture for knowledge of the natural world: the function of the Bible is to teach us how to go to heaven, not how the heavens go, in the aphorism attributed to Baronius. God has given us reason and the senses to enable us to come to understand the world around us. Attempting to teach the underlying structures of natural process would have baffled the readers of Scripture and defeated its obvious purpose. Galileo produced a number of convergent lines of argument to the effect that Scripture is simply not relevant to the concerns of the sciences to begin with.

The implications of these two quite different hermeneutic principles were, of course, altogether different for the resolution of the Copernican debate.[9] But that is not my concern here. More to my purpose is to note that the first principle has one quite disastrous consequence: it sets theologians evaluating the validity of the arguments of the natural philosophers, and natural philosophers defending themselves by composing theological tracts. Either way, there will be immediate charges of trespass. The theologian challenges the force of technical scientific argument; scientists urge their own readings of Scripture or their own theories as to how Scripture, in general, *should* be read. In both cases, the professionals are going to respond, quite predictably: what right have you to intrude in a domain where you lack the credentials to speak with authority? The assessment of theory strength is not a simple matter of logic and rule but requires a long familiarity with the procedures, presuppositions, and prior successes of a network of connected domains, and a trained skill in the assessment of particular types of argument.

Transposing from the Galilean to the Darwinian debate demands some care, yet there are obvious morals to be drawn. Neither of Galileo's principles is entirely adequate for regulating disputes of this general kind. One ought not to require that a scientific case be demonstrative before it has any standing in the face of an apparently contrary Scriptural assertion. On the other hand, one cannot (as Plantinga correctly says) simply rule out conflicts of this kind by laying down that Christian doctrine can have *no* implications for matters that fall under scientific jurisdiction. Galileo was right to maintain that the Bible was not intended as (in part) a manual of natural knowledge. The biblical writers simply made use of the language and the cosmological beliefs of their own day while telling the story of human salvation. But that story itself does require certain presuppositions about human nature, about freedom and moral responsibility, for example, that would clash with psychological theories affirming the unreality of our claim to freedom of moral action. So it is not as though the two domains are, in principle, so safely walled off from one another that no conflict can possibly arise.

Nevertheless, Scripture scholars would be in a large measure of agreement today that the domain of such potential conflict is quite limited. In particular, the creation narratives of the first two chapters of Genesis are not to be read as literal history. The points they are making lie deeper and can only be reliably discerned by investigating the wider literary context of that day, on the one hand, and the later theological appropriations of those narratives, on the other.[10] It is not as though the texts are to be taken literally unless and until a conclusive scientific account of origins can be constructed. Rather, no likelihood is to be attached in the first place to the literal construal of the story, say, of the separate creation of the animals. To interpret it literally or quasi-literally is to misunderstand the point that the writers of those narratives were trying to make, the great majority of contemporary Scripture scholars would agree.[11]

An interesting feature of Plantinga's argument is that he explicitly brackets the reference to Genesis that one would expect to find, given the primacy he accords to Scripture. Did he originally plan to return to the text of Genesis at the end of his paper to clinch his case? ("Suppose we temporarily set to one side the evidence, whatever exactly it is, from early Genesis.") I kept waiting for him to turn finally to the biblical narratives of creation as the strongest reason for distrusting the evolutionary story. Historically, these narratives provided the main warrant for the traditional Christian belief that God intervened in a special way to bring to be the first members in the lineage of each natural kind. Those who, like Plantinga, have urged the superiority of special creation over evolution have almost always relied upon a direct appeal to Genesis, unless (as we have seen) they were prevented, as the recent creation-science advocates were, by political constraints.

Plantinga is under no such constraints, however. Since he evidently believes that a case can be made for special creation without any overt appeal to Genesis, he may have felt it better to avoid the controversies that surround the literalist approach to the Genesis text. He already has the scientists on his hands. Why open a second front and take on the theologians too? There is no rhetorical advantage to be gained by making explicit that he can expect little support for the thesis of special creation on the part of contemporary biblical scholars.

Despite his silence in regard to Genesis, I do not think that a linkage between his argument and the more traditional Genesis-based argument can be denied. Without the latter, would anyone think it a priori more likely that the God of the salvation story would intervene to originate natural kinds instead of allowing them to appear gradually and in a "natural" way? And if biblical theologians are right in holding that the cosmological references in the Old Testament ought be understood as conveying fundamental theological truths about the dependence of the natural and human worlds on their Creator, rather than explaining how exactly these worlds first took shape, then perhaps one ought be just as wary of drawing a cosmological moral from the salvation story as a whole as from the controversial passages in Genesis.

What must be disputed, to my mind, is a modern analogue of the first of Galileo's principles,[12] which would, equivalently, reaffirm the presumption that the biblical text was partially intended as a cosmology, so that in cases of apparent conflict between the biblical and current scientific accounts we should evaluate the strength of the scientific account as a means of deciding which of the two "competitors" to accept. Plantinga proposes such a "balancing of likelihoods" methodology: a literalist understanding of God's making of the ancestors of the main natural kinds, he concludes, should be preferred unless and until a far stronger case can be made for the evolutionary alternative.

What I am urging is that it is potentially destructive (as the Galileo case amply shows) to treat the biblical and the scientific as competitors in the realm of cosmological explanation. The cosmological implications (if any) of the Scripture story are to be discovered by *theological* study, not by assessing the credentials of the supposedly competing scientific account.

Even if the theory of evolution could be entirely dismissed on scientific grounds, this would not of itself give us any warrant for supposing that the biblical account of origins ought, therefore, be taken literally. It might well be that, in the absence of a plausible evolutionary account, the only reasonable alternative for the Christian would be something like special creation. But even this would not warrant the supposition that special creation, in the literal sense, is what we ought properly infer from the biblical texts, whether the accounts of Creation in Genesis, or the story of Israel leading up to the coming of Christ. The interpretation of these texts is primarily a hermeneutic problem for the theologian; criticism of supposedly competing scientific theories will rarely be relevant.[13]

Where the theologian is unsure of the best interpretation to give a text, it is not inappropriate, of course, to take into account that some of the possible interpretations may be closed off by the findings of the natural or social sciences. But even in such a case (as Augustine's own practice might easily be made to illustrate) primary weight should be given to the *hermeneutic* issue as to what the disputed text was originally intended to convey and the theological issue of what the tradition has made of it. This way of handling relationships between Scripture and the sciences does not close them off from one another entirely, as we have already seen. But it encourages us to resist the temptation to construe the two as normally belonging to the same order of explanation or historical claim. As an illustration of how Scripture could "correct current science," Plantinga remarks: "If, for example, current science were to return to the view that the world has no beginning, and isn infinitely old, then current science would be wrong."[14] I do not believe that Scripture *does* prescribe that the universe had a beginning in time, in some specific technical sense of the term, "time"; the point of the Creation narratives is the dependence of the world on God's creative act, to my mind, not that it all began at a finite time in the past.[15] A world that has always existed would still require a Creator.

4. THE THESIS OF COMMON ANCESTRY

Plantinga dismisses the evidence ordinarily presented in support of what he calls the Thesis of Common Ancestry (TCA) as inconclusive, after a rather cursory review. His conclusion: "It isn't particularly likely, given the Christian faith and the biological evidence, that God created all the flora and fauna

by way of some mechanism involving common ancestry." Though my disagreement with him centers especially on the conclusion he draws from
Christian faith in regard to the antecedent likelihood of special creation, I am
going to spend some time on the scientific issues first. The credentials of a
thesis encompassing as much of past and present as TCA does cannot, of
course, be dealt with satisfactorily in a few pages.[16] This is particularly true
when these credentials are being *denied*, contrary to the firm conviction of
the great majority of those professionally engaged in the many scientific
fields involved.

Though a full-scale defense of TCA cannot be attempted here, and
would in any event be beyond my competence, it may be worthwhile to indicate how in a general way such a defense might proceed.[17] First, an important distinction, one alluded to by Plantinga. TCA is a *historical* claim that
the kinds of living things originated somehow from one another. On the other
hand, the various theories of evolution are an attempt to *explain* how that
could have occurred.[18] The dominant theory of evolution at the present time
is the so-called "modern synthesis," associated with such figures as Simpson,
Dobzhansky, and Mayr. It has its critics: Goldschmidt and Schindewolf a
generation ago, for example, Gould and Kimura today. Though all of these
have found fault with the Darwinism of the modern synthesis and have proposed alternatives to it, none would for a moment question TCA. Their confidence in TCA does not depend, then, on a similar degree of confidence in
the explanatory adequacy of a specifically Darwinian account of the origin
of species. Is it, perhaps, that they implicitly reject God's existence, and thus
TCA is for them (in Plantinga's phrase) "the only game in town"? I don't
think it is quite as simple as this, although the implicit setting aside of a theistic alternative obviously could play a role.

Much of the evidence for TCA functions independently of the *detail* of
any specific evolutionary theory. Plantinga mentions three such categories of
evidence, so I will confine myself to those. There is the fossil record which
has already yielded innumerable sequences of extinct forms, where the
development of specific anatomical features can be traced in detail through
the rock-layers. Paleontologists have traced the development of eyes in no
less than forty *independent* animal lineages ("lineages" being determined by
overall morphological similarities).[19] They continue to uncover stage after
stage in crucial "linking" forms, such as the therapsids, for example, the
forms that relate reptiles with the earliest mammals. In cases like these (and
there are a *lot* of them), paleontologists can point to a variety of morpholog-

ical features that gradually shift over time, retaining a basic likeness (a so-called *Bauplan*) throughout. Gould's objection regarding the rarity of transitional forms (quoted by Plantinga) has to be taken in context. Gould would not deny the morphological continuities of the fossil record; like thousands of other researchers he has given too much of his time to tracing these continuities for him to underrate their significance. What he *would* say (and what many defenders of the modern synthesis would now be disposed to admit) is that species often make their appearance in the record without the prior gradual sequence of modifications one would have expected from the traditional gradualist Darwinian standpoint. But this leaves untouched the implications, overall, of the fossil record for TCA. It *does*, of course, affect the sort of theory that could account for the sequence found in the record.[20]

Instead of scrutinizing the fossil record, we might look to the living forms around us, and there discover all sorts of homologies and peculiar features of geographical distribution, which are best understood in terms of TCA. The arguments here are long familiar and I will not dally on them. But there is a further category of evidence which has taken on a great deal of importance in the last twenty years. This comes from molecular biology.[21] Comparison of the DNA, as well as of the proteins for which DNA codes, between different types of organisms shows that there are striking similarities in chemical composition between them. Cytochrome C, for example, found in all animals, is involved in cell respiration. It contains 104 amino-acids, in a sequence which is invariable for any given species. For humans and rhesus monkeys, the sequence is identical except in one position; for horses and donkeys the sequence also differs in only one position. But for humans and horses, the difference is 12; for monkeys and horses, the difference is 11. If instead of cytochrome C another homologous protein is chosen, similar (though not necessarily identical) results are found. These very numerous resemblances and differences between the macromolecules carrying hereditary information can be explained by supposing a very slow rate of change in the chemical sequences constituting these molecules, and thus a relationship of common descent among the organisms themselves. Thus, the "molecular" differences between any two species become (on this hypothesis) a rough indication of how long since the ancestors of these species diverged; rather more securely, one can infer the relative order of branching between three or more species; one can infer whether A branched from B before C did. What is impressive here is the *coherence* of the results given by examining many different macromolecules in this light.

But much more impressive is that these results conform reasonably well with the findings of both paleontology and comparative anatomy in regard to the ancestral relations between species, the postulated tree of descent that had already been worked out in some detail in these other disciplines. The fit, as one would expect, is not exact in each case in regard to the "closeness" between the species, but it is nevertheless quite good. When a single explanatory hypothesis (TCA) underlies the binding together of three domains so diverse in character, we have the sort of consilience that carries more weight with scientists than does, perhaps, underlay another virtue of theory.

It should be underlined that specific theories of evolution are not yet involved. The support given TCA by these diverse types of evidence does not depend on any particular explanatory account of *how* species-change takes place. One could reject natural selection as the primary agent of evolutionary change, for example, and still find this argument for TCA convincing.[22] Of course, a satisfactory explanatory account of how evolutionary change occurred would greatly strengthen the case for TCA. But in the light of the continuing debates about the adequacy of this or that feature of the neo-Darwinian model, it is important to us that there is a vast body of evidence for common descent that does not depend for its logical force on the further issue of how *exactly* the transitions from life-form to another came about.

Plantinga raises one objection that bears on TCA directly. Does there not seem to be an "envelope of limited variability" surrounding each species, so that a deviation of more than a small amount from the central species-norm leads to sterility? Would one not expect to find evidence of new species now and then appearing in the present (or perhaps being deliberately produced) if TCA is true? The first and simplest response is to note that in the plant world (in the forest, for example) new species have indeed been observed. And production of fertile hybrids is an important part of agricultural research. The ability of populations of microorganisms to alter their structures quite basically over relatively short times under the challenge of antibiotics is all too well-known. But defenders of the modern synthesis themselves insist on the extraordinary stability of the genotype, in the animal realm particularly; this stability is essential to the maintenance of species differences, and some progress has been made toward an understanding of its molecular basis in the constellations of genes.

TCA does not require rapid change. The presumption is that the kind of species-change that would sustain TCA could take thousands of generations to accomplish. The rate of change required (as has been shown in detail in recent studies in population genetics) is far too slow for the sort of direct evidence to accumulate that Plantinga is asking for. But even more fundamentally, there are serious problems with the species concept itself, the concept underlying this objection. Ought it, for example, be based on the morphological difference (of the kind that paleontologists or comparative anatomists can attest to), or ought it be based on interbreeding boundaries (as naturalists have long preferred to maintain)?[23] If we were to find the fossil remains of animals as different as a St. Bernard and a Chihuahua in the rock strata, we should assuredly label them as different species. But if we adopt the biological species concept according to which "species are groups of interbreeding natural populations that are reproductively isolated from other such groups,"[24] how are we to apply this to populations that are widely separated in space or time? Mayr emphasizes that such application always involves complex and indirect forms of inference.[25] The moral is not that the species-concept is so ambiguous as to be unusable, but only that such notions as species-change are far more difficult to handle than at first sight they seem to be. And more specifically, the claim that an "envelope of limited variability" surrounds each species has no precise empirical foundation.

I suspect that in the end this claim simply begs the question against TCA. It asserts that the sort of change TCA would require does not occur. But this is just the issue, and this is what is challenged by the three kinds of evidence described above, all of them pointing to TCA as the most reasonable explanation. What does Plantinga make of these? He deals with them, to my mind, in a quite unsatisfactory way: "Well, what would prevent [God] from using similar structures?" referring to the argument from homologies; and: "As for the similarity in the biochemistry of all life, this is reasonably probable on the hypothesis of special creation." Any attempt to reconstruct the past on the basis of traces found in the present can, of course, always be met with the objection: but God *could* have disposed matters so as to make it look as though it happened that way, even though it didn't. If TCA is correct, one would *expect* the sort of coherences that molecular biology is now turning up in such abundance. I can see no reason whatever to suppose that the hypothesis of special creation would antecedently have led us to expect this same range of evidence. Recalling the lines of a famous debate long ago about fossils, the God of the Christian tradition is surely not one who would deceive us by strewing around what would amount to misleading clues!

Let me stress once again the criterion of consilience. Evidence from three quite disparate domains supports a single coherent view of the sequence of branchings and extinctions that underlie TCA. If TCA is *false*, if in fact the different kinds of organisms do not share a common ancestry, this consilience goes entirely unexplained. It is all very well to say: "but God *could* have. . . ." This hypothesis leaves the consilience exhibited by TCA an extraordinary coincidence. So it is not as though allowing the theistic alternative into the range of possible explanations alters the balance of probability drastically, as Plantinga supposes. TCA is, of course, a *hypothesis*, as any reconstruction of the past must be. But it remains by far the best-supported response, even for the theist, to the fast-multiplying evidence available to us.

5. THEORIES OF EVOLUTION

What about the objections to the neo-Darwinian theory of evolution, as such, as distinct from TCA? Plantinga outlines a familiar objection to any theory which relies on natural selection as the primary mechanism of evolutionary change. There is no plausible evolutionary pathway (he argues) linking an eyeless organism, say, with an organism possessing the complex structures of the mammalian eye, such that *every* single stage along the way can be *shown* to be adaptively advantageous. This is the oldest of objections to Darwin's theory; it was the primary criticism raised by Mivart in his *Genesis of Species* (1871). Darwin's own first response was to emphasize that his theory did not rely on natural selection alone.[26]

Among the other processes that he proposed, one in particular is still emphasized: change of function, where a structure that originally developed because of the adaptive advantage offered by one particular function takes on (especially under the impact of change of habitat or the like) a new function. Another process whose importance has only recently come to be recognized is genetic drift. In the isolated and often small populations that furnish the likeliest starting-point for the speciation-process, there can be a sort of genetic random sampling error that eventually marks off the smaller population from the parent population. And there can be "hitchhiker" effects of all sorts due to genetic linkage. These processes do not operate independently of natural selection, but they can easily bring about results that the adaptive-advantage-at-every-step model of evolutionary change could not.[27] Defenders of the modern synthesis are as quick as Darwin was to insist that they are *not* limited in their explanatory strategies to the selectionist model only.[28]

Nevertheless, to some critics of the modern synthesis, these concessions are not enough. Gould, for example, has criticized what he calls the "adaptationist program" for its failure to take seriously the many alternatives to trait-by-trait selection on the basis of adaptive advantage. As his own favored alternative he notes the constraints that the integrity of the structure of the organism as a whole sets on possible pathways of change, so that the outcome is explicable rather more by the nature of the constraints than by the application of selectionist norms to individual traits.[29] Kimura has developed a controversial molecular-level theory according to which most changes in gene-frequencies are of no selective advantage, but are neutral. More radical challenges come from those who rely on macro-mutations (saltations) to bridge major discontinuities in the fossil record; theories of this sort, it is generally thought, face intractable problems.[30]

Where does all this leave us? The confidence of the defenders of the modern synthesis is based on the substantial explanatory successes of their model. They have no illusions about having explained everything; in particular, they concede that the processes responsible for the origin of the main phyla are not well understood.[31] Their explanatory model has already been substantially reshaped over the last fifty years, while retaining the original emphasis on the transformative powers of selection operating on individual differences. Undoubtedly, more such reshaping lies ahead. Like any other active scientific theory, the modern synthesis is incomplete, but its exponents argue, in great detail, that there are no *in-principle* barriers to its continued successful extension to the difficult cases. A minority has proposed that a more radical transformation is needed, one which abandons either the gradualism or the heavy reliance on selection that have marked the Darwinian approach.[32] The most extreme view is represented by Michael Denton, who argues that *all* current theories of evolution are in principle inadequate to handle macroevolution, and that we have to await another quite different sort of theory.

Where does the burden of proof lie in a matter of this sort? The claim that principles of a broadly Darwinian sort are capable of explaining the origins of the diversity of the living world rests on the successes of the theory to date. These are very considerable; they span many fields and have shown intricate linkages between those fields. In particular, the theory has shown an extraordinary fertility as it has been extended into new domains; even when it has encountered anomalies, it has shown the capacity to overcome these in creative ways that are clearly not *ad hoc*.[33] This is the sort of thing that impresses those who are actually in touch with the detail of this research. And it gives a *prima facie* case for supposing that the theory can be further extended to contexts not yet successfully treated. But, of course, this cannot in the strong sense be *proved*; it can only be made to seem more (or less) plausible.

On the other side is the claim that theories of a Darwinian type are in *principle* incapable of handling certain classes of data: gaps in the fossil record, the origin of complex organs like the eye, the origin of the broad divisions of the living world (the phyla), or the like. Claims of this sort are hard to establish because they cannot anticipate the trajectory that the theory itself may follow as it is reworked in the light of new challenge. (Could the changes of the last century leading up to the modern synthesis have been foreseen?) This is not to say that such claims can *never* be established, or at least shown to be strongly supported. So it is not that the burden of proof falls to one side rather than the other. Rather, it is a matter of weighing up the merits of the case on each side, and making some kind of comparative assessment, informed by parallels from the earlier history of science, and a very detailed knowledge of the history and contemporary situation of the various fields where the evolutionary paradigm is applied.

Plantinga formulates a second sort of objection to theories of evolution in general: they can never tell the *whole* story of the genetic changes involved, the rates of mutation, the links between gene adaptation, and so forth: "Hence we don't really know whether evolution is so much as biologically possible." But first of all, evolutionary explanation begins at the level of the biological individual and the population, not the gene; natural selection operates on adaptations of whose genetic basis we may be (and usually are) entirely unaware. And the explanation is none the less real for that. But, more important, evolutionary explanation is of its nature *historical*, and historical explanation is not like explanation in physics or chemistry. It deals with the singular and the unrepeatable; it is thus *necessarily* incomplete. One must be careful to apply the appropriate criteria when assessing the merits of a particular explanation. An evolutionary explanation can never be better than plausible; the real problem lies in discriminating between different degrees of plausibility. The dangers of settling for a very weak sort of plausibility are real (Gould's "just so" stories). But the dangers of requiring too strong a degree of confirmation before allowing *any* standing to an evolutionary explanation ("Hence we don't really *know* . . .") are just as great.

The presumed inadequacy of current theories of evolution is part of what leads Plantinga to propose his own alternative. What *exactly* is it? Is it that God brought to be in a miraculous way *each* of the millions of species that have existed since life first appeared on earth? More than 99.99% of these are now extinct. May one ask why God would have created them? The thesis that Plantinga deems more probable than TCA is simply that "God created mankind, as well as many kinds of plants and animals, separately and specially." Perhaps he means that God just created the phyla (including the ones that have gone extinct?). As we have seen, it is the manner in which the major divisions of the living world came to be that has provided the theory of evolution with its largest challenge. But why not *all* species? How is Plantinga to decide just which thesis *is* more probable than TCA? Presumably by checking to see what evolutionary theory has, in *his* view, been able to explain successfully. And then whatever is left over, God is more likely to have brought about miraculously.

God of the gaps? It certainly *sounds* like that. Whatever science cannot currently explain, or, more exactly, whatever one can make a case for holding that science could never in principle explain, is to be deemed the "special" work of God. One is reminded of eighteenth century natural theology. But Plantinga's intent is not apologetic, as that of natural theology was. It is not that he is using the supposed gaps in evolutionary explanation to support belief in the existence of a God who could plug the gaps. Rather, he considers it *antecedently* probable that God would intervene in ways like this; his critique of evolutionary theory is intended to locate the spots at which He is most likely to have intervened. Whenever evolutionary theory is unable to explain in a totally convincing way the origins of a particular kind, the hand of God is to be seen at work.

Plantinga claims that the Christian believer "has a freedom not available to the naturalist," because he or she is "free to look at the evidence . . . and follow where it leads." This might be correct if he were to hold only that the believer holds open an extra alternative that allows him or her to be more critical of the shortcomings of the scientific theory. But he holds something much stronger than that: there is an antecedent *likelihood* of "special" intervention of this kind in cosmic process, and hence unless the scientist has a strong case, the hypothesis of Divine intervention has to be allowed the higher likelihood. Recall the two hermeneutic principles sketched by Galileo: the "confrontation" principle suggests that unless a clear case can be made for the scientific theory, the theological alternative should take preference. I am not sure that this *does* in the end allow the Christian believer more freedom than the naturalist. But whatever of that, it certainly ensures conflict; it is likely to maximize the strain between faith and reason.

6. THE INTEGRITY OF GOD'S NATURAL WORLD

Plantinga's argument relies first and foremost on the premise that God's "special" intervention in cosmic process is antecedently probable. Here is where he and I really part ways. My view would be that from the theological and philosophical standpoints, such intervention is, if anything, antecedently *improbable*. Plantinga builds his case by recalling that "according to Scripture, [God] has often intervened in the working of his cosmos." And the examples he gives are the miracles of Scripture and the life, death, and resurrection of Jesus Christ. I want to recall here a set of old and valuable distinctions between nature and supernature, between the order of nature and the order of grace, between cosmic history and salvation history. The train of events linking Abraham to Christ is not to be considered an analogue for God's relationship to His creation generally. The Incarnation and what led up to it was unique in its manifestation of God's creative power and His loving concern for His universe. To overcome the consequences of human freedom, a different sort of action on God's part was required, a transformative action culminating in the promise of resurrection for the children of God, something that (despite the immortality claims of the Greek philosophers) lies altogether outside the bounds of nature.

The story of salvation is a story about men and women, about the burden and the promise of being human. It is not about plants and animals; it provides no warrant whatever for supposing that God would have brought the ancestors of the various kinds of plants and animals to be outside the ordinary order of nature. The story of salvation *does* bear on the origin of the first humans. If Plantinga were merely to say that God somehow "leant" into cosmic history at the advent of the human, Scripture would clearly be on his side. How this "leaning" is to be interpreted is, of course, another matter.[34] But his claim is a much stronger one.

To carry the argument a stage further: what would the eloquent texts of Genesis, Job, Isaiah, and the Psalms lead one to expect? What have theologians made of these texts? This is obviously a theme that far transcends the compass of an essay such as this one. I can make a couple of simple points. The Creator whose powers are gradually revealed in these texts is omnipotent and all-wise, far beyond the reach of human reckoning. His Providence extends to all His creatures; they are all part of His single plan, only a fragment of which we know, and that darkly. Would such a Being be likely to "intervene" in His creation in the way that Plantinga describes? (I am uncomfortable with this language of "likelihood" in regard to God's action, as though we were somehow capable of catching the Creator of the galactic universe in the nets of our calculations. But let that be.) If one can use the language of antecedent probability at all here, it surely must point in the opposite direction.

St. Augustine is the most significant guide, perhaps, to the proper theological response to this question. He was the first to weave from biblical texts and his own best understanding of the Church's tradition the full doctrine of creation *ex nihilo*, as Christians understand it today. And in the *De Genesi ad litteram*, his commentary on the very texts in Genesis where the writer speaks of the coming to be of the plant and animal world on the fifth and sixth "Days" of Creation, he enunciated the famous theory of the *rationes seminales*, the seed-principles which God brings into being in the first moment of creation, and out of which the kinds of living things will, each in its own time, appear.[35] The "days," said Augustine, must be interpreted metaphorically as indefinite periods of time. And instead of God inserting new kinds of plants and animals ready-made, as it were, into a preexistent world, He must be thought of as creating in that very first moment the potencies for all the kinds of living things that would come later, including the human body itself:

> In the seed, then, there was invisibly present all that would develop in time into a tree. And in this same way we must picture the world, when God made all things together, as having had all things which were made in it and with it when day was made. This includes not only the heavens with sun, moon, and stars . . . but also the beings which water and earth contained in potency and in their causes, before they came forth in thetile course of time.[36]

Augustine, for one, would not have attributed an antecedent probability to God's "intervening" to bring the first kinds of plants and animals abruptly to be, rather than having them develop in the gradual way that seeds do.

But what are we to make of Plantinga's objection that having life coming gradually to be according to the normal regularities of natural process is "semi-deistic," that it attributes too much autonomy to the natural world? He says:

> God could have accomplished this creating in a thousand different ways. It was entirely within his power to create life in a way corresponding to the Grand Evolutionary Scenario . . . to create matter . . . together with laws for

its behavior, in such a way that the inevitable[37] outcome of matter's working according to these laws would be first, life's coming into existence three or four billion years ago, and then the various higher forms of life, culminating as we like to think, in humankind. This is a semi-deistic view of God and his workings.

He contrasts this alternative with the one he favors:

Perhaps these laws are not such that given enough time, life would automatically emerge. Perhaps he did something different and special in the creation of life. Perhaps he did something different and special in creating the various kinds of animals and plants.

His characterization of the first alternative as "semi-deistic" is intended to validate the second alternative as the appropriate one for the Christian to choose. But why should the first alternative be regarded as semi-deistic? He allows that it was within God's power to bring about cosmic evolution, but then asserts that to say He *did* in fact fashion the world in this way would be semi-deistic. This is puzzling. It would be semi-deistic in an extended sense perhaps, if we *already* knew that God had intervened in bringing to be some kinds of plants and animals, in which case the "Grand Evolutionary scenario" would attribute a greater degree of autonomy to the natural world than would be warranted. But this is exactly what we *don't* know. And to assume that we *do* know it would beg the question.

The problem may lie in the use of the label, "semi-deistic." A semi-deist, Plantinga remarks, could go so far as to allow that God "starts everything off," and "constantly sustains the world in existence," and even maintain that "any given causal transaction in the universe requires specific divine concurrent activity." All this would, apparently, not be enough to make such a view orthodox from the Christian standpoint. What more could be needed? Defining God's relationship with the natural order in terms of creation, conservation, and *concursus*, has after all been standard among Christian theologians since the Middle Ages. Perhaps what still needs to be made explicit is that God *could* also, if He so chose, relate to His creation in a different way, in the dramatic mode of a grace that overcomes nature and of wonders that draw attention to His covenant with Israel and ultimately to the person of Jesus. The possibility of such an "intrusion" on God's part into human history, of a mode of action that lies *beyond* nature, must not be excluded in advance, must indeed be affirmed. I take it that the denial that such a mode of action *is* possible on the part of the Being who creates and may even also conserve and concur is what constitutes semi-deism, in Plantinga's sense of that term.

But someone who asserts that the evolutionary account of origins is the best supported one is *not* necessarily a semi-deist in this sense. Some defenders of evolution—notably those who deny the existence of a Creator and are, therefore, not deists of *any* sort—would, of course, exclude special creation in this in-principle way. But there is no intrinsic connection whatever between the claim that God did, in fact, choose to work through evolutionary means and the far stronger claim that He *could* not have done otherwise. Nor, of course, is there any reason why someone who defends the evolutionary account of origin should go on to deny that God might intervene in the later human story in the way that Christians believe Him to have done.

In sum, then, at least *four* alternatives would have to be taken into account here. There are those who defend the evolutionary account of origins, and, rejecting the existence of God, would (if pressed) say that life could not *possibly* have come to be except through evolution. There may be those who maintain that God created, conserves, and concurs in the activity of the universe, but that He *could* not "intervene" in its history to bring new kinds of animals and plants to be, for example. These (if there are any such) are the semi-deists Plantinga describes. Then there are those who prefer the evolutionary account of origins on the grounds of evidence that this is in fact most probably the way it happened, but are perfectly willing to allow that it was within the Creator's power to speed up the story by special creation of ancestral kinds of plants and animals, even though (in their view) this was not what He did. This is a view that a great many Christians from Darwin's day to our own have defended; it is the view I am proposing here. It is *not* semi-deistic. And finally, there is the option of special creation: that God *did*, in fact, intervene by bringing various kinds of living things suddenly to be.

When Plantinga presents two alternatives only, the second being that God might "perhaps" have intervened as defenders of special creation believe He did, he must be supposing that the other alternative, the "Grand Evolutionary scenario," is one that excludes such a "perhaps," i.e., that excludes, *in principle*, the possibility that God could have intervened in the natural order. What I am challenging is this supposition. The Thesis of Common Ancestry can claim, as we have seen, an impressive body of evidence in its own fight. It need not rely on, nor does it entail any in-principle claim about what God could or could not do.[38]

So, finally, how *should* the Christian regard this thesis? Perhaps better, since there are evidently "distinctive threads in the tapestry of Christianity," in Plantinga's evocative metaphor, how might someone respond who sees in the Christian doctrine of creation an affirmation of the integrity of the natural order? TCA implies a cousinship extending across the entire living world, the sort of coherence (as Leibniz once argued) that one might expect in the work of an all-powerful and all-wise Creator. The "seeds," in Augustine's happy metaphor, have been there from the beginning; the universe has in itself the capacity to become what God destined it from the beginning to be as a human abode, and for all we know else.

When Augustine proposed a developmental cosmology long ago, there was little in the natural science of his day to support such a venture. Now that has changed. What was speculative and not quite coherent has been transformed, thanks to the labors of countless workers in a variety of different scientific fields. TCA allows the Christian to fill out the metaphysics of creation in a way that (I am persuaded) Augustine and Aquinas would have welcomed. No longer need one suppose that God added plants here and animals there. Though He *could* have done so, the evidence is mounting that the resources of His original creation were sufficient for the generation of the successive orders of complexity that make up our world.

Thus, common ancestry gives a meaning to the history of life that it previously lacked. In another perspective, this history now appears as preparation. The uncountable species that flourished and vanished have left a trace of themselves in us. The vast stretches of evolutionary time no longer seem quite so terrifying. Scripture traces the preparation for the coming of Christ back through Abraham to Adam. Is it too fanciful to suggest that natural science now allows us to extend the story indefinitely further back? When Christ took on human nature, the DNA that made him son of Mary may have linked him to a more ancient heritage stretching far beyond Adam to the shallows of unimaginably ancient seas. And so, in the Incarnation, it would not have been just human nature that was joined to the Divine, but in a less direct but no less real sense all those myriad organisms that had unknowingly over the eons shaped the way for the coming of the human.[39]

Anthropocentric? But of course: the story of the Incarnation *is* anthropocentric. Reconcilable with the evolutionary story as that is told in terms of chance events and blind alleys? I believe so, but to argue it would require another essay. Unique? Quite possibly not: other stories may be unfolding in very different ways in other parts of this capacious universe of ours. Terminal? Not necessarily: we have no idea what lies ahead for humankind. The transformations that made us what we are may not yet be ended. Antecedently probable from a Christian perspective? I will have to leave that to the reader.

NOTES

1. The most obvious difference scarcely needs be stated. Plantinga is one of the most highly respected philosophers in the U.S., justly renowned for the quality of his scholarship and the care and rigor of his arguments. I bracket him here with the creation-science group, incongruous as such an association may seem, only because of the broad similarity of their theses in regard to special creation. I very much fear that this similarity may be sufficient to encourage creation-scientists to co-opt his essay to their own purposes.

2. For a taxonomy of the ways in which faith and knowledge have been related by different Christian thinkers, see James Kellenberger, *Religious Discovery, Faith, and Knowledge* (Englewood Cliffs, NJ: Prentice-Hall, 1972), ch. 10.

3. William B. Provine, review of *Trial and Error: The American Controversy over Creation and Evolution*, Academe 73, no. 1 (1987): 50–52.

4. See McMullen, "The Rise and Fall of Physico-theology," section 4 of "Natural Science and Belief in a Creator," in *Physics, Philosophy, and Theology*, ed. R. J. Russell et al. (Rome: Vatican Observatory Press, 1988), 63–67.

5. Plantinga is using the term "myth" here in a technical sense, he reminds us, one that should not of itself be made to connote falsity or fiction.

6. Maurice Finocchiaro provides a new translation of the Letter in his *The Galileo Affair* (Berkeley: University of California Press, 1989), 87–118.

7. Galileo introduces one further way of dealing with tensions between Scripture and natural science, suggesting that the biblical authors accommodated themselves to their hearers. This does not, in practice, reduce to either of the principles above. The notion of accommodation had already been hinted at by theologians as diverse as Thomas Aquinas and John Calvin. But this is not the place for an exhaustive analysis of the logical complexities of the famous Letter. See my "Galileo as a Theologian," Fremantle Lecture, Oxford, 1983 (unpublished), and Jean Dietz Moss, "Galileo's Letter to Christina: Some Rhetorical Considerations," *Renaissance Quarterly* 36 (1983): 547–76.

8. Finocchiaro, *The Galileo Affair*, 94.

9. See my Introduction to *Galileo, Man of Science* (New York: Basic Books, 1967), 33–35.

10. There is an abundant literature on this topic. See, for example, Robert Clif-

ford S.J., "Creation in the Hebrew Bible," in *Physics, Philosophy, and Theology: A Common Quest for Understanding*, ed. R. J. Russell, W. R. Stoeger and G. V. Coyne S.J. (Notre Dame, IN: University of Notre Dame Press, 1988), 151–70; Dianne Bergant CSA and Carroll Stuhlmueller CP, "Creation According to the Old Testament," in *Evolution and Creation*, ed. Ernan McMullen (Notre Dame, IN: University of Notre Dame Press, 1985), 153–75; Bernhard W. Anderson, "The Earth Is the Lord's: An Essay on the Biblical Doctrine of Creation," in *Is God a Creationist?* ed. I. M. Frye (New York: Scribner, 1983), 176–96.

11. There is a larger issue here of deciding on the proper approach to Scripture generally. Plantinga characterizes the Reformed Christian as one who takes "Scripture to be a special revelation from God himself." Thus, for example, the story of Abraham, including the details of where he lived and journeyed and how he came to father a son, becomes a matter for history in the modem sense of that term, to be construed (in Plantinga's view) as having the standing of science. There is an implicit literalist presumption here that an Unreformed Christian like myself, someone unsympathetic, that is, to the constraints of the "*sola scriptura*" maxim, would surely question. But to debate this would lead us far afield indeed.

12. I am reluctant to label it "Augustinian," despite its obvious basis in the text of Augustine's *De Genesi ad litteram*. Augustine himself was not bound by it in practice. He did not require a conclusive demonstration over against the literal reading of the story of the Six Days before abandoning such a reading and espousing a highly metaphorical one. And he stressed the importance of literary norms in general in the understanding of the import of the biblical text. The presumption in favor of literalism that we have seen to be the main source of conflict ("the text is to be interpreted literally unless a contrary reading can be established from an extrinsic source such as natural science") would be much more characteristic of later theology, notably the post-Reformation theology of Galileo's own day.

13. In his *Letter to Christina*, Galileo cited Augustine to warn against the dangers of opposing "unbelievers" (read: experts) on the basis of inadequate scientific knowledge (Finocchiaro, *The Galileo Affair*, 112). I suppose that this is what worries me most about the strategy Plantinga urges on his Christian readers. Though he stresses the importance of scholarship and the patient effort to understand, the reader who proceeds on his advice to do battle with defenders of evolution all too easily risks causing the sort of "laughter" that Augustine deplores, because of its negative effects on the credibility of the Christian message generally.

14. As an illustration of how complex the notion of temporal beginnings has become, the Hawking model does not imply that the universe is infinitely old (as that phrase would ordinarily be understood) but rather that as we trace time backwards to the Big Bang, the normal concept of time may break down as we approach the initial singularity some fifteen billion years ago. The history of "real time" (as Hawking

calls it) would still be finite in the same terms as before, as he explicitly points out (Stephen Hawking, *A Brief History of Time* [New York: Bantam Books, 1988], 138).

15. The question of whether or not the time elapsed in cosmic history is finite or infinite depends, in part, on the choice of physical process on which to base the time-scale, particularly on whether it is cyclic or continuous. The question of the finitude or infinity of past time, so much debated by medieval philosophers and theologians, cannot straightforwardly be answered in absolute terms. The notion of time-measurement is far more complex and theory-dependent than earlier discussions allowed. But the theological point of the biblical account of creation remains untouched by technical developments such as this. See McMullen, "How Should Cosmology Relate to Theology?" in *The Sciences and Theology in the Twentieth Century*, ed. A. R. Peacocke (Notre Dame, IN: University of Notre Dame Press, 1981), 35.

16. As Plantinga himself recognizes: "There isn't the space here for more than the merest hand waving. . . . "But when the stakes are as high as they become by the end of his essay, one may fairly question whether hand waving is likely to be enough.

17. I would like to acknowledge my debt to the many who in discussion have helped me overcome the bafflement that evolutionary theory induces in the non-expert. In particular, my thanks go to Phil Sloan, Bill Charlesworth, Francisco Ayala, Bob Richards, and John Beatty.

18. Plantinga distinguishes between the Thesis of Common Ancestry and the attempt to explain common ancestry by some mechanism or other. But he calls the latter "Darwinism," which might confuse, since non-Darwinian explanations of common ancestry have, of course, also been proposed. And he says that TCA "is what one most naturally thinks of as the Theory of Evolution." What he may mean here is that TCA is theoretical and it implicitly involves evolution in some guise. But it is preferable, I would suggest, not to equate TCA and "the Theory of Evolution" because for most readers "the" theory of evolution is Darwin's.

19. See L. von Salvini-Plawen and E. Mayr, "On the Evolution of Photoreceptors and Eyes," *Evolutionary Biology* 10 (1977): 207–63.

20. In his most recent discussion of the relation between microevolution and macroevolution, Mayr writes: "Almost every careful analysis of fossil sequences has revealed that a multiplication of species does not take place through a gradual splitting of single lineages into two and their subsequent divergence but rather through the sudden appearance of a new species. Early paleontologists interpreted this as evidence for instantaneous sympatric speciation [speciation over a single area], but it is now rather generally recognized that the new species had originated somewhere in a peripheral isolate and had subsequently spread to the area where it is suddenly found in the fossil record. The parental species which had budded off the neospecies showed virtually no change during this period. The punctuation is thus caused by a localized event in an isolated founder population, while the main species displays no

significant change" (*Toward a New Philosophy of Biology* [Cambridge, MA: Harvard University Press, 1988], 415). This theory of allopatric speciation (speciation involving a second—in this case a geographically isolated but adjoining—territory) allows Mayr to modify the gradualism of the original Darwinian proposal, while retaining the basic Darwinian mode of explanation and avoiding the (to him) objectionable "punctual" events of the Gould-Eldredge scenario. But the debate is by no means closed.

21. For a brief review of this evidence, see Francisco Ayala, "The Theory of Evolution: Recent Successes," in *Evolution and Creation*, 59–90.

22. In this regard, the position adopted by Michael Denton, perhaps the most sweeping critic of evolutionary theory now writing, is quite puzzling. On the one hand, he finds the sort of consilience described above altogether remarkable: "It became increasingly apparent as more and more sequences are accumulated that the differences between organisms at a molecular level corresponded to a large extent with their differences at a morphological level; and that all the classes traditionally identified by morphological criteria could also be detected by comparing their protein sequences. . . . The divisions turned out to be more mathematically perfect than even the most die-hard typologists would have predicted" (*Evolution: Theory in Crisis* [Bethesda, MD: Adler and Adler, 1986], 276, 278). But the distances between the molecular sequences characteristic of different species can only be explained (he argues) by postulating a remarkably uniform "molecular clock" marking the rate of change in the constituents of particular kinds of molecules (and varying from one kind to another), and such a "clock" (he maintains) is impossible to understand on neo-Darwinian principles. What would seem, at best, to follow from this is that neo-Darwinian theory can't explain the uniformity of the postulated "clock." But he assumes that he has also justified TCA, while providing no hint himself as to how the correspondences he finds so remarkable might be explained by something *other* than common ancestry.

23. These are only two of the many possibilities. There is an enormous literature on this topic. See, for example, the papers gathered in Section VII of *Conceptual Issues in Evolutionary Biology*, ed. Elliott Sober (Cambridge, MA: MIT Press, 1984), and Ernst Mayr, *Animal Species and Evolution* (Cambridge, MA: Harvard University Press, 1963), 400–23.

24. Mayr, *Toward a New Philosophy of Biology* (TNPB), 318.

25. A further problem is suggested by the notion of a "natural" population. Reproductive isolation in the animal world is due, in the first instance, to behavioral barriers, which are the main isolating mechanisms (Mayr, *TNPB*, 320). Under artificial circumstances, such barriers can be overcome, but this will not necessarily give rise to new biological species. Likewise, deliberate interbreeding to produce new varieties of domestic dog, for example, will not produce a natural population with its own behavioral barriers to outbreeding.

26. Indeed, he showed some uncharacteristic indignation in his comment in the last edition of the *Origin of Species* (1872): "As my conclusions have lately been much misrepresented, and it has been stated that I attribute the modification of species exclusively to natural selection, I may be permitted to remark that in the first edition of that work, and subsequently, I placed in a most conspicuous position?namely, at the close of the Introduction—the following words: 'I am convinced that natural selection has been the main but not exclusive means of modification.' This has been of no avail. Great is the power of misrepresentation" (395).

27. For a useful review, from the point of view of the modern synthesis, see Ernst Mayr, "The Emergence of Evolutionary Novelties," in *Evolution after Darwin,* vol. 1: *The Evolution of Life,* ed. Sol Tax (Chicago: University of Chicago Press, 1960), 349–80.

28. Mayr, for instance, repudiates what he calls "selectionist extremism," and says that "much of the phenotype is a by-product of the evolutionary past, tolerated by natural selection but not necessarily produced under current conditions. . . . The mere fact of the vast reproductive surplus in each generation, together with the genetic uniqueness of each individual in sexually reproducing species, makes the importance of selection inescapable. This conclusion, however, does not in the least exclude the probability that random events also affect changes of survival and of the successful reproduction of an individual. The modern theory thus permits the inclusion of random events among the causes of evolutionary change. Such a pluralistic approach is surely more realistic than any one-sided extremism" (*TNPB*, 136, 140). Still, he also wants to say that the modern synthesis for which he is perhaps the leading spokesman "was a reaffirmation of the Darwinian formulation that all adaptive evolutionary change is due to the directing force of natural selection on abundantly available variation" (*TNPB*, 527; emphasis mine).

29. See S. J. Gould and R. Lewortin, "The Spandrels of San Marco and the Panglossian Paradigm: A Critique of the Adaptationist Programme," *Proc. Royal Society London* B205 (1979): 581–98.

30. One such problem is that a mutation affecting the phenotype in a major way would require co-ordinated change in hundreds of genes; another is that a macromutation in a single individual would not be enough, in a sexually reproducing species, to establish a new kind right away. The role of mutations in evolutionary change is much less dramatic than is often conveyed in popular accounts; they serve mainly to augment the stock of variations in a population upon which recombination can work. (Recombination is the blending of fraternal and maternal DNA in each new biological individual in a sexually reproducing species; it is responsible for the fact that each such individual is different from all others.)

31. In the early stages of life's development on earth, sixty or seventy different phyla (morphological types) developed, most of which became extinct. Not a single

new phylum has originated since the Cambrian period, more than four hundred million years ago. It would seem that the genetic structures of this early period were not as fixed as they later became. Selection may thus have had fewer constraints then than later on when highly cohesive genotypes developed; the rate of species-change might thus have been quite rapid, lowering the chances of an adequate fossil record of the changes.

32. The differences between the "punctuated equilibrium" model of Gould and Eldredge and the standard one of the modem synthesis are not nearly as great as was originally claimed. In particular, Gould's original assertion that only a "non-Darwinian" theory could handle the evidence from the fossil record was quite clearly based on a very narrow construal of what ought to count as "Darwinian." Mayr has to my mind convincingly shown that Gould's own model is compatible with Darwinian principles (*TNPB*, chapter 26).

33. Denton's comparison of the modern synthesis to late Ptolemaic astronomy with its profusion of epicycles, and his conclusion that it is a paradigm in crisis (*Evolution*, chapter 15) cannot, I think, be sustained. The crucial disagreement between us would be as to what constitutes and *ad hoc* modification (what he, oddly, calls a "tautology").

34. "God fashioned man from the dust of the earth and breathed into his nostrils the breath of life" (Gen. 2:7). The "fashioning" here could be that of a billion years of evolutionary preparation of that "dust" to form a being that for the first time could freely affirm or freely deny his Maker. Pius XII in his encyclical *Humani Generis* (1950) allowed that such an evolutionary origin of the human body was an acceptable reading of the Genesis text. But he added that the human soul could not be so understood; it had to be specially "infused" by God, presumably not just in the case of the first humans, but all humans since. Many theologians today would find the Platonic-sounding dualism underlying this assertion troubling. The uniqueness of God's covenant with men and women and of the promise of resurrection does not require that there be a naturally immortal soul, distinct in its genesis and history from its "attendant" body. But it is unnecessary to develop this issue here, since Plantinga's challenge extends to the evolutionary account of the plant and animal worlds, and not simply of the human.

35. For a full discussion, see "Augustine's 'seed principles,'" section 4 of my *Introduction to Evolution and Creation*, 11–16.

36. *The Literal Meaning of Genesis*, 2 vols., trans. by J. H. Taylor (New York: Newman, 1982), v, 23; 175 (translation slightly modified).

37. "Inevitable" is a word that defenders of evolution, whether theists or not, would be uneasy with. It suggests that the evolutionary process is at least in a general way deterministic or predictable. But this is just what nearly all theorists of evolution would deny.

38. There is one further perspective on this matter of semi-deism that I have deliberately set aside above. The occasionalists of the fourteenth century maintained that God is the only cause, strictly speaking, of what happens in the world. What appears to be causal action within the world isf for them no more than temporal succession. Things do not have natures that specify their actions; rather the fact that they act according to certain norms must be directly attributed to God's intentions. There is not reasons why God should not, for example, suddenly make new kinds of plants and animal appear, if he so wishes; since there is no *order* of nature, God is committed only to the reasonable stability of (more or less) regular succession on which human life depends. The issue that separated the nominalists from the Aristotelian defenders of real causation in nature is brought out very well in the essay by Alfred Freddoso cited by Plantinga: "Medieval Aristotelianism and the Case against Secondary Causation in Nature," in *Divine and Human Action*, ed. T. V. Morris (Ithaca, NY: Cornell University Press, 1988).

In this perspective, the issue of "special creation" comes to be posed in a quite different way. Any view which affirms the sufficiency of the natural order for bringing about the origins of life might be dubbed by the occasionalist as "semi-deist." When I read the paragraph in which Plantinga says that someone who maintains that God creates, conserves, and concurs in the activity of, the universe is "semi-deistic," my first reaction was to assume that this committed him to occasionalism, since it is *only* from the occasionalist perspective that this view of God's relationship with the natural order would be classed as "semi-deist." But Plantinga is quite evidently *not* an occasionalist; his treatment of natural science implies that he believes in the operation of secondary causation in nature. Thus, I have assumed in the discussion above that Plantinga must have had something else in mind, namely, the openness of creation to a supernatural order of grace and miracle. Incidentally, the occasionalist *would* be likely to believe that special creation is antecedently more probable, and (in Berkeley's version, at least) might tend to question a theory, like the theory of evolution, which depends on the reality of such causes as genetic mutation.

39. Though the alert reader will have caught echoes of the theology (not the biology; see section 5 above) of Teilhard de Chardin, the affinities with the Christology of Karl Rahner are more immediate perhaps. See, for example, his "Christology within an Evolutionary View of the World," *Theological Investigations* (Baltimore: Helicon, 1961, 1979), 5:157–91.

THOMAS AQUINAS VS.
THE INTELLIGENT DESIGNERS

What Is God's Finger Doing in My Pre-Biotic Soup?

MICHAEL W. TKACZ

WHERE ARE THE THOMISTS?

A few years ago I received a phone call from a professor of philosophy at a nearby private religiously affiliated college. He had just returned from an international conference devoted to challenges to evolutionary biology from Intelligent Design Theory. There was a bit of urgency in the professor's tone, so I agreed to meet him. As it turned out, he had something of a complaint to make, for he opened our meeting by showering me with a series of questions: Where are the Thomists? Where are the Catholics? How come you Thomist guys are not out there defending us Intelligent Designers? After all, we are on the same side, are we not? Asking the professor the occasion of this outpouring of questions, he explained that he and the other organizers of the conference had invited several Thomists to participate and he was dismayed that, far from expressing sympathy with the Intelligent Design Movement and its challenge to Darwinism, they were

Michael W. Tkacz, "Thomas Aquinas vs. The Intelligent Designers: What Is God's Finger Doing in My Pre-Biotic Soup?" Lecture at Gonzaga University, Fall 2005.

quite critical of the Movement. Perhaps feeling a bit betrayed, he wanted to ask me, a Thomist, just what was going on.

The debate between Creationists and Evolutionists has been going on for a long time now and neither side has been especially interested in what Thomism—a minority position to be sure—has had to contribute to the discussion. To the extent that philosophers working in the Thomistic tradition are considered at all, both sides seem to have been dissatisfied. Secular Darwinians often view Thomists as just another species of literalists attempting to substitute the Book of Genesis for good biology—indeed, the only difference between Thomists and Protestant Creationists, on their view, is that Thomists do it in Latin. On the other hand, Protestant Creationists have often viewed Thomists as already half-way to secularism and naturalism—no doubt due to insufficient attention to the reading of scripture.

Now come the Intelligent Designers who have revived the debate with evolutionary biology on scientific grounds. This new challenge to Darwinism attempts to show that the biological evidence supports gradual evolution of species less than it does direct creation by a Divine Designer. Given the philosophical sophistication of their arguments, it is perhaps natural that Intelligent Designers would assume that they had allies among traditional Thomists who are known for their systematic defense of the doctrine of creation. Yet, Thomists have not generally been quick to jump onto the Intelligent Design bandwagon. As my philosophy professor friend discovered, the Intelligent Design Movement has, overall, not been well-received in Thomistic circles. So, the question is: Why? Why have Thomists, who share with Intelligent Designers so many of the same concerns about the secularization of our society, not been more supportive of the Movement? Why have so many Thomists hesitated to join Intelligent Design theorists in their campaign against Darwinism? Why do some Thomists, far from being supportive, appear even a bit hostile to the Intelligent Design project?

A bit of attention to the Thomistic philosophy of creation may help to answer these questions. More importantly, investigating the coolness of Thomism toward Intelligent Design Theory may help to move the debate away from its polarized Creation vs. Evolution state toward a discussion that is more philosophically productive. A look at the Thomistic understanding of God's relationship to nature may even suggest a third alternative to the already well-known positions of the Darwinians and Intelligent Designers.

THOMAS AQUINAS ON CREATION

Back in the days of Thomas Aquinas himself, there was a scientific revolution that seriously challenged the traditional Christian doctrine of creation. From the time of the early Church, orthodox Christians have held that the universe was created by a transcendent God who is wholly responsible for its existence and the existence of everything in it. In fact, this is a teaching that Christians inherited from the Jews and shared with those of the Islamic faith. At the beginning of the thirteenth century, however, a great historical change came to Western Europe as the works of the ancient Greek natural philosophers and mathematicians became available in the Latin language for the first time. Especially important among these works were those of Aristotle who had worked out the basic principles of nature and developed a methodology for scientific research that promised, in time, to unlock the secrets of the universe.

This scientific revolution caused great excitement among the Latin-speaking scholars in the then new universities of Europe. They avidly pursued research in many of the natural sciences and, essentially, founded the historical tradition of experimental science that continues today. It was not long before progress was being made in such fields as mathematical astronomy, optics, meteorology, botany, zoology, and other sciences. At the same time, the new science was a cause for concern, for some theologians saw in it a challenge to the doctrine of creation. Specifically, many held that there is a fundamental incompatibility between the claim of the Greek naturalists that something cannot come from nothing and the Christian teaching of creation *ex nihilo*. Indeed, the Greek philosophers used their fundamental principle as grounds for arguing that the universe is eternal: there can be neither a first nor a last motion. It certainly appeared to many of the contemporaries of Thomas Aquinas that one cannot have his Christian cake and scientifically eat it too; Christianity and natural science seemed to be incompatible and one must choose between the two.

Into this medieval debate came Thomas Aquinas. He pointed out that the Christian conception of God as the author of all truth and the notion that the aim of scientific research is the truth indicates that there can be no fundamental incompatibility between the two. Provided we understand Christian doctrine properly and do our science well, we will find the truth—not a religious truth and another scientific truth—but the truth, the way things actually exist and function. Yet, what about the apparent conflict between the notion of creation from nothing and the scientific principle that for every nat-ural motion or state there is an antecedent motion or state?

Thomas pointed out that the judgment that there is a conflict here results from confusion regarding the nature of creation and natural change. It is an error that I call the "Cosmogonical Fallacy." Those who are worried about conflict between faith and reason on this issue fail to distinguish between cause in the sense of a natural change of some kind and cause in the sense of an ultimate bringing into being of something from no antecedent state what-soever. "Creatio non est mutatio," says Thomas, affirming that the act of cre-ation is not some species of change. So, the Greek natural philosophers were quite correct: from nothing, nothing comes. By "comes" here is meant a change from one state to another and this requires some underlying material reality, some potentiality for the new state to come into being. This is because all change arises out of a pre-existing possibility for that change residing in something. Creation, on the other hand, is the radical causing of the whole existence of whatever exists. To be the complete cause of some-thing's existence is not the same as producing a change in something. It is not a taking of something and making it into something else, as if there were some primordial matter which God had to use to create the universe. Rather, creation is the result of the divine agency being totally responsible for the production, all at once and completely, of the whole of the universe, with all its entities and all its operations, from absolutely nothing pre-existing.

Strictly speaking, points out Thomas, the Creator does not create some-thing out of nothing in the sense of taking some nothing and making something out of it. This is a conceptual mistake, for it treats nothing as a something. On the contrary, the Christian doctrine of creation *ex nihilo* claims that God made the universe without making it out of anything. In other words, anything left entirely to itself, completely separated from the cause of its existence, would not exist—it would be absolutely nothing. The ultimate cause of the existence of anything and everything is God who creates, not *out of some nothing*, but *from nothing at all*.

In this way, one can see that the new science of the thirteenth century, out of which our modern science developed, was not a threat to the tradi-tional Christian doctrine of creation. To come to know the natural causes of natural beings is a different matter from knowing that all natural beings and operations radically depend on the ultimate cause for the existence of every-thing: God the Creator. Creation is *not* a change. Creation *is* a cause, but of a very different, indeed unique, kind. Only if one avoids the Cosmogonical

Fallacy, is one able to correctly understand the Christian doctrine of creation *ex nihilo*.

THOMISM AND THE AUTONOMY OF NATURE

Two implications of this distinction between change and creation are worthy of note here. One is that God creates without taking any time to create; he creates eternally. Creation is not a process with a beginning, a middle, and an end. It is simply a reality: the reality of the complete dependence of the universe on God's agency. The other implication is the radical otherness of God's agency. God's productive causality is unlike that of any natural cause, for God not only produces what he produces all at once without any process, but also without requiring anything pre-existing or any preconditions what-soever. God does not act as part of a process, nor does God initiate a process where there was none before. There is no *before* for God; there is no pre-existing state from which God's action proceeds. God is totally and immediately present as cause to any and all processes.

On the basis of these implications for the correct understanding of creation, modern Thomists distinguish between the existence of natural beings and their operations. God causes natural beings to exist in such a way that they are the real causes of their own operations. Indeed, if this were not the case, then it would not have been that God created *this* natural being, but some other. Salmon swim up stream to spawn. In creating such a natural being, God created a fish that reproduces in *this* way. If God created salmon without their natural reproductive agency, then he did not create salmon, but something else.

Consider another example: a large quadrapedic mammal, such as a hippopotamus, gives live birth to its young. Why? Well, we could answer this by saying that "God does it." Yet, this could only mean that God created hippopotamuses—indeed the mammalian order, the whole animal kingdom, and all of nature—such that these animals have the morphology, genetic make-up, etc. that are the causes of their giving live birth. It cannot be that God "reaches into" the normal operations of hippopotamuses to cause them to give live birth. Were one to think that "God does it" must mean that God intervenes in nature in this way, one would be guilty of the Cosmogonical Fallacy.

Now, if this distinction between the being of something and its operation is correct, then nature and her operations are autonomous in the sense that nature operates according to the way she is, not because something outside of her is acting on her. God does not act on nature the way a human being might act on an artifact to change it. Rather, God causes natural beings to be in such a way that they work the way they do. Hippopotamuses give live birth because that is the sort of thing they are. Why are there such things as Hippopotamuses? Well, nature produced them in some way. What way did nature produce them and why does nature produce things in this way? It is because God made the whole of nature to operate in this way and produce by her own agency what she produces. Thus, God remains completely responsible for the being and operation of everything, even though natural beings possess real agency according to the way they were created.

INTELLIGENT DESIGNERS AND THE COSMOGONICAL FALLACY

In light of this sketch of the Thomistic account of creation and natural cause, one can perhaps understand the reluctance of contemporary Thomists to rush to the defense of the Intelligent Designers. It would seem that Intelligent Design Theory is grounded on the Cosmogonical Fallacy. Many who oppose the standard Darwinian account of biological evolution identify creation with divine intervention into nature. This is why many are so concerned with discontinuities in nature, such as discontinuities in the fossil record: they see in them evidence of divine action in the world, on the grounds that such discontinuities could only be explained by direct divine action. This insistence that creation must mean that God has periodically produced new and distinct forms of life is to confuse the fact of creation with the manner or mode of the development of natural beings in the universe. This is the Cosmogonical Fallacy.

Among the most sophisticated attempts of Intelligent Design theorists to counter the Darwinian account of the formation of organisms is the Irreducible Complexity Argument of biochemist Michael Behe. He argues that there are specific life forms and biotic subsystems which are irreducibly complex and which could not possibly be brought about by means of natural selection. Irreducibly complex systems and forms reveal intelligent design in nature and, therefore, indicate the reality of an Intelligent Designer of the universe. Intelligent Design theorists are often perplexed and, even a bit put out, that Thomists do not acknowledge the cogency of Behe's argument. After all, Thomists are quite open to the notion that creation provides evidence for the existence of the Creator—cosmological arguments for the existence of God based on the order and operation of nature have long been the special preserve of Thomism.

Why, then, have Thomists not been among Behe's most ardent supporters? First of all, they would agree with many biologists who have pointed out that Behe's claims of irreducible complexity fail to distinguish between the lack of a known natural explanation of the origin of complex systems and the judgment that such explanation is in principle impossible. Thomists, however, would go even further than most biologists by identifying the first claim as epistemological and the second as ontological. Now, a Thomist might agree with Behe's epistemological claim that no current or foreseeable future attempt at explanation for certain biological complexities is satisfactory. Yet, a Thomist will reject Behe's ontological claim that no such explanation can ever be given in terms of the operation of nature. This ontological claim depends on a "god of the gaps" understanding of divine agency and such an understanding of God's action is cosmogonically fallacious.

CONCLUSION

There is, of course, much more to be said on this topic. Let me be the first to admit that this presentation provides, at best, a sketchy account of the issues. For one thing, a complete treatment of the relationship of Thomism and Intelligent Design Theory must take account of the variation of views on each side. Nonetheless, what has been presented here regarding the identification of the Cosmogonical Fallacy provides some insight into the reasons for fundamental disagreement between Thomists and Intelligent Design theorists. The careful distinctions of Thomas Aquinas clarifying the Christian doctrine of creation *ex nihilo* exclude certain ways of conceiving of God's relation to the natural world. Thus, despite their many shared cultural and religious concerns, those who do philosophy in the Thomistic tradition and those who have devoted themselves to the Intelligent Design Movement find themselves on opposite sides of the crucial issue of the nature of divine agency.

BIBLIOGRAPHIC NOTE

There is a growing body of literature on Intelligent Design Theory. Consult the bibliographies available on the website of the Discovery Institute (www.discovery.org) for a list of titles. For the Thomistic reaction to Intelligent Design Theory, see *Aquinas on Creation*, trans. Steven E. Baldner and William E. Carroll (Toronto: Pontifical Institute of Mediaeval Studies, 1997); William E. Carroll, "Creation, Evolution, and Thomas Aquinas," *Revue des Questions Scientifiques* 171 (2000): 319–47; Marie I. George, "On Attempts to Salvage Paley's Argument from Design," in *Science, Philosophy, and Theology*, ed. John O'Callaghan (South Bend, IN: St. Augustine's Press, 2006). For theists, much of the debate over evolutionary biology is related to issues concerning the proper way to understand the opening lines of the Book of Genesis. For a fine discussion of the Genesis text in the context of the evolution debate see Leon R. Kass, "Evolution and the Bible: Genesis 1 Revisited," *Commentary* (November 1988): 29–39.

GENESIS AND GOD

HOLMES ROLSTON III

There is a metaphysical version of the if-functional-then-not-true argument. [Edward O.] Wilson argues that if something has evolved in natural history, then it cannot be the work of transcendent deity.

1. If E (evolved), then not T (transcendent).
2. E.
3. Therefore not T.

"No species, ours included, possesses a purpose beyond the imperatives created by its genetic history. . . . We have no particular place to go. The species lacks any goal external to its own biological nature."[1] "There is no transcendental guide or extra-somic set of universal principles to follow."[2] As before, the logic is valid, but are the premises sound? "If x emerged in historical time, then x is not divine"? If from genes, then not from God?

Holmes Rolston III, "Genesis and God," in *Genes, Genesis and God: Values and Their Origins in Natural and Human History,* The Gifford Lectures, University of Edinburgh, 1997–1998 (Cambridge: Cambridge University Press, 1999), chapter 5.

That fails to consider whether one purpose of God might be this Earth history: the creation and its redemption. This amounts to claiming, in the traditional vocabulary of theologians, that immanence cannot combine with transcendence, that the beyond cannot be in our midst. Theologians almost unanimously think otherwise, on the evidence of religious experience, critically evaluated. So one will need to know what it is about biology, about genetics, that authorizes this conclusion that the historical cannot be the immanent location of a transcendent divine presence. We humans do not particularly want some goal "external to our biological nature"; we wish one consistent with it, but we might want to maintain that, metaphysically, neither our biological nor our sociological natures are self-explanatory.

Wilson insists, "The evolutionary epic is probably the best myth we will ever have."[3] We agree, but the question is whether the dramatic events on this Earth contain no hint of larger, more universal powers in which they are embedded. Perhaps, rather, culture and biology are finding out in their historical domains what Kurt Gödel found for the much simpler domains of mathematics and logic, that systems to be completely understood require reference to other systems at a higher level of organization. Against the reductionists, religious persons have to be compositionists, to move up, not down, to get the interpretive level needed to frame and complete lower level truths. Nature and history have been creative, making more out of less. The essential characteristic of narrative is that events have to be understood in the light of the complexities to which they lead, not just in the light of the origins from which they flow. The event structures toward which things climb, their endings, are as significant as the matter-energy out of which they arise, their beginnings.

We have no cause to think that the startling genesis on Earth, recorded in the genes, recorded in the cultural heritages, including the religions, is not sacred; nor that humans, funded by their evolved perceptual and cognitive equipment, can never detect that sacred presence. The idea of God has been among the most fertile in shaping history. That is the fertility that ultimately needs to be explained.

That returns us to the global claims of religion, claims that are transcendent at least in the sense of detecting a divine power in, with, and under the genesis on Earth. Contra Wilson, does biology leave space for such claims or even invite such claims as complementary explanations? Genes record only a portion of the history that has taken place: they do not, for instance, record the prelife cosmological story; nor do they record the postgenetic cultural story. Still, vital to the Earth epic is this fertility intimately linked with the genes, the means by which all the more complex structures on Earth, living things, are formed. There are no such genes on the moon, nor Jupiter, nor Mars. Genes remember, research, and recompound discoveries, and the storied achievements, the values achieved, rise, over several billion years, to spectacular levels of attainment and power. The cosmic universals give way to the particulars of Earthen natural history.

ACTUAL AND POSSIBLE NATURAL HISTORY

What can we say about how the possible becomes actual over evolutionary time? Here, one must increasingly pass from bioscience to metaphysics. We return, at the end, to questions faced earlier, about the increase of complexity and diversity, about contingency and inevitability in such increase, about progress, now with questions looming about the possibility of divine presence. This is the fertility question in its metaphysical form, the generation of the actual out of the possible, and the generation of those possibilities, and even a Generator of such possibilities. The possibility route to be found is not so much logical, or empirical, or even physical; it is historical. What possibility spaces are needed to get from beginnings to where we have now arrived, in Earth history?

At the other extreme from those emphasizing the contingency, there are eminent biologists—though they tend to be molecular biologists rather than paleontologists—who find this storied natural history to be inevitable, at least in outline, and therefore predictable. Christian de Duve concludes: "Life was bound to arise under the prevailing conditions, and it will arise similarly wherever and whenever the same conditions obtain. There is hardly any room for 'lucky accidents' in the gradual, multistep process whereby life originated." After life arises there is contingency as to its directions and species, but this is "constrained contingency" so that the general trends in the development of life—cellular organisms, multicellular organisms, solar energized organisms, increasingly diverse and complex organisms, and intelligent organisms—are likewise inevitable. "Life and mind emerge not as the results of freakish accidents, but as natural manifestations of matter, written into the fabric of the universe. I view this universe [as] . . . made in such a way as to generate life and mind, bound to give birth to thinking beings."[4]

"This universe breeds life inevitably," concludes George Wald.[5] Life is an accident waiting to happen, because it is blueprinted into the chemicals, rather as sodium and chlorine are preset to form salt, only much more startlingly so because of the rich implications for life and because of the openness and information transfer also present in the historical life process. Whatever place dice throwing has in its appearance and maturation, life is something arranged for in the nature of things. The dice are loaded.

When the predecessors of DNA and RNA appear, enormously complex molecules appear; bearing the possibility of genetic coding and information, they are conserved, writes Melvin Calvin, "not by accident but because of the peculiar chemistries of the various bases and amino acids. . . . There is a kind of selectivity intrinsic in the structures." The evolution of life, so far from being random, is "a logical consequence" of natural chemistries.[6] Manfred Eigen concludes that "the evolution of life . . . must be considered an *inevitable* process despite its indeterminate course."[7] Life is destined to come as part of the narrative story, although the exact routes it will take are open and subject to historical vicissitudes. [Stuart] Kauffman agrees: "I believe that the origin of life was not an enormously improbable event, but law-like and governed by new principles of self-organization in complex webs of catalysts."[8]

Such accounts suggest that the possibilities are always there, latent in the physics and chemistry, although the resulting Earth history is not so "fine-tuned" as astrophysics and nuclear physics have found in their cosmologies. But even in Earthen biology, the possibilities must, or almost must, become actual. Alternately put, there are few possibilities beyond those that do actualize. But of course all such possibilities are seen only retrospectively. What does happen, can happen. But we are wondering how it comes about that these events can happen. If, *per impossibile*, some scientist had under observation the elementary particles forming after the first three minutes, nothing much in them suggests anything specific about the coding for life that would take place, fifteen billion years later, on Earth. After Earth forms, the lifeless planet is irradiated by solar energy, as are other planets as well. The events in physics and chemistry there are to a considerable extent lawlike and predictable, at least statistically, although in geology and meteorology the system is quite complex as a result of shifting initial conditions, possibly even at times chaotic. Still, in orogeny and erosion, or the shifting of the tectonic plates, the possibilities always seem there.

At the microscopic levels, quantum physics depicts an open system and nested sets of possibilities, but, at first, all the atoms and molecules take non-living tracks. Only later do some atoms and molecules begin to take living tracks, called forth as interaction phenomena when cybernetic organisms appear. If there is some "inside order" to matter that makes it pro-life, it is in the whole system and not just in the particles. Despite the anthropic principle, such order is not generally evident in the systemic astronomy, since by far the vastest parts of the universe are lifeless. Life is an Earth-bound probability. Nor, on Earth, are the meteorological or geomorphological systems all that suggestive of inevitable life. They mostly seem kaleidoscopic variations on geophysical and geochemical processes.

Only in biology do there open up entirely unprecedented levels of achievement and power. Such possibilities are not inside the atoms and molecules apart from their systemic location, since atoms and molecules would not even be collected into a "thin hot soup" except for the Earth world in which this is possible, nor can this or that sequence of DNA code for anything unless there is an environment in which to behave this way or that, with a niche to fill. Even if there is some "selectivity intrinsic in the structures," this does not rule out a universe of myriad options, only some of which are realized.

Physics and chemistry, unaided, do not get us very near to life and mind. There really isn't much in the physics and chemistry of atoms and molecules, prior to their biological assembling, that suggests that they have any tendencies to order themselves up to life. Even after things have developed as far as the building blocks of life, there is nothing in a "thin hot soup" of disconnected amino acids to predict that they will connect themselves or be selected along upward, negentropic though metastable courses into proteins, nor that they will arrange for DNA molecules in which to record the various discoveries of structures and metabolisms specific to the diverse forms of life.

All these events may occur naturally, but they are still quite a surprise. Recent microbiology has been revealing their enormous complexity. We do not know that life, if it occurs on some other planet, there built too of the same atoms, must select these same biochemistries, although the amino acids found on meteorites and the prebiotic molecules guessed to be present in interstellar dust clouds can suggest that the potential for life is omnipresent in matter. Laws are important in natural systems, whether extraterrestrial or terrestrial. But natural law is not the complete explanatory category for nature, any more than are randomness and chance. In nature, especially on this historical Earth, there is creativity by which more comes out of less.

Science does not handle historical explanations very competently, especially where there are emergent novelties; science prefers law-like explanations in which there are no surprises. One predicts, and the prediction comes true. If such precision is impossible, science prefers statistical predictions, probabilities. One predicts, and, probably, the prediction comes true. Biology, meanwhile, though prediction is often possible, is also full of unpredictable surprises—like calcium endoskeletons in vertebrates after millennia of diatomaceous silica and chitinous arthropod exoskeletons. A main turning point in the history of life fused once-independent organisms into the cell and its mitochondria, which became the powerhouses for life. Another critical symbiosis introduced free-living chloroplasts into the plant cell, again producing the energy vital for all life.

There is no induction (expecting the future to be like the past) by which one can expect, even probably, trilobites later from prokaryotes earlier, or dinosaurs still later by extrapolating along a regression line (a progression line!) drawn from prokaryotes to trilobites. There are no humans invisibly present (as an acorn secretly contains an oak) in the primitive eukaryotes, to unfold in a law-like or programmatic way. The ancient ancestral forms are not protovertebrates or preterrestrials, nor are gymnosperms about-to-be angiosperms, as though the descendant forms were latent among the functions of the predecessors. Originating events often become what they become only retrospectively: "Vertebrates began (possibly) with the notochords of primitive chordates." "Eyes began with. . . ." Nevertheless, there is the epic story—eukaryotes, trilobites, dinosaurs, primates—swarms of wild creatures in seas and on land, followed by humans who arrive late in the story.

Making this survey, can one insist that the probabilities, or at least the possibilities, must always have been there? Can one claim that what did actually manage to happen must always have been either probably probable, or, minimally, improbably possible all along the way? Push this to extremes, as one must do, if one claims that all the possibilities are always there, latent in the dust, latent in the quarks. Such a claim becomes pretty much an act of speculative faith, not in present actualities, since one knows that these events took place, but in past probabilities always being omnipresent. Is the claim some kind of induction or deduction, or most-plausible-case conclusion from present actualities? Speculation about such possibilities that are always there is easy, provided one does not have to specify any of the details. But this perennial and vast library of possibilities is mostly imaginary.

For in fact, on Earth, there really isn't anything in rocks that suggests the possibility of *Homo sapiens*, much less the American Civil War, or the World Wide Web, and to say that all these possibilities are lurking there, even though nothing we know about rocks, or carbon atoms, or electrons and protons suggests this is simply to let possibilities float in from nowhere.[9] Unbounded possibilities that one posits ad hoc to whatever one finds has in fact taken place—possibilities of any kind and amount desired in one's metaphysical enthusiasm—can hardly be said to be a scientific hypothesis. This is hardly even a faith claim with sufficient warrant. It is certainly equally credible, and more plausible, and no less scientific to hold that new possibility spaces open up en route.

Karl Popper concludes that science discovers "a world of propensities," open to historical innovation, the possibility space ever enlarging.

> In our real changing world, the situation and, with it, the possibilities, and thus the propensities, change all the time. . . . This view of propensities allows us to see in a new light the processes that constitute our world: the world process. The world is no longer a causal machine—it can now be seen as a world of propensities, as an unfolding process of realizing possibilities and of unfolding new possibilities. . . . New possibilities are created, possibilities that previously simply did not exist. . . . Especially in the evolution of biochemistry, it is widely appreciated that every new compound creates new possibilities for further new compounds to synthesize: possibilities which previously did not exist. The possibility space . . . is growing. . . . Our world of propensities is inherently creative.[10]

The result is the evolutionary drama. "The variety of those [organisms] that have realized themselves is staggering." "In the end, we ourselves become possible."[11]

But—the reply comes—since all those things did come in subsequent evolutionary and cultural history, their possibilities must have been there all along. You were not listening when we discovered that matter is self-organizing, autopoietic. That posits enormous possibilities, there from the start, and nothing in the historical drama ought to take by all that much surprise one who believes in self-organizing nature. Thomas R. Cech, a molecular biologist, reviews the origin of life:

> If intrinsic to these small organic molecules is their propensity to self-assemble, leading to a series of events that cause life forms to originate, that is perhaps the highest form of creation that one could imagine. . . . At least

from the perspective of a biologist, I have given an account of how possibilities did, in times past, become actual. When this happened, life originated with impressive creativity, and it does not seem to me that possibilities floated in from nowhere; they were already present, intrinsic to the
chemical materials.[12]

True, matter—energized as it is on Earth—is now self-organizing. But
that leaves open the question whether, on the adaptive landscapes on which
organisms struggle to increase their fitness for survival, landscapes which
themselves shift as the organisms make their discoveries, there are changing
possibility spaces coming in through evolutionary history. In creating themselves, the creatures need possibility space, opportunity space, transformational space. Evolving into *Homo sapiens* is, we can suppose, in the possibility space of *Homo habilis* (or whatever the hypothetical ancestor). But it
takes considerable imagination to find *Homo* in the possibility space of trilobites (or whatever the remote ancestor in that epoch). The creatures do have,
over time, the possibility of speciating and respeciating. But it is not so clear
that the creatures, in their self-actualizing, do have, or generate all by themselves, all these other kinds of selves into which they are transformed. There
is enormously more out of less, and enormous space for the introduction of
novelties that do not seem "up to" the faculties of the organism. One can say,
if one likes, that a dinosaur is lurking in the possibility space of a microbe,
or that microbes self-transform into dinosaurs, which self-transform into primates. But that really is not a claim based on anything we know about the
biology or ontology of microbes.

The self-creating is more a holistic, systemic affair; it is what happens to
microbes when they are challenged in their habitats and after a very long
time. This requires the creation of new possibility spaces. From a God's-eye
view, perhaps the possibilities are always there,[13] but we humans have no
such viewpoint. We do view results and know that the possibilities both got
there and got actualized, but it is quite as much an act of faith to see
dinosaurs in the possibility spaces of quarks as to see dinosaurs in the possibility space of God.

Looking at a pool of amino acids and seeing dinosaurs or *Homo sapiens*
in them is something like looking at a pile of alphabetical letters and seeing
Hamlet. In fact *Hamlet* is not lurking around a pile of A–Z's; such a play is not
within their possibility space—not until Shakespeare comes around, and in
Shakespeare plus a pile of letters, *Hamlet* does lurk. By shaking a tray of

printer's type, one can get a few short words, which are destroyed as soon as they are composed. If sentences begin to appear (an analogue of the long, symbolically coded DNA molecules and the polypeptide chains) and form into a poem or a short story (an analogue of the organism), one can be quite sure there are some formative, even irreversible, constraints on the sorting and shaking that are catching the up-thrusts and directionally organizing them.

It hardly seems coherent to hold that nonbiological materials are randomly the more and more derandomized across long structural sequences and thus ordered up to life. That is quite as miraculous as walking on water. Something is introducing the order, and, further, something seems to be introducing layer by layer new possibilities of order, new information achieved, not just unfolding the latent order already there from the start in the setup.

Some will reply that all actual events materialize in a global possibility space, and while the former become over time, the latter does not. The possibility space is always there. There is no such thing as the creation of possibilities that were not there. New doors may open but only into rooms that previously existed, albeit unoccupied and with no furniture. One does not need to get possibilities from nowhere because there are infinite possibilities everlastingly, or at least since the Big Bang. The proof of this lies in what has subsequently happened.

But surely the possibility space of serious alternatives does enlarge and shrink. There are times of opportunity, in which taking one direction opens up new possibilities and taking another shuts them out. Along the way, new possibility space for genetic engineering is brought into the picture, and this is linked with the appearance of new information, to which we next turn.

THE GENESIS OF INFORMATION

The story becomes memorable—able to employ a memory—only with genes (or comparable predecessor molecules). The story becomes cumulative and transmissible. The fertility possibilities are a hundred times recompounded. If the DNA in the human body were uncoiled and stretched out end to end, that slender thread would reach to the sun and back over half a dozen times.[14] That conveys some idea of the astronomical amount of information soaked through the body. In nature, in the Newtonian view there were two metaphysical fundamentals: matter and energy. Einstein reduced these two to one: matter-energy. In matter in motion, there is conservation of matter, also of energy; neither can be created or destroyed, although each can take diverse forms, and one can be transformed into the other. In the biological sciences, as we have emphasized, the novelty is that matter-energy is found in living things in diverse information states. The biologists still claim two metaphysical fundamentals: matter-energy and information. Norbert Wiener insists, "Information is information, not matter or energy."[15]

In living things, concludes Manfred Eigen, this is "the key-word that represents the phenomenon of complexity: information. Our task is to find an algorithm, a natural law that leads to the origin of information. . . . Life is a dynamic state of matter organized by information."[16] Bernd-Olaf Küppers agrees: "The problem of the origin of life is clearly basically equivalent to the problem of the origin of biological information."[17] George C. Williams is explicit:

> Evolutionary biologists have failed to realize that they work with two more or less incommensurable domains: that of information and that of matter. . . . Matter and information [are] two separate domains of existence, which have to be discussed separately in their own terms. The gene is a package of information, not an object. . . . Maintaining this distinction between the medium and the message is absolutely indispensable to clarity of thought about evolution.[18]

John Maynard Smith says: "Heredity is about the transmission, not of matter or energy, but of information. . . . The concept of information is central both to genetics and evolution theory."[19] The most spectacular thing about planet Earth, says Dawkins, is this "information explosion," even more remarkable than a supernova among the stars.[20] And, adds, Klaus Dose,

> More than 30 years of experimentation on the origin of life in the fields of chemical and molecular evolution have led to a better perception of the immensity of the problem of the origin of life on Earth rather than its solution. . . . We do not actually know where the genetic information of all living cells originates.[21]

When sodium and chlorine are brought together under suitable circumstances, anywhere in the universe, the result will be salt. This capacity is inlaid into the atomic properties; the reaction occurs spontaneously. Energy inputs may be required for some of these results, but no information input is needed. When nitrogen, carbon, and hydrogen are brought together under suitable circumstances anywhere in the universe, with energy input, the spontaneous result may be amino acids, but it is not hemoglobin molecules or lemurs—not spontaneously. The essential characteristic of a biological molecule, contrasted with a merely physicochemical molecule, is that it contains vital information. Its conformation is functional. With the typical protein, enzyme, lipid, or carbohydrate this is structural, keyed by the coding in DNA. The coding here is information about coping in the macroscopic world that the organism inhabits. The information (in DNA) is interlocked with an information producer-processor (the organism) that can transcribe, incarnate, metabolize, and reproduce it. All such information once upon a time did not exist but came into place; this is the locus of creativity.

Nevertheless, on Earth, there is this result during evolutionary history. The result involves significant achievements in cybernetic creativity, essentially incremental gains in information that have been conserved and elaborated over evolutionary history. The know-how, so to speak, to make salt is already in the sodium and chlorine, but the know-how to make hemoglobin molecules and lemurs is not secretly coded in the carbon, hydrogen, and nitrogen. Life is a local countercurrent to entropy, an energetic fight uphill in a world that typically moves thermodynamically downhill (despite some negentropic eddies, and despite irreversible thermodynamics). Thermodynamics need be nowhere violated, because there is a steady "downhill" flow of energy, as energy is irradiated onto Earth from the sun, and, eventually, reradiated into space.

But some of this energy comes to pump a long route uphill. This is something like an old-fashioned hydraulic ram, where the main downstream flow is used to pump a domestic water supply a hundred yards uphill through a pipe to a farmhouse—except of course that the ram pump is deliberately engineered and the "life pump" spontaneously assembled itself as an open cybernetic system several thousand times more complex and several billion years long. Life is a river that runs uphill, and even if it nowhere runs uphill very steeply (if we look at its incremental assembly bit by bit), the river as a whole runs far uphill, and each living creature in the stream is quite highly ordered. Some forces are present, some force, some Force! that sucks order in superseding steps out of disorder. Organisms must be constructed along a long negentropic pathway. This requires the continual introduction of information not previously present.

The central dogma of molecular and evolutionary biology is that random variations are introduced into the replication of this information, that rarely such variations prove beneficial in the sense that they improve performance with the result that more offspring are produced, and that such variations in result increase proportionately in the gene pool. The classical view emphasizes that such variations occur at random and without regard to the needs of the organisms. Contemporary genetics is increasingly inclined to interpret this process as a kind of information search using random variations in problem solving and to see the search space as more constrained by the prior achievements of the organism; nevertheless the random element remains prominent. Here is where possibilities lie and where actual novelties are generated out of such possibilities.

John Maynard Smith and Eörs Szathmáry analyze "the major transitions in evolution" with the resulting complexity, asking "how and why this complexity has increased in the course of evolution." "Our thesis is that the increase has depended on a small number of major transitions in the way in which genetic information is transmitted between generations." Critical innovations have included the origin of the genetic code itself, the origin of eukaryotes from prokaryotes, meiotic sex, multicellular life, animal societies, and language, especially human language. But, contrary to de Duve, Eigen, Calvin, Kauffman, or Cech, they find "no reason to regard the unique transitions as the inevitable result of some general law"; to the contrary, these events might not have happened at all.[22] So what makes the critical difference in evolutionary history is increase in the information possibility space, which is not something inherent in the precursor materials, nor in the evolutionary system, nor something for which biology has an evident explanation, although these events, when they happen, are retrospectively interpretable in biological categories. The biological explanation is modestly incomplete, recognizing the importance of the genesis of new information channels.

The philosophical, metaphysical, and theological challenge, left over after the current scientific accounts, is the query what is the most adequate account of the origin of these information channels and the genetic information thereby discovered. In the course of evolutionary history, one would be disturbed to find matter or energy spontaneously created, but here is information floating in from nowhere. For the lack of better explanations, the usual turn here is simply to conclude that nature is self-organizing (autopoiesis), though, since no "self" is present, this is better termed spontaneously organizing. An autopoietic process can be just a name, like "soporific" tendencies, used to label the mysterious genesis of more out of less, a seemingly scientific name that is really a sort of mystic chant over a miraculously fertile universe.

What is inadequately recognized in the "self-organizing" accounts is that, though no new matter or energy is needed for such spontaneous organization, new information is needed in enormous amounts and that one cannot just let this information float in from nowhere. Over evolutionary history, something is going on "over the heads" of any and all of the local, individual organisms. More comes from less, again and again. A more plausible explanation is that, complementing the self-organizing, there is a Ground of Information, or an Ambience of Information, otherwise known as God.

THE GENESIS OF VALUE

Another way of interpreting this genesis of information arises from looking at its result: the generation, transmission, and deepening of values. Scientists and philosophers have been much exercised about the generation of values, about how an *ought* comes out of an *is*, but it seems pretty much fact of the matter that, over evolutionary history, values have been generated, startling though this may also be. "Survival value" figures large in evolutionary theory. Something is always dying, and something is always living on. For all the struggle, violence, and transition, there is abiding value. The question is not whether Earth is a well-designed paradise for all its inhabitants, nor whether it was a former paradise from which humans were anciently expelled. The question is whether it is a place of significant value achievement.

Scientists have sometimes tried to portray nature as a valueless place, and that can seem so in the emptiness of outer space, or the frozen wastes of Antarctica, or the sands of the Sahara. But where there is life, value is always at stake. Once humans might have thought that even biological nature is valueless, with value lighting up as, and only as, humans take an interest in what is going on. But such anthropocentrism has become increasingly incredible in Darwin's century. The same evolutionary science that discovered nature red in tooth and claw discovered the value in teeth and claws, the vitality flowing in the blood, the world as a sphere of the contest of values, generated in this perpetual contest. These biological scientists and their evolutionary and ecological sciences are a witness to the genesis of values, in the biodiversity they describe and wish to protect, in the insights into human origins and possibilities they seek to gain, in the morality they urge, at the same time that their theory is incompetent to warrant, support, or appraise such values.

Evaluating Earth, the appropriate category is not *moral* goodness, for there are no moral agents in nature; the appropriate category is some one or more kinds of *nonmoral* goodness, better called its *value*, its worth. One must evaluate phenomena such as the achievement of diversity and complexity out of simplicity; the discovery of sentience, cognition, experience; the mixture of order and contingency, of autonomy and interdependence. This epic of vital ascent is the rare expression point, on Earth, of a peculiar power in cosmic nature. Something divine is embodied (incarnate) in the story. Any struggle and suffering can only be interpreted in the context of such creativity.

According to a long dominant paradigm, there is no value without an experiencing valuer, just as there are no thoughts without a thinker, no percepts without a perceiver, no deeds without a doer, no targets without an aimer. Valuing is felt preferring by human choosers. Possibly, extending this paradigm, sentient animals may also value, using their teeth and claws, or maybe even plants can value as they, nonconsciously, defend their lives with thorns and propagate their kind with seeds. But, in an evolutionary account, the value story becomes systemic, more holistic, ecological, global. Earth is a value-generating system, value-genic, valuable, value-able, that is, able to generate values that are widely "distributed," "dispersed," "allocated," "proliferated," "divided," "multiplied," "transmitted," "recycled," and "shared" over the face of the Earth.

It is true that humans are the only evaluators who can reflect about what is going on at this global scale, who can evaluate what has happened in natural and cultural history, who can deliberate about what they ought to do conserving these events. When humans do this, they must set up the scales, and humans are the measurers of things. Animals, organisms, species, ecosystems. Earth cannot teach us how to do this evaluating. But they can display what it is that is to be valued and evaluated. The axiological scales we construct do not constitute the value, any more than the scientific scales we erect create what we thereby measure.

Humans are not so much lighting up value in a merely potentially valuable world as they are psychologically joining ongoing planetary natural history in which there is value wherever there is positive creativity. Although such creativity can be present in subjects with their interests and preferences, it can also be present objectively in living organisms with their lives defended, and in species that defend an identity over time, and in systems that are self-organizing and that project storied achievements. The valuing subject in an otherwise valueless world is an insufficient premise for the experienced conclusions of those who value natural history. Conversion to an evolutionary and ecological view seems truer to world experience, more logically compelling, better informed.

From this more objective viewpoint, there is something subjective, something philosophically naive, and even something hazardous in a time of ecological crisis, for humans to continue to live (as in an age of science they have often done) as though nature were valueless and everything previously generated in natural history were only to be evaluated relative to its potential to produce benefit for humans. When Earth's most complex product, *Homo sapiens*, becomes intelligent enough to reflect over this earthy wonderland, everyone is left stuttering about the mixtures of accident and necessity out of which we have evolved. But nobody has much doubt that this is, recalling the way that the astronauts phrased it, "a small pearl in a thick sea of black mystery" (Mitchell), "to be treasured and nurtured, something precious that *must* endure" (Collins. . . .). Almost as if to dispute Wilson's claim that nothing Earth-bound can be transcendent, Mitchell adds, "My view of our planet was a glimpse of divinity."[23]

Those are astronauts, not biologists, but what they see is the home planet, the living planet in all its startling possibilities, of which evolutionary history is the most indisputable evidence. We have earlier heard Edward Wilson celebrating that biodiversity, finding it in its own way "miraculous,"[24] and urging its conservation, even when he could find no such divinity. Here again is the fertility, which generates religion. Earth is dirt, all dirt, but we find revealed what dirt can do when it is self-organizing under suitable conditions with water and solar illumination. We will not be valuing Earth objectively until we appreciate this marvelous natural history.

Life persists because it is provided for in the ecological Earth system. Earth is a kind of providing ground, where the life epic is lived on in the midst of its perpetual perishing, life arriving and struggling through to something higher. One may think, as we near a conclusion, that biology produces many doubts; here are two more: I doubt whether one can take biology seriously, the long epic of life on Earth, the prolific fecundity that surrounds us on this planet, without a respect for life, and the line between respect for life and reverence for life is one that I doubt that you can always recognize. If anything at all on Earth is sacred, it must be this enthralling generativity that characterizes our home planet. "The world is sacred." That is the conclusion of even so resolute a naturalist as Daniel Dennett, which not even Darwin's "universal acid" can dissolve, dissolve God though this acid can.[25] So the secular—this present, empirical epoch, this phenomenal world, studied by science—does not eliminate the sacred after all; to the contrary, the secular evolves into the sacred. If there is any holy ground, any land of promise, this promising Earth is it.

But then why not say that here, if anywhere, is the brooding Spirit of God? One needs an adequate explanation for generating the sacred out of the secular. Indeed, why not even go on to say that this genesis of value is the genesis of grace, since the root idea in "grace" (Latin: *gratia*) is pleasing, favorable, praiseworthy; essentially, again, the idea of something valuable, now also a given. In this genesis, nature is a sequence of gifts; we are given what has "sprung forth" and find that, in this springing forth, values are created. Whatever else has happened, there has been the genesis of values; each of us is a remarkable instance of that.

"The essence of religion," said Harald Höffding, "consists in the conviction that value will be preserved."[26] That helps us to understand Mayr's remark that most biologists are religious. If one finds a world in which value is given and persists over time, one has a religious assignment. A central function of religion is the conservation of value, and value generated and conserved is the first fact of natural history, as well as the principal task of culture. Frederick Ferré defines religion, "One's religion . . . [as] one's way of valuing most intensively and most comprehensively."[27] At the metaphysical level, science neither describes nor evaluates the genesis of value adequately, although the descriptions of biological science—those of evolutionary history eventuating in cultural history—present an account that demands evaluating, intensively and comprehensively. Religion is about the finding, creating, saving, redeeming of such persisting sacred value in the world. In this sense, whatever the quarrels between religion and biology, there is nothing ungodly about a world in which values persist in the midst of their perpetual perishing. That is as near as Earthlings can come to an ultimate concern; such benefit, such "blessing," is where, on Earth, the Ultimate might be incarnate.

DETECTING THE TRANSCENDENT

The universe existed for ten or fifteen billion years without any biological information present, so far as we know. The divine presence in that epoch will need to be found in the setup, in the fine-tuned universe, or, along the way, in, with, and under the physics, astrophysics, and chemistry. Such presence continues during the biological epoch on Earth. But now the creativity is more notably that generating the information vital to life. Again, one can appeal to the set-up. In our corner of the universe, the interplay of matter and energy accumulated into a solar system with one lucky planet. Perhaps there are other such planets; we do not know whether they are common or rare. But at least there is this one.

Located at a felicitous distance from the sun. Earth has liquid water; atmosphere; a suitable mix of elements, compounds, minerals; and an ample supply of energy. Radioactivity deep within the Earth produces enough heat to keep its crust constantly mobile in counteraction with erosional forces, and the interplay of such forces generates and regenerates landscapes and seas—mountains, canyons, rivers, plains, islands, volcanoes, estuaries, continental shelves. Geochemistry is as relevant as chemistry. The properties of the elements—hydrogen, carbon, and so on—are necessary but not sufficient. The properties of the Earth system, a kind of cooking pot, are also necessary, and, together with the physicochemical properties, perhaps these are sufficient to make life probable, even inevitable.

Detecting the transcendent asks whether God underlies that setup. God lies in, with, and under the forces that created Earth as the home (the ecosystem) that could produce all those myriads of kinds. God, the Ground of the Universe, is also the Good Fortune of the Planet. "Let the earth bring forth living creatures according to their kinds" (Genesis 1.24). The Earth-system does prove to be prolife; the story goes from zero to five million species in five billion years, passing through perhaps five billion species that have come and gone en route. The setup, first on cosmological levels and later on planetary levels, mixes chance and order in creative ways. If, once, there was a primitive planetary environment in which the formation of living things had a high probability, for such living things to become actual would require not so much interference by a supernatural agency as the recognition of a marvelous endowment of matter with a propensity toward life. So the molecular biologists were earlier arguing. Such a natural performance could be congenially seen, at a deeper level, as the divine creativity.

But one still has to give an account of the information appearing ex nihilo, that is, where no such information was present before. One may indeed need a fortunate endowment of matter with a life propensity (helped perhaps by the anthropic principle in astrophysics) and at the same time still need something to superintend the possibilities during evolutionary history. That there are complementary explanations does not always mean that one is superfluous. Here one can posit God as a countercurrent to entropy, a sort of biogravity that lures life upward. God would not do anything in particular but be the background, autopoietic force energizing all the particulars. The particulars would be the discoveries of the autonomous individuals. God would be the lift-up (more than the setup) that elevates the creatures along their paths of cybernetic and storied achievement. God introduces new possibility spaces all along the way. What theologians once termed an established order of creation is rather an order that dynamically creates, an order for creating.

One should posit, says Daniel Dennett, "cranes," not "skyhooks," for the building up of evolutionary history.[28] That contrast of metaphor seems initially persuasive, appealing to causes more natural than supernatural, more immanent than transcendent. When we pinpoint the issue, however—what account to give of this remarkable negentropic, cybernetic self-organizing that characterizes the life story on Earth—the metaphor becomes more pejoratively rhetorical than analytically penetrating. There is the repeated discovery of information how to redirect the downhill flow of energy upward for the construction of ever more advanced, higher forms of life, built on and supported by the lower forms. Up and down are rather local conditions (down, up a few miles); it does not matter much which direction we imagine this help as coming from—east or west, from the right or left, from below or above, high or deep, immanence or transcendence, skyhooks or cranes. The Hebrew metaphor was that one needs "wind" as well as "dirt." The current metaphor is that one needs "information" as well as "matter" and "energy."

Stripped of the rhetoric, what the "skyhook" metaphor means, Dennett says, is explanations that are more "mindlike," and the "cranes" metaphor posits "mindless, motiveless mechanicity." Dennett holds that Darwinian science, extrapolated philosophically, has discovered cranes upon cranes "all the way down" and building up and up with "creative genius." "There is simply no denying the breathtaking brilliance of the designs to be found in nature."[29] But if the secret of such creativity is information possibilities opening up and information searched and gained, then the kind of explanation needed can as plausibly be said to be mind-like as mindless mechanicity.

One might look to the potential deep in matter, "cranes all the way down." There is a kind of bottomless bootstrapping, as if lifting oneself up and up by one's own bootstraps were not remarkable, matter lofting itself up into mind. Such cranes, piling up higher and higher, are still pretty "super," quite imposing with their endless superimposing of one achievement on another. One can just as well look to some destiny toward which such matter is animated and inspired (skyhooks). Even after an infinite regress of cranes, or a regress ending in nothing at all, or in informationless matter-energy, or in a big bang, one might not find that explanations are over. The issue is where the information comes from by which matter and energy become so superimposingly informed across evolutionary history that this brilliant, "sacred" (Dennett) output arises from a beginning in mindless chaos; how "out of next to nothing the world we know and love created itself."[30]

In this "world of propensities," concludes Karl Popper, the "inherently creative" process with its "staggering" biodiversity is neither mechanistic nor deterministic. "This was a process in which both *accidents* and *preferences*, preferences of the organisms for certain possibilities, were mixed: the organisms were in search of a better world. Here the preferred possibilities were, indeed, allurements."[31] Cranes or skyhooks, evolutionary development is "attracted to" (in the current "chaos" metaphor) cumulating achievements in both diversity and complexity, and this attraction needs explanation. Attractors, or, at a more metaphysical level, even an Attractor, seem quite rational explanations.[32]

Returning to the metaphor of the alphabet and Shakespeare, the question is whether, in the introduction of these possibilities, one needs an author as well as an alphabet. What is required to get *Hamlet* is a great deal of information input into the letters. Perhaps the alphabet-author analogy is flawed. That analogy places all the creativity in the author working with an inert alphabet. One needs rather to posit a self-organizing alphabet, and a maker to start up and sustain such a self-organizing alphabet. Still, the elemental materials are not evidently an alphabet from the beginning; they have to be taken over for alphabetic functions. Some story has to be generated with these materials-become-alphabet. That requires information input into such alphabetic materials, or, if not "input," information generation in some way or other. The skeptic will protest that there is no need for an author at all. One can have law without lawgivers, history without historians, creativity without creators, information without an informer, and stories without storytellers.

Change the analogy: the elements are more like "seeds" than "letters." The root meaning of "nature" is "generating," and nature has all these possibilities "seeded" into it. The problem with such a model is that we now know what is in seeds as the secret of their possibilities—information—and there is no such information inside amino acids, much less hydrogen and carbon atoms, much less electrons and protons. The creation of matter, energy, law, history, stories, of all the information that generates nature, to say nothing of culture, does need an adequate explanation: some sources, source, or Source competent for such creativity. Seeds need a source. In the materializing of the quantum states, bubbling up from below; in the compositions of prebiotic molecules; in the genetic mutations, there are selective principles at work, as well as stabilities and regularities, forming and in-forming these materials, which principles order and order up the story.

This portrays a loose teleology, a soft concept of creation, one that permits genuine, though not ultimate, integrity and autonomy in the creatures. We have in the life adventure an interaction phenomenon, where a prolife principle is overseeing the affairs of matter. The divine spirit is the giver of life, pervasively present over the millennia. God is the atmosphere of possibilities, the metaphysical environment in, with, and under first the natural and later also the cultural environment, luring the Earthen histories upslope. God orchestrates such self-organizing, steadily elevating the possibilities, making for storied achievements, enriching the values generated.

God could sometimes also be in the details. The general picture is not one of divine micromanagement; rather of secular integrity and creaturely self-organizing. The extent to which divine inspiration enters into particulars might be difficult to know, especially if God operated with the resolve to maximize the creaturely autonomy, to prompt rather than to command. Dennett concedes, for example, that no Martian biologists, examining "a laying hen, a Pekingese dog, a barn swallow, and a cheetah," could prove, simply from an examination of the organisms, that the former were the product of deliberate, engineered artificial selection, as well as of natural selection, and the latter were the product of natural selection only. "If the engineers chose to conceal their interventions as best they could . . . there may be no foolproof marks of natural (as opposed to artificial) selection."[33]

If there has been divine selection, this will not be detectable as any gap in or perforation of the natural order; it might be detectable in the resulting genesis, or creativity. If the roulette wheels at Las Vegas spin at random most of the time, but once a year God loaded the dice, that would be difficult to detect. Chance is an effective mask for the divine action. Still, God could be slipping information into the world. One might suspect such divine presence if the resulting story, in the lotteries of natural history, produced the epic adventures that have in fact actually managed to happen. An "information explosion" on our Earth, rare in the universe, might be a clue that "inspiration" is taking place.

Perhaps it is a mistake to look for God in the particulars of information discovery. God does not intervene as a causal force in the world, not at least of such kind as science can detect. "God" is not among the entries to be found in the index of a biology text. God perennially underlies the causal forces in the world, and God gives meaning to the world, which science is incompetent to evaluate. That does require the introduction of channels for information, and information in those channels, which arrives in the particulars of genetic trial and error. Such information is not a mere cause, not in any physicochemical sense, but a novel "cause" that puts meanings into events, that generates all the richness of evolutionary history.

God is an explanatory dimension[34] for which contemporary biology leaves ample space, as we have seen as biologists stutter over the origins of the information that generates complexity and diversity, over any selection for progress, over what to make of randomness, over the introduction of possibilities. If one adds the desire of a Creator not so much to conceal such complementing selective activity as to optimize the integrity, autonomy, and self-creativity of the creatures—letting them do their thing, generating and testing, discarding what does not work and keeping what does—with divine coaching on occasion, then a conclusion that there is a divine presence underneath natural history becomes as plausible as that there is not. The question becomes not so much a matter of conclusive proof as of warranted faith.

There once was a causal chain that led to vertebrae in animals, where there were none before, an incremental chain no doubt, but still a chain by which the novelty of the vertebral column was introduced on Earth. Such a chain is constructed with the emergence of more and more information; this information, coded in DNA, informs the matter and energy so as to build the vertebral cord. The cord is constructed because it has a value (a significance, here a precursor of meaning) to the organism. It makes possible the diverse species of life that the vertebrate animals defend. Continuing the development of the endoskeleton, it makes possible larger animals with mobility, flexibility, integrated neural control. When such construction of valuable biodiversity has gone on for millennia, the epic suggests mysterious powers that signal the divine presence.

The question, the biologists will say, is of the selective forces. Yes, but the answer comes, partly at least, from seeing the results, with ever more emerging from what is earlier less and less. One seeking to detect the divine inspiration will notice how there are occasions—seasons, contexts, events, episodes, whatever they are called—during which critical information emerges in the world, breakthroughs, as it were, incremental and cumulative though these can also be. This will be true in culture, perhaps the inspiration that underlies the Ten Commandments or the Sermon on the Mount. It can as well be true in nature, in some inspiration that first animates matter and energy into life; or launches replication and genetic coding, or eukaryotes, or multicellular life, or sexuality; or energizes life with mitochondria and chloroplasts, or glycolysis and the citric acid cycle; or moves life onto land; or invents animal societies or acquired learning; or endows life with mind; and inspires culture, ethics, religion, science.

The skeptic's reply is always to emphasize that evolution is not elegant. It is wasteful, blundering, struggling. Evolution works with what is at hand and makes something new out of it. The creatures stumble around, and if there is a God who "intervenes," God ought to do better than that. There is only a "blind watchmaker."[35] Still, consider again the remarkable results, and the providence appropriate to a God who celebrates an Earth history, who inspires self-creativity. The word "design" nowhere occurs in Genesis,[36] though the concept of creativity pervades the opening chapters. There is divine fiat, divine doing, but the mode is an empowering permission that places productive autonomy in the creation. It is not that there is no "watchmaker"; there is no "watch." Looking for one frames the problem the wrong way. There are species well adapted for problem solving, ever more informed in their self-actualizing. The watchmaker metaphor seems blind to the problem that here needs to be solved: that informationless matter-energy is a splendid information maker. Biologists cannot deny this creativity; indeed, better than anyone else biologists know that Earth has brought forth the natural kinds, prolifically, exuberantly over the millennia, and that enormous amounts of information are required to do this.

The achievements of evolution do not have to be optimal to be valuable, and if a reason that they are not optimal is that they had to be reached historically along story lines, then we rejoice in this richer creativity. History plus value as storied achievement in creatures with their own integrity is better than optimum value without history, autonomy, or adventure in superbly designed marionettes. That is beauty and elegance of a more sophisticated form, as in the fauna and flora of an ancient forest. The elegance of the thirty-two crystal classes is not to be confused with the grace of life renewed in the midst of its perpetual perishing, generating diversity and complexity, repeatedly struggling through to something higher, a response to the brooding winds of the Spirit moving over the face of these Earthen waters.

NOTES

1. Edward O. Wilson, *On Human Nature* (Cambridge, MA: Harvard University Press, 1978), 2–3.

2. Edward O. Wilson, "Comparative Social Theory," vol. 1 of *The Tanner Lectures on Human Values, 1980,* ed. Sterling M. McMurrin (Salt Lake City: University of Utah Press, 1980), 70.

3. Wilson, *On Human Nature,* 201.

4. Christian de Duve, *Vital Dust: Life as a Cosmic Imperative* (New York: Basic Books, 1995), xv–xvi and xviii.

5. George Wald, "Fitness in the Universe: Choices and Necessities," in *Cosmochemical Evolution and the Origins of Life*, ed. J. Oró et al (Dordrecht, Netherlands: D. Reidel, 1974), 9.

6. Melvin Calvin, "Chemical Evolution," *American Scientist* 63 (1975): 176 and 169.

7. Manfred Eigen, "Selforganization of Matter and the Evolution of Biological Macromolecules," *Interdisciplinary Science Reviews* 13 (1971): 519 and Manfred Eigen, *Steps Towards Life: A Perspective on Evolution,* with Ruthild Winkler-Oswatitsch (New York: Oxford University Press, 1992).

8. Stuart A. Kauffman, *The Origins of Order: Self-Organization and Selection in Evolution* (New York: Oxford University Press, 1993), xvi.

9. Against the caution of Alfred North Whitehead, *Process and Reality,* corrected edition (New York: Free Press, 1929, 1978), 46.

10. Karl R. Popper, *A World of Propensities* (Bristol, UK: Thoemmes, 1990), 17–20.

11. Ibid., 26, 19.

12. Thomas R. Cech, "The Origins of Life and the Value of Life," in *Biology, Ethics, and the Origins of Life,* ed. Holmes Rolston III (Boston: Jones and Bartlett, 1995), 33.

13. "My frame was not hidden from thee, when I was being made in secret, intricately wrought in the depths of the earth. Thy eyes beheld my unformed substance" (Psalm 139:15–16).

14. Estimated from data in James M. Orten and Otto. W. Neuhaus, 1982. *Human Biochemistry,* 10th ed. (St. Louis: C. V. Mosby, 1982), 8 and 154.

15. Norbert Wiener, *Cybernetics* (New York: John Wiley, 1948), 155.

16. Eigen, *Steps Towards Life,* 12, 15.

17. Bernd-Olaf Küpper, *Information and the Origin of Life* (Cambridge, MA: MIT Press, 1990), 170.

18. Quoted in John Brockman, *The Third Culture* (New York: Simon and Schuster, 1995), 43.

19. John Maynard Smith, "Life at the Edge of Chaos?" *New York Review of Books* 52, no. 4 (March 2, 1995): 28.

20. Richard Dawkins, *River Out of Eden: A Darwinian View of Life* (New York: Basic Books, 1995), 145.

21. Klause Dose, "The Origins of Life: More Questions Than Answers," *Interdisciplinary Science Reviews* 13 (1988): 348.

22. John Maynard Smith and Eörs Szathmáry, *The Major Transitions in Evolution* (New York: W. H. Freemand, 1995), 3.

23. Kevin W. Kelley, ed., *The Home Planet* (Reading, MA: Addison-Wesley, 1988), photograph 52.

24. "The flower in the crannied wall—it *is* a miracle." In Edward O. Wilson, *The Diversity of Life* (Cambridge, MA: The Belknap Press of Harvard University Press, 1992), 345.

25. Daniel C. Dennett, *Darwin's Dangerous Idea* (New York: Simon and Schuster, 1995), 520–21.

26. Harald Höffding, *The Philosophy of Religion* (London: Macmillan and Co., 1906), 14.

27. Frederick Ferré, *Basic Moden Philosophy of Religion* (New York: Charles Scribner's Sons, 1967), 82.

28. Dennett, *Darwin's Dangerous Idea*, 73–80.

29. Ibid., 74, 76, 155.

30. Ibid., 185.

31. Popper, *A World of Propensities,* 26, 20.

32. "To me the most fascinating property of the process of evolution is its uncanny capacity to mirror some properties of the human mind (the intelligent Artificer) while being bereft of others." (Daniel C. Dennett, *The Intentional Stance* [Cambridge, MA: MIT Press, 1987], 299). It seems important to Dennett that the design is a mirage. Or, more accurately, the design isn't a mirage, for there is a designing system, but that there is a Designer of the designing system is a mirage. One needs no supernature, and the evidence for this is that we can plunge into subnature, and subsubnature, and subsubsubnature, simplifying all the way down until there is nothing at all. Although creativity is forbidden from above, it is welcomed from below. But set aside the above-below imagery, still the "attraction" to something out of chaos, the "genesis" of something out of nothing, of more out of less— such brute fact remains as evident as ever, and as demanding of explanation.

33. Dennett, *The Intentional Stance,* 284–85.

34. A cause in the Aristotelian, though not the scientific sense.

SCIENCE AND REASON, REASON AND FAITH

A Kantian Perspective

ALFRED I. TAUBER

REASON IN DISPUTE

During the week before Christmas, Judge John E. Jones III, sitting in the Federal Middle District of Pennsylvania, ruled against teaching a new form of creationism in the public high school. The case arose from a suit brought by parents against the Dover school board, which, in 2004 had instructed teachers to read a short statement about the inconclusive status of neo-Darwinian evolution theory and suggest that Intelligent Design might be entertained as an alternative explanation. After a long trial that delved into the nature of scientific theory and the questions of what constituted scientific knowledge, the judge ruled Intelligent Design was a ploy to bring religion into the classroom and accused certain board members of duplicity. Judge Jones only confirmed what the voters had already accomplished by throwing the errant board members back to church.

Alfred I. Tauber, "Science and Reason, Reason and Faith: A Kantian Perspective," The Herbert H. Reynolds Lecture in the History and Philosophy of Science, Baylor University, Waco, TX, February 21, 2006.

The country was riveted on the courtroom drama, some comparing it to Scopes circus of 1925, when Clarence Darrow confronted William Jennings Bryan in the famous Tennessee "monkey trial." The 1960 movie, *Inherit the Wind*, so well enacted by Spencer Tracy and Fredric March, captured my own imagination as a youngster, and then, as now, I was fascinated with the arguments about God's presence or absence in nature. I can well understand how religionists regard nature with awe, and to find coherence, and perhaps more importantly, meaning, in the cosmos, they cannot abide placing their God outside His handiwork. If He is present in their daily lives, why should He be omitted from designing the greatest of creations, human intelligence? After all, the Bible describes how Adam was made in the image of God. Accordingly, His intelligence, like our own, must have some engineering capability dwarfing even our wildest conceptions. True believers maintain that orthodox scientists are blind to a deeper Reason, because they have yet to see His fingers at work. So what looked to Darwin and his followers as only a contingent, blind evolutionary process, is, in fact, only understandable as an act of deliberate design.

The Dover case took on a special luster during the summer of 2005, when in *The New York Times*, Cardinal Schönborn wrote a controversial op-ed piece. He claimed that he was protecting "rationality" against an ideological science:

> The Catholic Church, while leaving to science many details about the history of life on earth, proclaims that by the light of reason the human intellect can readily and clearly discern purpose and design in the natural world, including the world of living things.
>
> Evolution in the sense of common ancestry might be true, but evolution in neo-Darwinian sense—an unguided, unplanned process of random variation and natural selection—is not. Any system of thought that denies or seeks to explain away the overwhelming evidence for design in biology is ideology, not science. . . . Now at the beginning of the 21st century, faced with scientific claims like neo-Darwinism and the multiverse hypothesis in cosmology invented to avoid the overwhelming evidence for purpose and design found in modern science, the Catholic Church will again defend human reason by proclaiming that the imminent design evident in nature is real. Scientific theories that try to explain away the appearance of design as the result of "chance and necessity" are not scientific at all, but as John Paul put it, an abdication of human intelligence.[1]

The slippage is evident: Schönborn propels his metaphysical reason, that which supports God's cosmological purpose, into the epistemological domain, where the preponderant scientific interpretation sees no design (and, incidentally, makes no comment about God's presence or absence). In other words, theological reason is conflated with scientific reason, and the boundaries are trespassed as if there were no difference. The Kantian lesson (discussed in detail below)—how reason must make way for faith—is simply ignored. Rather than provide divine presence and teleology with its own reason, the Cardinal insists on projecting his faith into the natural world. In short, because his reasoned theology (as in the Church's persecution of Galileo) apparently could not accommodate neo-Darwinian blind evolution, Schönborn must dispute dominant scientific opinion. Given his first allegiance to his own religious tenets he had no other option.

What I am calling "slippage" is a result of these competing metaphysics, and here we come face to face with the challenge in its starkest terms: Schönborn's metaphysics demands divine intervention; science embraces a naturalism whose metaphysics are defined independently of teleology. Reason is simply the tool used by each to support its respective agenda. Unfortunately, "reason" is used by like-minded theologians as some kind of universal solvent for dissolving problems without acknowledging that it is not reason that is in dispute, but rather the metaphysics in which reason functions. The question of whether Intelligent Design might take its place in the scientific menu does not strike me as particularly interesting at this point.[2] We have witnessed endless and convincing rebuttal, but what intrigues me, and the question upon which I will focus, concerns the character of reason. Both sides claim a rational discourse, and, indeed, intelligent people espouse Intelligent Design, but given the presuppositions of each system, the conclusions of the respective positions are irreconcilable. Argument is stultified, because pre-suppositions are, as R. G. Collingwood described them, the suppositions that are closed to further analysis or revision.[3] They are the bedrock of the conceptual apparatus they support. Start with different presuppositions and logical progression will bring the disputants to very different ends. More to the point, scientific method, specifically its notions of objectivity coupled to empiricism, has asserted its own program at the expense of other modes of knowing. Indeed, scientific facts are not at issue, but rather their interpretation, so that we should recognize the instrumentality of reason: Science may be used by anyone; its technology applied for diverse social pursuits; its knowledge perhaps designed for one purpose, applied to another; its findings interpreted to support one metaphysics, or another.[4]

And now we come to the heart of the matter. The Intelligent Design case exemplifies not only how science is in tension with different worldviews, but more deeply how the metaphysics in which science functions as an instrument of inquiry is in conflict with others. The drama is not about science per se, but about the metaphysics in which science functions. The classic examples are the religious disputes arising from Galileo's astronomical findings and Darwin's theory of common descent. In each instance, a religious orthodoxy disputed the science. Galileo's case has been settled, but Darwin's still lingers, not in the particulars of evolutionary findings, but as in the case of the Cardinal, the meaning of those findings.[5] When the fossil record is placed within a fundamentalist reading of the Bible, a "meta-theory" has supplanted the scientific one. And the irony of our age is not that science cannot trump fundamentalist arguments, but rather that the wondrous picture science presents may be translated into religious terms and effectively employed against those who supported and developed the system for very different ends.[6] We will not settle the matter by argument, rational or otherwise. The best we can do is support the liberalism which allows communities with different belief systems to thrive next to each other. To that end I will direct my comments.

Since science's understanding of the universe and our place in it, may or may not include a divine presence, God is beside the matter. If one wishes to impose a secondary layer of divine interpretation upon those findings, fine, but do not conflate two ways of knowing. Each has its place, and therein, its authority. This is my theme.

THE PROBLEM

Neo-Darwinism's non-teleological, materialistic view may be interpreted as denying major assertions of Christian theology, and much else. Indeed, each form of materialistic theory—from evolution to the origin of the universe, from the heart's beating to the brain's functions—rests on a denial of design, and consequently, a displacement of a master divinity. More than just rejecting religious doctrine, neo-Darwinism asserts its own metaphysical picture in contrast to it: a stark, materialistic universe with no *telos*. Such a view leaves humans the chore of defining significance and meaning within a human construct. I believe that challenge lies at the base of the conflict between secularism and religious ideology. In a sense, Nietzsche's challenge ("God is dead!") remains an abiding unresolved question: Can, or even should, Man define his cosmos? Beyond naturalistic explanation, can the values which govern society be truly based upon, or even derived from, human deliberation? Can we successfully assert our own significance? Can we meaningfully exist without divine revelation and live in a world navigated and created by human intentions and will?

These questions have rested at the heart of the secular enterprise throughout modernity. Indeed, they largely define the humanistic project, and when liberal society is confronted by such expressions of discontent as the Dover case, we are reminded that for a vast proportion of Americans, the world science presents cannot provide meaning that satisfies their existential needs. Indeed, they are correct. I readily admit that science requires some "framing"—aesthetic, spiritual, moral—to integrate its worldview with human experience. The fundamentalists aspire to integrate a scientific picture—evolution—with deeply held religious commitments. I also seek seamless connections between a materialistic universe governed by laws that have no personal enchantment and the various dimensions of my subjectivity. So I share with the fundamentalists a humane aspiration to understand my own identity—psychologically, sociologically, spiritually, and so on—as my identity is refracted from different perspectives. In short, all of us seek some kind of "placement." The difference between fundamentalists and me is that they have a scheme, revealed and doctrinaire, and I do not, at least not as a dogma. Instead, I firmly reside within a humanist tradition that attempts to provide responses to these existential questions within the framework of "Man as the final measure."

On this view, science not only provides the basis for technological advances, but answers to its deepest commitments of exploring nature as a response to our metaphysical wonder. In this, science and religion are closely aligned, but quickly separate, not so much because of reason, but rather as a result of differing metaphysical presuppositions.[7] In contrast to a cosmos revealed by revelation, science was born as natural philosophy, and thus committed to a vast program of empirical *discovery*. Indeed, science as a branch of philosophy still adheres to the humanist tradition, and despite deep tensions, their broader agenda of promoting liberal inquiry must bring them again into close proximity. From this vantage, the science-humanist alliance, melded in philosophy, must be seen again as a key bulwark of modernity and its liberal program.

The tack taken here is guided by a sighting of reason; the winds are coming from starboard; we require a steady compass to hold our course. I suggest we find our bearings by looking back to the port from which we embarked. That safe harbor is the Enlightenment. From there, we must chart our present predicament. So let us begin with a review of some history.

THE CALL OF THE ENLIGHTENMENT

What is Enlightenment? Kant's famous answer, *"Enlightenment is mankind's exit from its self-incurred immaturity"* or as he further extolled, "Have the courage to use your *own* understanding. . . ."[8] The essay goes on to celebrate the virtues of an independent mind, guided by rationality, moral forthrightness, and above all, a vision of personal freedom, which captures these moral and epistemological virtues of the *philosophes*. This is only a partial answer and we will have occasion to visit this conceptual question again, but for now, let me ask a simpler historical question: What is *the* Enlightenment? That, also, turns out not to be a trivial question, as I learned about fifteen years ago, long before I attained my present level of alarm. I was presenting a report to a group of physicians, and dropped the phrase, "the Enlightenment," probably as a dangling participle to no good effect. In any case, the chief medical officer, a man in his mid-40s at the time (that is, a man about my own age), South African (and thus possessing an accent that smacked of erudition), and a rather general haughty air about him (no doubt from the authority of his position), stopped me by asking, "What is *the* Enlightenment?" I paused, not sure of his intention, but soon discerned that he was genuinely perplexed from a state of utter ignorance. At that moment, there in the boardroom of the big city hospital, I realized that we were in trouble, deep trouble. Shortly thereafter I initiated my career shift into philosophy, where despite encountering a universe of different kinds of problems, at least my colleagues knew such turn of phrases as "the Enlightenment" and could respond with a kindly nod or a disapproving frown. They knew how we are the products of that cultural moment, and how those values developed and continue to guide liberalism and the specific endeavor we call education.

I have often contemplated how I might have answered my physician inquisitor. Instead of sputtering some incoherent mumblings, I wish I could have quickly listed the key components of *the* Enlightenment: celebration of an unfettered reason; the relentless questioning of authority and doctrine; the promotion of individuality and free-choice; the centrality of selfhood and moral agency; the confidence in progress; the sanctity of secularism. In short, these precepts, refracted into the worlds of politics, law, social mores, and perhaps most evidently in theology, marked modernity's coming of age. Science played a singular role in promoting this enterprise and, in turn, was indebted to it. I would have explained that the clinical science that he practices is a product of a new way of thinking, born during the "Century of Genius"[9] as an expression of a form of rationality that had become a tool for open-ended inquiry. Indeed, I would have emphasized the open-ended character of truth-seeking; the agnosticism about the divinity; and, not least, the fallibility of knowledge.

Modern science in many ways exemplifies the Age of Reason; specifically I am referring to its program of truth-seeking. Somewhat chastened by the postmodern critique of any final Truth, I still believe we make an important distinction between an understanding of reason that serves a predetermined goal (for instance one defined by religious faith that is constrained *a priori* by presuppositions deemed immune in advance to questioning), as opposed to the use of enlightened reason that is open-ended. Inquiry in this latter formulation has no *telos* other than the inquiry itself. In this sense, scientific knowledge is neutral; the process of study is putatively immune to bias and prejudice (at least in its theoretical prime state); fallibilism is assumed; objectivity is sought. I will be making the case that this view of epistemic accomplishment is fundamental to liberal thought and that this characteristic binds science firmly to the humanities. Each share the same critical values, and, in many respects, the same methods of analysis and tireless questioning of the fruits of their respective studies. That alliance may be directed towards secular ends, but not necessarily so.

Returning to my doctor colleague, I would have explained that his ignorance was symptomatic (a word he would undoubtedly have understood and would hopefully peek his interest) of the troubled status of this humanist-science alliance. Let us briefly review that recent history.

SCIENCE AND REASON'S DIVISION

Almost half a century ago, the growing separation between science and the humanities prompted C. P. Snow to describe academic culture as comprised of "Two Cultures."[10] He described mutual illiteracy, which prevented scien-

tists and humanists from engaging each other across the boundaries separating their respective disciplines. Because of its success and its independence of the larger philosophical context from which it emerged, science was
regarded as an unruly adolescent: full of itself; brimming with confidence
and even arrogance; overflowing with its power and promise. As Wilfred
Sellers noted (writing as a philosopher):

> The scientific picture of the world *replaces* the common-sense picture . . .
> the scientific account of "what there is" *supersedes* the descriptive ontology
> of everyday life. . . . [I]n the dimension of describing and explaining the
> world, science is the measure of all things, of what is that it is, and of what
> is not that it is not.[11]

Here, "common-place" is a placeholder for all those modes of knowing
eclipsed by the triumph of science's worldview.

Humanists feared an imbalance in two domains. The first was intellectual: Scientism was viewed as imperialistic, assuming to apply its methods
and logic in arenas where, because of its authority, caution is required.
Humanists were suspicious of claims that are by their very nature fallible and
which history has repeatedly demonstrated are infected by pernicious cultural determinants. A particularly invasive scientific philosophy, positivism,
asserted a rigid factuality to what constituted knowledge, and that standard
as applied to the human sciences,[12] would de-value other hermeneutical
forms of inquiry. Thus, as a purely intellectual conflict, most scientists and
humanists found themselves on different sides of the demarcation lines outlined by the positivist program.

The second domain of controversy arose from the political and social
consequences of the first. Despite the achievements of science, humanists
rightly feared the imbalanced influence of the science "lobby," whose
authority rested on the economic bounty indebted to scientific advances. The
Two Culture divide was consequently also an expression of how science,
largely as a result of its material success, increasingly dominated public
policy decisions and education resources. The social apparatus that supported the scientific enterprise ranged from the educational reform stimu-
lated by the Sputnik challenge to scientific industries promoting their vested
interests. Beyond the technology sold to the domestic West, these were
prominently energized by, what Eisenhower menacingly described, a
"military-industrial complex," which prominently displayed its products in

Vietnam and later in Iraq. Many were troubled by the danger of misplaced applications (like nuclear power) and, even more, a kind of political arrogance, which seemed to accompany the power of unbridled technology. These matters, while germane, are not our subject. Here, suffice it to note that by the end of the 1950s, science education dominated other forms of knowing, so that a gentle species of scientism seeped into the schools educating new generations of citizens.

Ironically, coincident with Snow's critique, the original cultural divide began to mend in an unpredictable way, only to be broken again along different fault lines. Bridged by inter-disciplinary studies of science, where philosophers, historians, and sociologists pursued an ambitious program to characterize the laboratory as an intellectual and cultural activity, science no longer was allowed to perform insulated from outside scrutiny. Indeed, science was wrenched back from its isolated status, and the Two Cultures were melded back to one, with a vengeance. The sacrosanct status of scientific rationality and claims to orderly progress was challenged by Thomas Kuhn's *Structure of Scientific Revolutions*,[13] which closely followed Michael Polanyi's exploration of a more comprehensive appreciation of scientific thinking than that offered by positivist philosophies of science. Indeed, Polanyi's *Personal Knowledge*[14] (1958, 1962) marks the beginning of a new movement to study science in a broadened humanistic context, which employed analytic tools quite alien to the then current "internal" approaches espoused by Rudolf Carnap and other logical positivists.

To place these developments in their historical context, I present a review of the original alliance of humanists and scientists, how they separated, and why a renewed effort to hold their common ground is incumbent on both. We begin with Kant, who responded to the eighteenth-century challenge of understanding the legitimate claims of science, moral discourse, and religion in the face of rapidly changing notions of the divine and its place in a secular, liberal society. Revelation had been displaced by a critical stance oriented by new standards of what is factual and what is not; what is knowledge and what is opinion; what is objective and what is subjective. He specifically sought to define reason in its various guises so that the pursuit of knowledge and the faith of belief might proceed on their respective courses, confident that neither would conflict with the other. This project articulated the Enlightenment's highest ideals.

We must also review some key historical features that highlight the parting of science from the humanities—very broadly and very briefly—and then I will return to explore the circumstances of a new alliance, now based on those who would still embrace the original Enlightenment values characterizing modernity. I am following the tradition initiated by Kant and then developed by Whitehead, Husserl, and Gadamer, each of whom, despite the radical differences of their respective philosophies, profoundly understood that the bifurcation of reason bestowed a conundrum that could only be addressed by a synthesis of science and its supporting philosophical critique.[15] Here, we will ponder in various ways how, reason must "be its own pupil"[16] and thus remain loyal to its own "character." I will first review some key historical features that highlight the parting of science from the humanities—very broadly and very briefly—and then I will return to explore the circumstances of their continued alliance.

THE FRACTURED ALLIANCE

I. History

"Natural philosophy" became "science" in the mid-nineteenth century, when practitioners, both natural and social scientists, distinguished their own technical and professional route from the more general concerns of humanists. The break was, however, already evident at the end of the eighteenth century, when both poets and physicists recognized a seeming chasm opening between them. Goethe, perceiving this division, sought a reunification of "science" and "poetry" in the realm of aesthetics.[17] This strategy proved futile. In the same period, Kant conceptualized the split by dividing human cognition into what he called "pure" and "practical" reason. "Pure" reason referred to the cognitive functions that humans apply to the natural world, and "practical" reason dealt with the moral realm (social or humanistic concerns). Kant's formulation provided a model by which science and religion might co-exist secure in their respective domains (discussed further below). To do so, a new lexicon was required to distinguish practitioners of one sort from the other.

The term "scientist" was coined by a British scientist and philosopher of science, William Whewell (1794–1866). In 1840, writing in the Introduction of his *Philosophy of the Inductive Sciences*, Whewell commented, "We need very much a name to describe a cultivator of science in general. I should incline to call him a *Scientist*."[18] What strikes me as noteworthy is not this definition, but the late date of its birth. After all, the word "science" is ancient. The

Latin *scientia* means "knowledge" as opposed to *sapientia*, wisdom. In other words, *scientia* is knowledge of, or cognition about, the world, as opposed to the more self-reflexive domain of wisdom. And, *sciens*, "knowing," originally meant "to separate one thing from another, to distinguish," which also points to analysis of a particular kind. Certainly this etymology closely adheres to what we broadly understand to be what science seeks.

In short, the word, "science," has an ancient etymology, but the word, "scientist," is distinctly modern. Indeed, Charles Darwin, who wrote during the same period as Whewell, referred to himself as a "natural philosopher." Darwin was very careful with his language and as a gentleman he had good reason to prefer the older designation. The term "philosophical" was not explicitly defined, but generally stood for an approach to the study of the natural world, which included the search for laws in biology, a dissatisfaction with teleological arguments, a certain speculative or intuitive attitude in method (especially rampant amongst the *Naturphilosophen*) and idealist approach.[19] In addition, "scientist" was too easily associated with commercial overtones of technical applications and thus the designation carried a pejorative connotation of someone who was inclined to look for the economic benefits of discoveries, in contrast to the pristine search for knowledge. Not until the end of the 19th century could the term scientist assume its current neutrality.

I mention all of this to make a simple point: Until the mid-nineteenth century, science was a category of philosophy. The examination of the natural world was part of what philosophers did. Only as the methods of scientific inquiry became increasingly technical and a new professionalism took hold in its various disciplines, did a scientist emerge as someone different from a philosopher. If one examines the Western intellectual world as late as the 1850s, the educated classes were comfortably conversant with the latest scientific findings, and many pursued, what we would call amateur science.[20] Chemistry and physics began to separate a bit earlier, but certainly natural history remained the province of a wide audience. And I am not referring to its popular mode: I mean specifically that gentlemen would go to natural history meetings well into the 1850s and 1860s without any professional encumbrances to their full participation. In short, until about 150 years ago, most scientists and most philosophers shared the same intellectual bed.

2. Methodological Separation

Advances in scientific techniques and methods of study required specialization. The techniques developed in the nineteenthcentury reflected a growing sophistication, both in terms of material investigations, as well as the mathematics supporting them. The field of 'biology' was invented as its own discipline in the first decade of the nineteenthcentury and by the 1820s, Claude Bernard and other physiologists were reducing organic processes to physics and chemistry. Concurrently, physics and chemistry were employing new mathematics, primarily statistical in nature, which by the 1870s created statistical mechanics and all that it spawned. In short, focused attention to the rapid growth of technical knowledge became a pre-requirement for active participation, and this demanded specialized training. Eventually this professional narrowing led to academic and professional segregation. By the 1870s, science was divided into various natural and social sciences, each of which assumed a high degree of technical competence and cognitive training.[21]

The fruits of that labor resulted in new industries derived from scientific findings and their successful application to material culture. Since the Renaissance, science has been sold as a package deal: Invest in scientific inquiry and the discoveries will be converted into economic, military, and social power. Indeed, the investment has been true to its promise, and few could dispute that the triumphs of technology are inseparably linked to the success of the underlying science. But I wish to note that technology is *not* science; the two are distinct. Technology builds on scientific insight, and much else, while science is based in another domain: Science seeks to discover the character of nature and is thus part of natural philosophy. On this view, technology is the *application* of knowledge for material innovation, while science underlies such engineering. It is the difference between second order and first order pursuits. But with the close identification of science and technology this distinction is often blurred. I mention it here to emphasize that science has been too often associated with its product as opposed to its deeper commitments to philosophical inquiry, albeit of a special kind.

More importantly, the intellectual discipline of each domain drifted apart. The hermeneutical methods used in the humanities, writ large, have their own standing. But the interpretations applied to human creativity are not suitable for the study of nature under the present scientific paradigm. The object of investigation determines different approaches and different truth criteria. Those who would separate science and the humanities would do so primarily on this difference. Indeed, these methodological differences are rooted in a deeper philosophical divergence.

3. Philosophical Divide

During the Enlightenment, those who pondered the nature of knowledge were struck by a growing separation of investigative methods employed by those who studied the natural world, on one hand, and those who commented on the social, spiritual, and psychological domains, on the other. Distinctions between opinion and knowledge, always a central concern of philosophy in one form or another, by the mid-eighteenthcentury had reached a critical crisis. David Hume, the great Scottish skeptic, drew these distinctions with particular sharpness. He presented Kant with the challenge of refuting a skepticism that placed in doubt the reality of the natural world, or at least the ability to know that world objectively. The place of reason, the role of emotions, the intuitions of the spiritual domain, and the ability to understand human psychology each required a model of the mind that would account for their respective claims to these particular forms of knowledge. On what basis could, for example, knowledge of the natural world or the moral universe be conceived as legitimate and well-grounded?

Kant began by offering a schema of the mind that made the natural world intelligible, and thus susceptible to scientific investigation. He conceptualized that to know the natural world and the moral domain required two different kinds of human cognition. He called these, respectively, "pure" and "practical" reason. "Pure" reason referred to the cognitive functions that humans apply to the natural world. Such knowledge is derived from appearances?the cognitive product or the *phenomenon* that we perceive. The *noumenon*, the thing-in-itself we cannot know, and thus our ontology is of a "second-order." Kant was satisfied: "What the things may be in themselves I do not know, and also do not need to know. . . ."[22] In contrast, 'practical' reason dealt with the moral realm, that is, with social or humanistic concerns. In other words, Kant thought that humans possess one faculty for knowing the material world, best exemplified by scientific inquiry; and he held that a second universe, the moral- spiritual-personal, was, in terms of the first form of understanding, unknowable. People might believe in the freedom of the will, the immortality of the soul, and God, but the means by which humans might *know* such metaphysical claims was not discernable by the same means humans knew the natural world. As Kant acknowledged:

"Thus I had to deny *knowledge* in order to make room for *faith*."[23] Faith refers to metaphysics, by which Kant meant the possibility of going beyond the science of appearances to address moral pursuits. Thus one kind of knowledge was differentiated from the other, and in fact, the argument followed a strong Christian tradition: "Faith is the assurance of things hoped for, the conviction of things not seen."[24]

The consequence of this division was, from Kant's perspective, a way to save Belief. But what he in fact did (for those so inclined) was to legitimatize one way of knowing as "real" and the other as "less real." In short, science could claim a special legitimacy, albeit the Kantian transcendental claims were immediately attacked[25] and the philosophical basis of Kant's theory of science led to unresolved debate.[26] Science thereby asserted its own agenda with more confidence, and some would say with arrogance. Any commitment to this configuration of reason still required that some balance be sought between what Kant called the reason of the empirical domain and the reason of the moral. Specifically, where does scientific inquiry end and other modes of knowing take over? For instance, the hermeneutical disciplines, those that interpret, as opposed to analyze, employ a legitimate countervailing method of knowing. From this perspective, only an interpretative stance makes any sense when assessing a work of art or determining the emotional meaning of behavior. Systems of justice, cultural practices, and the meaning of behaviors cannot be reduced to strict objective inquiry (the standards simply do not exist), but rather rest on different kinds of assessment and interpretation. And when religious knowledge makes its claims, on what basis might a scientific attitude allow for the spiritual?

These questions will not rest and, indeed, they frame the basic issues regarding the place of science in our pluralistic society. The general point, and the one to which I will return, is simply that when science is viewed circumspectly it becomes only one of several modes of inquiry, albeit with its particular strengths, but also with its limitations. The line separating objectivity from subjectivity is highly dynamic, historically contingent, and continuously contested. Despite the obvious importance of making these distinctions, the history of science is marked by the controversy of defining those margins. Indeed, from a philosophical point of view, this is a key component of science's epistemological mission.

Kant's warnings not to trespass into a realm best left to others were naïve. Analytically, we can separate the epistemological and metaphysical concerns of a philosophy of nature, but as modern science developed its distinctive epistemology, a new metaphysics also emerged. Indeed, it is disingenuous to insist that science has no metaphysics: As a branch of philosophy it has first principles, pre-suppositions, which dwell in the deep reaches of its conceptual structure. I call this aspect of science's metaphysics its "logical" structure and it includes such precepts as 1) the world is ordered; 2) we might discern this order by detached empirical observation, neutral rational description and objective analysis; 3) laws will emerge from this inquiry and they remain inviolable; 4) why nature corresponds to our human mathematical and objective descriptions is mysterious, but the empirical product of that method has been highly successful and thus approximates a depiction of the real as truth, and so on. Indeed, the technical product of this methodological logic, and the power of its predictability points to a new mastery of nature shared by all.

A second dimension of science's metaphysics concerns the abiding questions that direct its inquiry. Within its ontological domain, science embraced the basic questions ancient philosophers had inherited from even more ancient myth and religion: What is the world? How is it organized? Where does Man fit into that universe? What is distinctly human? Science presented cogent answers in its distinctive voice in terms decidedly non-metaphysical. Yet, while the terms of engagement had been radically altered and the ontological voice muted, the original metaphysical inquiry remained embedded (but hardly dormant) in the scientific enterprise. Given that the metaphysical questions remained, it is not surprising that the results science offered were construed as alternatives to traditional religious beliefs. Indeed, by the mid-nineteenth century, Whewell could assert with arrogant confidence, "Man is the interpreter of Nature, Science the right interpretation."[27]

Into our own era, competing metaphysical positions have provoked conservative theologians to accommodate themselves to science's claims, when the integration of empirical study did not clearly coincide with the rational constructions of their dogmas. Discontent with a scientific worldview that had relinquished divine guidance, left fundamentalists resenting the scientist's independence (or better, insularity). In the United States this independence of religion led stalwart promoters of secularism (like the Robert Ingersoll and Cornell's founding president, Andrew Dickson White[28] to denounce religion as an offense against science. Darwin's prescient early journal musings (July 1, 1838) soon became commonplace sentiments: "Origin of man now proved.—Metaphysic must flourish.—He who understands baboon <will> would do more toward metaphysics than Locke."[29]

The answers science provided were hardly neutral, inasmuch as the secularists regarded investigative findings with one set of lenses, while the religionists peered through another. In short, the borders were violated by both parties as they sought to bolster their own programs. Theoretically, a strictly neutral science would posture itself towards neither camp, but given its historical and cultural affinity with the humanist tradition, science became a powerful instrument of secularization. Moreover, since neutrality was never a viable option, science found itself caught in the cross fire of an ideological war that has been waged for over five centuries. And no wonder, for no less than The Truth was at stake.

BINDING THE SCIENCES TO THE HUMANITIES

The project of protecting liberal education requires the alignment of science with its humanistic origins, or what I am calling, science's deeper philosophical project. "Humanism," (like the word "scientist") was coined in the nineteenthcentury to apply to the re-discovery of the classical tradition in the medieval period. Humanists were originally concerned with a general education, which spans the classics to modern science. But humanists accorded particular importance to the liberal agenda: freedom of thought, tolerance, revision and correction of opinion, open communication, and a self-critical attitude. These underlying values tie together the central concerns of the humanities and science into a powerful alliance. In fact, one could argue that these values captured much of philosophy's pride and business. Accordingly, the scientific worldview could make its claims based on a long history of coupling its particular concerns to this much larger agenda.

Today the humanities are the direct heir of the original humanistic disciplines, and science seems far distant from those origins. But recall that science also originated as a contributing member of the humanistic faculty, and on this broad view, science is part of a larger historical development of humanistic thought. Although we are usually struck by how science followed a naturalistic philosophy, even its empiricism is based on a rationality that had deep roots in philosophy. Through ruthless self-criticism, the frame of reference is always in doubt; the historical record reveals fallibility; the place of objective knowledge as opposed to subjective opinion is tested and contested. And when opinion is held, it is open to revision through free argument.

These are the deepest values of science and the underlying philosophy guiding its methods and defining its aims. Science is sustained, indeed instantiated, by a self-critical philosophy, tested against the investigations of nature. Nature devoid of human value and human caprices demanded stark answers to starkly posed questions. In short, although science and humanities pursue different objects of inquiry, they support each other in common purpose and the same philosophical self-critical attitude. And beyond this kinship we find other aspects that link them.

Subordinate the difference of science's object of study, the natural world, as well as differing methodologies (the empirical basis of scientific investigations), and we are left with an essentialist core: Science, like the humanities, is a human-centered focus of inquiry—"human-centered" in two senses.

First, the standards of discourse are human-derived (as opposed to divinely inspired). Revelation has been displaced by a critical stance oriented by new standards of what is factual and what is not. What is knowledge and what is opinion? What is objective and what is subjective? The second component refers to knowledge directed at developing human industry. "Industry" does not refer here to material culture, but rather the more general understanding of industry as the systematic labor to create value. The study of nature is deeply committed to a personal comprehension of the world, a picture of reality that offers insight, and thereby an orientation, of Man in Nature.

Scientific findings alone are insufficient for determining significance, and thus interpretation is required.[30] Commentators from Goethe to Whewell to Michael Polanyi have understood that raw knowledge, a fact, is essentially meaningless.[31] What is the significance of a scientific fact or larger theory unless it may be applied to human understanding? "Understanding" entails many layers of interpretation, and here the linkage to the humanistic disciplines becomes most evident. Science influences its supporting culture, the values that govern its use, and ultimately the sense of meaning and significance ascribed to the scientific portrait of the world. Polanyi called this final step "personal knowledge" when he wrote about the same time as Thomas Kuhn about the limits of positivism. Both recognized, as did an entire generation following them, that scientific knowledge was ultimately human-centered in the sense discussed here. On this broad view, science is part of a larger historical development of humanism, and finds itself, ultimately, in its service.

Certain conclusions beckon: First, the 'package deal' of *doing* science and *placing* science within its intellectual and social contexts argues that science and its study as a human activity cannot be separated. This interdisciplinary effort arises, because the boundaries of science cannot be circumscribed to the laboratory or technical discourse.[32] The findings seep into applications, which affect our material culture, medicine, the military, and virtually all aspects of our society. Only an educated public can make appropriate use of the fruits of scientific labor, thus a close coordination between scientists and lay public is required to reap the greatest harvest from the investment made in research. The University mediates that discussion.

Second, the critique of science is essential to its flourishing. Science gains its place at the table precisely because of its power to define a competing worldview. The "naturalization" of man, from the evolution of species to the biological character of the mental testifies to how successfully scientific explanations have been translated into potent theories of Man and Society. (For instance, how much of human behavior is determined by the genetic dimension? Why should we preserve natural resources? When does a fetus become an individual? Can vaccines be developed to prevent AIDS? To what use should nuclear energy be applied? And on, endlessly.) Notwithstanding the effective penetration of scientific theory into notions about the nature of our social and psychological existence, a careful scrutiny is required to apply the conceptual lessons appropriately. Closely linked to that application, the converse operation is also necessary, namely a critical view of the truth claims made by scientists. With these critiques, philosophy and history of science find their most pressing calling.

Perhaps not surprisingly, as science assumed its new independent standing, the disciplines of history and philosophy of science matured. They filled a gaping hole. After all, as Thomas Kuhn noted 40 years ago, scientists were not interested in their own histories, much less the philosophy undergirding their discipline.[33] In turn, the humanists lamented the scarcity of meaningful dialogue between themselves and their scientific colleagues. The sociologies of each group had radically diverged. But beyond this professional separation, the respective mode of discourse seemed foreign to the other and thus cross-fertilization had become increasingly barren.

The mission of the humanistic disciplines to critique science, interpret its development, and assist efforts made from within the scientific establishment in its own self-critical evaluations seem to warrant historians and philosophers the status of bona fide adjuncts in science faculties. And more, the ability to translate scientific discoveries and theories into wider conceptual and social contexts, where their significance might be more fully appreciated, also requires an intimacy between the laboratory scientist and her humanist commentator. After all, science is only one system of investigation within that larger arena of human study of nature, man and society. As such it has proven to be a crucial means of discovering our world and characterizing our relationship to it. But like any mode of philosophical study, it is subject to criticism, and in that critique, scientific method itself is scrutinized and thereby improved. One might even say that self-critical scientists are themselves engaged in the philosophical project of "natural philosophy" by carefully examining their methods and truth claims. This essentially philosophical self-criticism is probably the most fundamental characteristic of science *and* philosophy as generally construed.

Third, beyond the material fruits of scientific labor, the most profound effect is science's worldview, or, as Heidegger[34] noted, that there *is* a worldview at all! The theories and methods that have demonstrated the worlds of molecular biology, tectonic plates, quantum mechanics, and so on, have markedly altered how we conceive the world in which we live and our relation to it. Further, the human sciences, for better and for worse, have bestowed their own theories on human character and conduct. Taking their lead from Goethe and Schiller, philosophers as diverse as Heidegger and Whitehead, Weber and Foucault, have repeatedly shown how science has effectively competed with earlier metaphysical systems, and thus has provided views of a reality replete with novel challenges for defining meaning and significance to human existence.

The crisis created by the ascendancy of a scientific material universe was aptly summarized by Schiller: "How are we to restore the unity of human nature . . ." in a disenchanted world?[35] Viewed from the secular perspective, science joined other cultural forces to offer alternative definitions of human identity and Man's relationship to the larger universe—cultural, natural, and supernatural. Of course, science's worldview is not necessarily incompatible with a divine presence, but protecting free inquiry and open interpretation remains a challenge that can only be successfully accomplished by the strong alliance of those committed to the larger liberal agenda.

AN UNHOLY ALLIANCE

Until fairly recently, investigating the natural world was of one piece with the rest of philosophy. Natural philosophy, that part of philosophy which focused on nature, was easily integrated with the other concerns. This fundamental kinship remains. What haschanged are the sociologies of science and the humanities, and the technical virtuosity of the modern scientist. But the intellectual drive is the same. At the foundations that set their respective agendas, scientists and humanists share the same set of basic values to govern their pursuits and their respective logics: a *telos* of inquiry that has no *telos*—the inquiry is done for itself. For those who wish to impose their own theological teleology on human knowledge, this position is unacceptable. Secularism is the object of dissension. And beneath that religious conflict, liberalism rests on the altar for sacrifice, a liberalism which advocates tolerance for each point of view.

Basically, science is agnostic about religious claims. It makes no attempt to address God, or to listen to Him. Whether the divine exists or not is simply not at issue, for science has no means to explore that dimension. Further, existence is mysterious enough to make room for both knowledge *and* belief. But science's neutrality is intolerable, to *both* secularists and religionists, and therein is the rub. Because the secularists were better able to employ science for their own ends, science was guilty by association in the eyes of the true believers. And, indeed, if science must choose, it has little choice but to move with the secularists, who make no theological demands on its truth claims.

Secularization signals God's retreat from the everyday world of common experience and activities, and also refers to a major realignment of social hierarchies and the rationale for new political structures. Science partook in this social revolution in at least three ways: 1) the technology based on scientific discoveries revolutionized the material culture, revealing mysterious forces and events as natural and thereby open to human understanding; 2) this naturalized world view placed divine intervention increasingly peripheral to human understanding; and 3) the logic and standards of knowledge as applied to the natural world were extended to the social and psychological domains of human experience, thereby rationalizing a redistribution of power and authority from monarchial and ecclesiastical centers to liberal institutions. These developments placed God under a new lens of inquiry, and as God's place in the universe shifted, so did Man's.

The power of science's discourse rests in its powerful epistemology. The empiricist measures his rational discourse against a natural object that "speaks" back to him in a public voice. Objectivity thus attains a new standing as communal witnessing has effectively replaced private inspiration and insight. Here we see the convergence of other cultural forces that combined in the rise of secularism: the re-alignment of authority; the autonomy of the individual; the claims for individuality; the rise of free agency. (And of course, strong arguments have been made as to how post-Reformation Protestantism also contributed to rise of modern scientific epistemology.)[36] Scientists embraced these new cultural values and enthusiastically declared that a more rigorous objectivity had replaced folk psychology, superstition, and other intimacies of the heart with a different logic and a different understanding of the world. And in this context, human nature also became increasingly naturalized at the expense of an older religious metaphysics. Scientific knowledge thus displaced *opinion* in every realm of *knowledge*.[37]

Instead of aligning science to the secularist project, the more judicious adopted an agnostic metaphysical orientation: Following Kant, science may allow a divine presence, but only one consistent with the best scientific interpretations. In short, various forms of *knowledge* must be differentiated from *beliefs*. Kant's formulation provided a model by which science and religion might co-exist secure in their respective domains. What we can know is one set of experiences, and what we feel, intuit, or opine is a set of different kinds of assertions. To know the difference and to keep them separate is the foundation of a liberal society. God may come and go as He likes, but Man must govern himself by human-derived standards and modes of knowledge that in our era reflect a certain kind of rationality. Kant thus alerted the natural philosopher not to probe into areas in which scientific method had no ready access. He thus left a domain for belief that would originate in different human faculties of thought and emotion. He profoundly understood that science would not ask for, and thus would not offer, a basis for religious belief, one way or the other. Science erected a neutral picture that tilts one way with God, and another without Him. But which way the cosmos tilts is dependent on individual choice. That pluralistic option threatened those who could not claim the same kinds of certainty science exhibited employing a different kind of rationality and a different basis for objective judgment.

Unfortunately, Kant's suggestion has had only mixed success, because the growing hegemony of a non-revealed worldview continues to be intolerable to those who steadfastly champion their particular religious beliefs. If science was regarded simply as a tool for technological advancement, the debate would have been quelled, but all understood that much more was at stake than material gain.

Belief falls into the domain of personal choice; knowledge is what we agree is universally accessible. Following Kant, we call such knowledge "objective" and we attain it by a form of reason fashioned by certain epistemological criteria. These may change, indeed, they do, but revelation is not one of them. Socrates specifically opposed reasoning directed to confirming revelation and opinion. By endless interrogation, he drove his interlocutors to face their complacent assumptions and lazy beliefs. He thus established the basic demand of philosophical inquiry. Fallibilism is the lynch pin of the entire enterprise, for the body of knowledge is assumed to be incomplete, if not in error.[38]

> [A]ny thinking . . . is under a standing obligation to reflect about and criticize the standards by which, at any time, it takes itself to be governed. . . . [This] is implicit in the very idea of a shaping of the intellect. . . . This does not mean that such reflection cannot be radical. One can find oneself called on to jettison parts of one's inherited ways of thinking; and [that the] weaknesses that reflection discloses . . . can dictate the formation of new concepts and conceptions. But the essential thing is that one can reflect only from the midst of the way of thinking one is reflecting about.[39]

The perfectionism of endless critique provides the scientist with the basic value of inquiry, a value which binds science to its philosophical antecedents. Doubt and skepticism remain the cardinal virtues of scientific theory as well as underlying its various modes of proof.

Derived from this self-critical foundation, science developed values that seek to legitimate interpretation by parsimony, coherence, and predictive capacities. And success is assessed by rationality oriented by criticism:

> Entertaining a doubt adds up to little more than applying a question mark, or raising one's eyebrows; serious criticism, by contrast, requires fashioning an argument. To doubt is to suspect something might be amiss, to criticize is to *argue* that it is. Skeptical discourse requires a supply of interrogatives, critical discourse requires rich background knowledge and a developed logic of problem-seeking and solving. Criticism necessarily presupposes doubt, but is also a necessary prerequisite for positive action. In the face of suspected imperfection the first step toward improvement will always be critical. Hence the term "constructive skepticism."[40]

Rationality on this view becomes a category of action, a means to expose and solve problems, and how inquiry might gauge its success or failure is determined by a larger set of goals, and thus rationality assumes an instrumental quality.

This understanding of rationality might be equally applied to religious argument and scientific dispute, but the key difference is the object of inquiry: The theologian probes the human heart and soul; the scientist explores the natural world. The difference is telling: The values by which science defines nature have evolved during the modern period to attain a powerful means to separate human prejudice and belief from an objective account. Kant established this crucial distinction by disallowing "pure reason" to impose its own categories upon the metaphysical universe, thus "saving" belief from the tyranny of science's power. By segregating religious insight from knowledge, he made room for belief. This lesson is a key precept of the liberal agenda, by leaving different kinds of rationality to explore distinctive domains.

Again we see the deep affinity of science and the humanities: Both must promote pluralism to protect free inquiry and critical analysis freed of doctrine. But with the vast social and intellectual forces that bestowed a unique mode of inquiry (and the rewards of technological success), science seemed to forget its humanistic origins. That amnesia has dire consequences given the new challenges of a postmodern era, where reason, in certain quarters, has been redefined by standards inimical to scientific ideals. Sharing a common ancestry, science and the humanistic disciplines are rivals and at the same time locked into the same "family," a family that has particular goals and characteristics.

I believe that in order to understand the current attacks on science, we best understand the character of scientific inquiry within its larger context and defend it on the basis of its crucial role as a liberal institution, one that instantiates our highest ideals of unfettered inquiry. Science, more than other intellectual activities, has provided us with those standards. It is time for humanists of all stripes to train their collective sights on the real enemy. Whether their protection of liberalism, intellectual freedom and pluralism will be steadfast and successful represents the crucial test in these days so painfully marked by the fundamentalist assaults of the Taliban and Cardinal Schönborn.

CONCLUSION

So in the end, how should we regard the religionists' project? Two attitudes beckon, one which is conciliatory, the other which is not. Let us begin with the latter, which is largely political, political in the broadest sense of the term. Like most Americans, I have become preoccupied with thinking about the fate of democracy since 9/11; about terrorism and torture; about our military exploits and conservative domestic politics; about stem cell research and creationism. From deeply blue Boston, I peer at the *New York Times* daily and conclude that it is hardly clear that the liberal program is thriving, or whether it can sustain assaults on its central role in democratic societies. Will the Enlightenment—with its commitment to the autonomy of reason— someday in the not-too-distant future be viewed as an anomalous event in world history? Can the values of tolerance, self-scrutiny and pluralism hold the ground against religious fundamentalism? In 1989, with the fall of the Berlin Wall, I doubt that many would have predicted the world in which we now live—a world full of ironies. Perhaps the view fromsome locations is more optimistic, but I can only share my own perspective that religious fundamentalism continues to haunt the liberal tradition, where pluralism protects free inquiry and critical analysis freed of doctrine. At stake is not only the standing of science in the American educational system, but the character of reason in a liberal society.

And on a more conciliatory note, I end by emphasizing that human reason apparently has a basic property, one demonstrated by myriad psychological and cognitive studies: Coherence of experience, coherence of belief, coherence of understanding seems to be a basic property of the human mind. Freud discovered numerous defense mechanisms to hold the psyche together; cognitive scientists have demonstrated the ability to screen out or forget data or experience conflicting with more dominant experience; and metaphysicians jealously guard their presuppositions to hold their world together. But as we gaze at the deep chasm of a materialistic universe, we do well to recognize that the metaphysical wonder that lies at the heart of the scientific query originates with the very same religious questions that evolved into philosophical ones, and then into the domain of science. In that evolution, the questions remained, but the answers became increasingly circumscribed, so that now science admits it cannot address the original query, at least not directly. Accepting its limits, science resides within its own metaphysical strictures, and we thereby acknowledge that the drive for coherence requires a different kind of understanding, one which acknowledges science's own domain. That challenge is to find a way of cohering a world that has no obvious coherence. I find no fruitful argument, nor productive debate. I simply accept a credo of our age: Many worlds comprise reality. May we engage each as best we can.

ACKNOWLEDGMENTS

I appreciate the invitation to deliver the 2006 Herbert H. Reynolds Lecture in the History and Philosophy of Science at Baylor University. This project helped to crystallize ideas that had been in suspension for some time, and the paper is part of a continuing dialogue with Menachem Fisch, whose work has inspired me to again re-visit the question of the relationship between science and religion in the context of debates about rationality and objectivity. Despite the differences we hold, I am much indebted to his delineation of these issues, and in dedicating this paper to him, I offer my sincere thanks for his constructive criticisms.

NOTES

1. *New York Times*, July 11, 2005.
2. The debate about the evolution of biological complexity has a long history (Michael Ruse, *Monad to Man: The Concept of Progress in Evolutionary Biology* [Cambridge, MA: Harvard University Press, 1996]), and a rich literature has recently developed on this question (Robert T. Pennock, ed., *Intelligent Design, Creationism, and Its Critics: Philosophical, Theological, and Scientific Perspectives* [Cambridge, MA: MIT Press, 2001]; Michael Ruse, *Darwin and Design: Does Evolution Have a Purpose?* [Cambridge, MA: Harvard University Press, 2003]; William A. Dembski and Michael Ruse, eds., *Debating Design: From Darwin to DNA* [Cambridge: Cambridge University Press, 2004]; for a succinct review, see George Nakhnikian, "It Ain't Necessarily So: An Essay Review of *Intelligent Design, Creationism, and Its Critics: Philosophical, Theological, and Scientific Perspectives*," *Philosophy of Science* 71 [2004], 593–604). In the spate of letters following Schönborn's editorial, Robert Cone succinctly noted that "natural selection may be unplanned, but it is not unguided. It is guided by need, whether for shelter, reproduction, food, safety, or other vital necessity." Indeed, in the course of random mutations, more complex options are offered and these may be chosen to accommodate the stresses of changing environments and competition among other species. On this view, biological diversity, initiating sometimes more complex, and at other times, more simple "solutions," have appeared. According to neo-Darwinism, "design" is an unnecessary element in explaining evolution. Complex structures evolve, according to this view, by a step-wise process, where structure A is used for one function and may then be used as the basis for the evolution to structure B that addresses a different function, and so on. In short, a complex biological structure

cannot appear de novo, but rather develops by myriad intermediate stages to appear as a complex entity.

3. R. G. Collingwood, *An Essay on Metaphysics* (Oxford: Clarendon Press, 1940).

4. Science's instrumentality has at least two dimensions: The first refers to how research is applied (perhaps, employed) to devise technologies. These might be put to constructive use (the usual case) or instead, employed as a tool for purposes quite at odds with the original intent of seeking knowledge for our social good. This instrumental quality of science (its technological power) holds one of its ironies: Instead of maintaining its original philosophical credentials, science, more precisely its technological progeny, too often has become so divorced from those earlier concerns that the basic research has become a tool that may be applied independently of the primary intent of the investigation. Co-opted by those whose own agenda has nothing to do with promoting the Western values that spawned science in the first place, we have painfully learned how powerful technologies may be used as an instrument of power for socio-political ends at odds with our own.

A second sense of instrumentality refers to science's intellectual activity, a mode of discovery and knowing, where the findings are used like a currency to buy different goods. The goods are findings or ideas, which are then placed into a conceptual context. The competing context may be differing scientific theories, but in this discussion, I am interested in religious contexts. For example, the sun assumes a certain meaning as conceptualized by a materialistic astrophysics, and a different one when regarded as Apollo racing across the heavens. The Greek myth has been eclipsed, but certain religious fundamentalists will contest the ontology of particle physics as "the cause" of the sun's birth, and instead refer to God's will and deliberate choice. Where the physicist will admit that knowledge reaches a limit, the true believer will push the universe's origins back into the divine act. The question at hand thus may be simply defined: Where does knowledge end and belief begin? That border has again become an active battlefield, for no less than the authority of knowledge is at stake. Simply, science without its supporting liberal, self-critical foundations becomes instrumental, solely a tool for technology, or, as a tool for ideologies, competing with liberalism.

5. The creationists pose a somewhat different kind of argument, not one that acquiesces to the scientific findings, but rather a dispute over the facts themselves. They have stubbornly opposed contemporary Darwinism by insisting that creationism is a bona fide theory of life and that the findings documented by evolutionists assume a different meaning in creationist theory. Students of this controversy have concluded, and I think fairly, that the argument cannot be won by evidence. (Elliott Sober, *Philosophy of Biology* [Boulder, CO: Westview Press, 1993]). The Darwinists point to mountains of molecular, paleontologic, and organismic data to

show blind evolution at work in the field and laboratory, as well as in the geological record. The creationists argue that God placed the history there by reason of His own wisdom; that evolution is directed and thus bestowed by God; that he created the world, or perhaps He continues to guide evolution, for His own purposes. Given the fundamentally different underlying presuppositions of each point of view, there is no meaningful debate.

6. Interpretation follows from a complex array of underlying suppositions and a tradition of supporting interpretations. For instance, in the nineteenth century those seeking a materialistic explanation of life to discredit vitalism measured heat production of contracting muscles to account for the energy exchange of muscle metabolism. Hermann Helmholtz, and others, could fully account for the biochemistry of this process to argue effectively against vitalist forces. That episode was in a long train of laboratory findings that followed a reductionist strategy to establish a materialistic science of life. It was part of a revolutionary *philosophical* program. (D. H. Galaty, "The Philosophical Basis for Mid-Nineteenth Century German Reductionism," *Journal of the History of Medicine and Allied Sciences* 29 [1974], 295–316; C. U. Moulines, "Hermann von Helmholtz: A Physiological Theory of Knowledge," in *Epistemological and Social Problems in the Early Nineteenth Century,* ed. H. N. Jahnke and M. Otte [Dordrecht, Netherlands: D. Reidel, 1981], 65–73.) Darwin's theory of evolution and Pasteur's microbiological demonstrations against spontaneous generation were battles fought in the same war. Needless to say, the vitalists held to a radically different philosophy of the organic, so their interpretations wildly differed. They simply argued that Helmholtz's experiments were still too insensitive to detect the vitalistic element. Indeed, vitalism, even in respectable scientific circles, would not fully expire until the turn of the century, and again, its demise was supported by a large intellectual project of support that brought not only biophysical findings to bear, but invoked a cultural environment accepting a nonvitalist interpretation. In our own era, science for the creationist, or for that matter anyone holding to a conflicting metaphysics, may use research findings as an instrument for support of their own agenda. (See note 4.)

7. For example, see J. Marcum, "Exploring the Rational Boundaries between the Natural Sciences and Christian Theology," *Theology and Science* 1 (2003): 203–20 and J. Marcum, "Metaphysical Foundations and Complementation of the Natural Sciences and Theology," *Journal of Interdisciplinary Studies* 17 (2005): 45–64.

8. Immanuel Kant, "What Is Enlightenment?" in *What Is Enlightenment?,* ed. James Schmidt (Berkeley: University of California Press, 1996).

9. Albert North Whitehead, *Science and the Modern World* (London: Macmillan, 1925).

10. C. P. Snow, *The Two Cultures* (Cambridge: Cambridge University Press, 1959).

11. Wilfred Sellers, *Empiricism and the Philosophy of the Mind* (Cambridge: Cambridge University Press, 1956, 1997), 82–83.

12. Auguste Comte, *The Positive Philosophy,* ed. Abraham S. Blumberg (New York: AMS Press, 1974).

13. Thomas Kuhn, *Structure of Scientific Revolutions* (Chicago: The University of Chicago Press, 1962).

14. Michael Polanyi, *Personal Knowledge: Towards a Post-Critical Philosophy*, corrected edition (1958, Chicago: University of Chicago Press, 1962).

15. H. Wein, "In Defense of the Humanism of Science: Kant and Whitehead" in *The Relevance of Whitehead*, ed. Ivor Leclerc (London: George Allen and Unwin, 1961); Whitehead, *Science and the Modern World*; Edmund Husserl, *The Crisis of European Sciences and Transcendental Phenomenology,* trans. David Carr (1932, Evanston, IL: Northwestern University Press, 1970); Hans-Georg Gadamer, *Reason in the Age of Science*, trans. Frederick G. Lawrence (1976, Cambridge, MA: MIT Press, 1981).

How science might require a philosophical self-consciousness is an old theme, and, at least for me, builds from Alfred North Whitehead's own commentary about the need for scientists to become more self-aware of their philosophical debts: "If science is not to degenerate into a medley of *ad hoc* hypotheses, it must become more philosophical and must enter upon a thorough criticism of its own foundations." (Whitehead, 24) I am not pursuing that agenda here except in the broadest sense, namely to remonstrate the place of science in the liberal university. Thus this essay might better be regarded as a contribution to the wider discipline of science studies.

16. Immanuel Kant, *Critique of Pure Reason,* trans. Paul Guyer and Allen W. Wood (1787, Cambridge: Cambridge University Press, 1998), 109.

17. A. I. Tauber, "Geothe's Philosophy of Science: Modern Resonances," *Perspectives in Biology and Medicine* 36 (1993): 244–57.

18. William Whewell, *Philosophy of the Inductive Sciences* (London: Macmillan, 1840), cxiii.

19. Philip F. Rehbock, *The Philosophical Naturalists: Themes in Early Nineteenth-century British Biology* (Madison: University of Wisconsin Press, 1983), 3–11.

20. Alfred I. Tauber, *Henry David Thoreau and the Moral Agency of Knowing* (Berkeley: University of California Press, 2001).

21. Roger Smith, *The Norton History of Human Sciences* (New York: W. W. Norton, 1997).

22. Kant, *Critique of Pure Reason*, 375.

23. Ibid., 117.

24. Heb. 11:1.

25. Frederick C. Beiser, *The Fate of Reason* (Cambridge, MA: Harvard University Press, 1987).

26. Gordon G. Brittan, *Kant's Theory of Science* (Princeton, NJ: Princeton University Press, 1978) and Michael Friedman, *Kant and the Exact Sciences* (Cambridge, MA: Harvard University Press, 1992).

27. Whewell, *Philosophy of the Inductive Sciences*, xvii.

28. Noah Feldman, *Divided by God: America's Church-State Problem—and What We Should Do About It* (New York: Farrar, Straus and Giroux, 2005).

29. Charles Darwin, *Charles Darwin's Notebooks*, eds. P. Barrett et al. (Ithaca, NY: Cornell University Press, 1987), 84e, 539. See Tess Cosslett, ed., *Science and Religion in the Nineteenth Century* (Cambridge: Cambridge University Press, 1984) for a rich compendium of the nineteenth century debate.

30. Tauber, "Goethe's Philosophy of Science: Modern Resonances"; Tauber, "From Descartes' Dream to Husserl's Nightmare" in *The Elusive Synthesis: Aesthetics and Science,* ed. Alfred I. Tauber (Dordrecht, Netherlands: Kluwer Academic Publishers, 1996), 289–312; Tauber, "Introduction" in *Science and the Quest for Reality*, ed. Alfred I. Tauber (New York: New York University Press, 1997), 1–49; Tauber, *Henry David Thoreau and the Moral Agency of Knowing*.

31. Tauber, "Goethe's Philosophy of Science: Modern Resonances"; Whewell, *Philosophy and the Inductive Sciences*; Polanyi, *Personal Knowledge*.

32. T. F. Gieryn, "Boundaries of Science" in *Handbook of Science and Technology Studies,* eds. S. Jasanoff, G. E. Merkle, J. C. Petersen, and T. Pinch (Thousand Oaks, CA: Sage Publications, 1995), 393–443.

33. Kuhn, *The Structure of Scientific Revolutions*.

34. Martin Heidegger, "The Age of the World Picture" in *The Question Concerning Technology and Other Essays*, trans. W. Lovitt (New York: Harper and Row, 1977), 115–36.

35. F. Schiller, *Letters on the Aesthetic Education of Man*, trans. E. M. Wilkinson and L. A. Willoughby, in *Essays*, eds. W. Hinderer and D. O. Dahlstrom (1801, New York: Continuum Publishing, 1993), 121.

36. Peter Harrison, *The Bible, Protestantism, and the Rise of Natural Science* (Cambridge: Cambridge University Press, 1998).

37. The enthusiasts even argued that scientific methods were applicable to all domains of human need. As discussed, this caused controversy within the academy, because scientism not only became a method of investigating the natural world, it was regarded by some as representing the way we best construct a worldview from one end of human experience to another. See Edward O. Wilson, *Consilience* (New York: Vintage Books, 1998).

38. Karl Popper, *Conjectures and Refutations: The Growth of Scientific Knowledge* (New York: Harper Torchbooks, 1963).

39. John McDowell, *Mind and World* (Cambridge, MA: Harvard University Press, 1994), 81.

40. Menachem Fisch, "Self Confronting Normativity and the Limits of Self-Criticism," Paper delivered at Notre Dame University, History and Philosophy of Science Colloquium, March 4, 2004.

CONTRIBUTORS

Elisabeth Bumiller is a reporter for the *The New York Times*.

Matt Cartmill is a professor with Duke University's Biological Anthropology and Anatomy institute.

Charles Darwin (1809–1882) was a British naturalist and author of *The Origin of Species*.

Daniel C. Dennett is Austin B. Fletcher Professor of Philosophy and Director of the Center for Cognitive Studies at Tufts University.

Barbara Forrest is a professor of philosophy in the Department of History and Political Scienceat Southeastern Louisiana State University.

Owen Gingerich is a Professor Emeritus of Astronomy and of the History of Science at Harvard University.

Stephen Jay Gould (1941–2002) was a member of the faculty at Harvard University for over thirty years where he was Alexander Agassiz Professor of Zoology, Professor of Geology, Biology, and the History of Science.

John Paul II (1920–2005) was the Supreme Pontiff of the Roman Catholic Churchfrom 1978–2005.

Philip Kitcher is a professor of philosophy at Columbia University.

Ernan McMullen is the John O'Hara Professor Emeritus of Philosophy at the University of Notre Dame.

Kenneth R. Miller is a professor of biology at Brown University.

Nancey Murphy is a professor of Christian philosophy at the Fuller Theological Seminary.

William Paley is the eighteenth century author of *Natural Theology* and the design argument for God's existence.

Robert T. Pennock is an associate professor of philosophy at Michigan State University.

Holmes Rolston III is the University Distinguished Professor of Philosophy at Colorado State University.

Michael Ruse is the Lucyle T. Werkmeister Professor of Philosophy at Florida State University.

Alfred Tauber is the Zoltan Kohn Professor of Medicine and Professor of Philosophy and Director of the Center for Philosophy and History of Science at Boston University.

Michael W. Tkacz is an associate professor of philosophy at Gonzaga University.

James Q. Wilson is the Ronald Reagan Professor for Public Policy at Pepperdine University.

Carl Zimmer is a science journalist whose writings have appeared in such publications the *New York Times*, *National Geographic*, *Science*, *Newsweek*, *Natural History*, and *Discover*, where he is a contributing editor.